SPIRITUAL FRIEND

SPIRITUAL FRIEND

Tilden H. Edwards

PAULIST PRESS
New York/Ramsey

ACKNOWLEDGMENTS

The quotation from Abraham Joshua Heschel is reprinted with the permission of Farrar, Straus and Giroux, Inc. from THE SABBATH. Copyright 1951 by Abraham Joshua Heschel.

Lines from "The Second Coming" are reprinted by permission of MacMillan Publishing Company Inc. from *Collected Poems* of William Butler Yeats copyright 1924 by MacMillan Publishing Company Inc. Revised 1952 by Bertha Georgie Yeats.

Library of Congress
Catalog Card Number: 79-91408

ISBN: 0-8091-2288-X

Published by Paulist Press
Editorial Office: 1865 Broadway, New York, N.Y. 10023
Business Office: 545 Island Road, Ramsey, N.J. 07446

Printed and bound in the
United States of America

Contents

In appreciation for the profound gifts to me of
 my closest friend, Ann
 my spiritual friend, Jerry
 my colleagues in Shalem
And for the naked faith that sustains us all.

Acknowledgments

The experience and insights of many people besides myself enter this book, people both living and dead to this life. I make no claim to any special private maturity in Christian spirituality and spiritual direction. I do, though, claim the maturity of the collective Christian tradition in many of these pages. But that maturity is not a static awareness; rather, it is a dynamic one always freshly appropriating the truth in the unfolding personal and historical moment of grace.

There are a few people who have been particularly helpful to me as supporters or stimulators in this book:

Those for whom I have been privileged to be spiritual friend.

The staff and participants of the Shalem spiritual directors program, and of Shalem spiritual development groups.

My doctoral committee for the Union Graduate School: Doctors Gerald May, Terrence Tice, Vincent Harding, Elaine Prevallet, and Helen Bonny.

Pattie Loy for her valiant work and long hours in deciphering my writing as she typed the manuscript, and Elise Snight, who typed the final draft.

Monica Maxon and Jan Cox of the Shalem staff for their help in protecting my time to write.

My wife Ann and children Jeremy and Jennifer for their patience and support during the countless hours I disappeared into the "pit" of our basement while writing.

T.H.E.

Introduction

A neighbor recently confided to me that she had been going through a "crisis of soul" for some time, but felt frustrated that there was no one she trusted to whom she could turn. She had been in therapy and knew that wouldn't suffice. She was a concerned social activist, but that did not alleviate the inner gnawing. She has a fine family, but they weren't prepared to be helpful here. She had been to Sunday liturgy, but that could not deal directly enough with her personal situation. She had considered seeing a priest or minister, but she was on the fringe of the Church, and anyway she vaguely sensed that most clergy don't have the time or, if they do, don't have the special gift or training to deal with her situation. So where could she turn?

This woman speaks for millions of people in our society today, especially if we expand the number to include not only persons with an immediate "soul crisis," but also ones who seek ongoing "soul-awareness" throughout their lives. The massive numbers of mental-health professionals available to us are prepared to help people cope more effectively with everyday problems of emotional life, but not usually to help with a deeper probing that is focused on one's underlying existential, value-laden purpose and way of life. This "religious-philosophical" area in our culture is not normally their domain.[1]

On the other hand, religious professionals, who are most accountable for this domain, have increasingly been given much the same kind of training and assumptions about hu-

1

man development as the mental-health professional, this together with a theological/philosophical preparation that
deals with human beings largely in broad abstractions. Missing is an adequate bridge that can link the depth of historical
and contemporary religious experience and interpretation
concretely with a person's unique situation.

In recent Roman Catholic and Anglican tradition, this
bridge most commonly has been called "spiritual direction"
and its theoretical discipline "spiritual theology," or "ascetical and mystical theology." In Protestant traditions there is
no shared term for this area; perhaps "faith development" or
"devotional life" comes closest, or it might be seen as a dimension of "pastoral theology."

Because the term "direction" has authoritarian connotations for some people, other older terms continued to live
alongside of it: spiritual friend or companion, soul friend (an
old Irish tradition), guide, and spiritual father or mother,
brother or sister. No term seems right for everyone, so I will
use these names interchangeably. The area of relationship
represented by all these terms is an ancient, enduring and
currently neglected area of human need, whatever we choose
to call it.

How can we best respond to this need today, as it reveals itself in our personal life, in our neighbors, and in the
society as a whole? How does it relate to our current psycho-
logical-religious-cultural situation? What does it say about
the institutional tasks of the Church in our society today?
How can it be met in groups as well as on a one-to-one basis?
Further, what is valuable for us today in different traditions
of guidance? How do we prepare people to be better spiritual companions for others?

These are some of the questions I want to address in the
following pages. My hope is that they will stimulate you to
further concern, thought, and practice in this area, that together we may reclaim the classic strengths of spiritual
friendship for the communities to which we belong and
adapt them to our historical moment. My conviction is that,
rightly appropriated and graced, spiritual friendship can
serve deeper personal spiritual life. Where such practice is

widespread, I believe it also can provide impetus for the corporate renewal of religious institutions, helping them to be more discerning instruments of service for their own members, as well as for the whole society.

This conviction rises from my own exploration of spiritual friendship over the past six years. I have struggled with each of the questions mentioned above, alone and with many others, and I have searched through the relevant historical and current literature. The Shalem Institute for Spiritual Formation in Washington, D.C. is one of the fruits of this effort. Shalem offers people opportunities to explore many facets of spiritual friendship and contemporary spirituality.[2]

A new Shalem project has been the immediate stimulus for this book: the mounting of an experimental two-year program for the better preparation of spiritual directors drawn from a variety of backgrounds.[3] The planning and execution of this program has led to a fresh struggle with all of those questions mentioned earlier.

I am aware that any "answers" offered here are "answers in process." I have dipped down into the ocean of knowledge and experience at a particular point in time and drawn up these findings. What will prove mere flotsam and what valuable treasure awaits your testing and my own in the years ahead.

For the sake of clarity and movement, I have kept most substantiating quotations and elaborations in notes rather than in the text. If you want the full value of this book, therefore, you might want to pay attention to the notes. If your primary interest is in context, theory, and history, you will want to pay special attention to Part I. If the concrete practice of spiritual direction is your primary concern, then you will find Part II most relevant.

Before going further, we will need to discuss the difficulties of communication we face in this area.

Language

A hearing-aid company recently asked in a commercial: "Are you hearing sounds but not words?" When we approach the touchy and fuzzy area of spirituality, our first problem is the communications barrier. I can give you endless "sounds," but if they don't carry the meaning intended, they remain meaningless words, or worse, misinterpreted ones.

We cannot overcome this problem completely, since we are dealing with an area primarily of *apprehension* rather than of comprehension. Spirituality refers to the most subtle dimension of our awareness, where we sense ourselves belonging beyond our ego image[4] to a larger, more valuable horizon of reality that impinges on all we are and do. We cannot "grasp" this horizon. It is always beyond any scientific instrument or description. Yet many people throughout history claim to "know" this reality more assuredly than any other. Such intuitive knowledge in Christian tradition is referred to as "experimental" knowledge of God. With our normal minds and senses, we can know only indirectly, by inference and trust.[5]

This means that any language I use will be subjected to your own screens of comprehension and experience. If, for example, I use the word "God" as the focal point of spirituality, that can mean different, even contradictory things to us. We can act as if we are talking about the same reality, yet in fact have no idea what each other is really talking about, no matter how closely I might try to define my terms.

Different responses have been made to this dilemma, perhaps summed up in the two classic, interrelated Christian spiritual paths: the "kataphatic" and the "apophatic." The kataphatic[6] underlines positive images of God and tries to clarify and affirm these images. This focus on the *via affirmativa* underscores the human capacity to reach God through creatures, images, and symbols. This is the dominant Western religious path.

The apophatic, on the other hand, underscores the *via negativa*, calling all particular expressions of God radically inadequate. God is "not this, not that." God is best known in obscure awareness. Meister Eckhart in the thirteenth century spoke with the frequently paradoxical language of this path when he said, "It is possible to be so poor that one does not even have a God."[7] Many Western mystics and their more dominant counterparts in Eastern Orthodoxy and Asian religions are classic examples of this path.

Both spiritual traditions overlap a third way of thinking about God, the *via analogia*, which identifies and enlivens spiritual life with metaphors, analogies, approximations. The apophatic path, though stripping away what God is not, nonetheless will use positive names for God, such as "Light," or "the Holy One." The apophatic path also involves a positive yearning for the True God and an all-encompassing clarity.

The apophatic path is currently undergoing something of a renaissance in the West, perhaps in reaction to the glibness, the overfamiliarity with which the names of God have been bandied about and sold in our slick, hungry, commercial culture. At the same time, perhaps, the reemergence of this path is a reaction to that skeptical or cynical philosophical alternative that assumes no ultimate reality behind any religious language.

The apophatic approach is an option, one that recognizes a reality behind the "holy words" but senses that reality as too much other, too much mystery to be mastered by thought or directly touched with our feelings. The rise of meditation practices today that emphasize the relativity of images to a larger "apprehension of reality" is perhaps a behavioral sign of this apophatic way.

Though some people would see an ultimate conflict between the apophatic and kataphatic, especially in their relative weighting of "negative" and "positive" languages, I think they are complementary and mutually corrective. The negative language prevents idolatry of particular word images, saving us for the larger Horizon of our lives; the positive language affirms points of contact, intimacy, and vocation that are particularly crucial in uniting, affirming, and moving people to action.[8] The apophatic and kataphatic, at their best, assume each other and need each other. Both lead, through grace, to the same shared, magnetic Source of our lives.

In this book I will use "religious language" when there

seems to be no adequate substitute that does not reduce the meaning to less than is intended. Our contemporary scientific, secular, scholarly, and humanistic languages do not always provide words adequate to the subtle dimensions of spirituality. Such languages today are so dominated by assumptions of an ego-centered man or physical universe-centered reality that they are impoverished in their capacity to express any other sense of reality.

On the other hand, much of our "religious" culture is dominated by an uncritical, sentimental religious language that trivializes, fixes, and fantasizes the infinite horizon of God to such an extent that it easily distorts, narrows, and obscures the Holy.

A much smaller educated religious leadership uses a different, more critical theological language, the heritage of two thousand years of Christian thought. There is great value in the careful, tested, constantly updated precision of this language, as there is in the language of any long-established discipline. But its historic danger is twofold: on the one hand, theological language can become so abstract, specialized, and complex that only another highly theologically educated person can fully understand it.

On the other hand, theological language largely has been cut off from its old roots in the theologian's "experimental knowledge of God" since the late Middle Ages. Therefore it is no longer a description or interpretation of experientially apprehended Mystery or a way into it, but more often than not a partial outsider's conceptual thinking around someone else's profound experience. The theologian has become scholar with no necessary personal cultivation of or reference to personal experimental knowledge.[9]

So there is our divided "linguistic leadership," as we may call it: scientific-humanistic, popular religious, scholarly theological (often suspicious of one another), in a culture whose only lingua franca appears to be technical assembly instructions (for things and people) and commercials. How can we speak of the unspeakably Holy, or of the subtle footsteps of the Holy in the life of a spiritual friend, in *this* situation?

Only one answer is totally clear: there is no easy way. Nevertheless, we press on. I will try to use different "languages" as they seem helpful: theological where only that will do, behavioral-scientific where its precision clarifies and broadens understanding, humanistic where metaphor and story best communicate, apophatic paradox and simile in places of deepest mystery. A certain awkwardness, a "stuttering about the divine," is inevitable in this area of apprehension, doubly so in a time lacking in adequate, shared linguistic symbols.

In so using different appropriate languages, I will be reflecting a spreading genre of "mixed communication media" while speaking of the transcendent dimension of our lives. At its worst, this mixture can reflect a shallow eclecticism that comes from much tasting in our cafeteria culture, but little lingering for special savoring and integration at some point along the way.

My own "lingering point" as an Episcopal priest and ecumenical educator is religious, one especially reflecting a Christian culture and language. Each of us approaches the transcendent out of some particular framework. This is mine. Yet I have tried to be open to the way the truth reveals itself at other stopping points along the line and to trust that ultimately all truth is one (even though in itself not every position is necessarily true or adequate). I increasingly identify myself, through and beyond my particularities, with the whole human family and its treasury of gifts from a generous Hand.

Simone Weil says this best for me: "Christ likes us to prefer truth to him because, before being Christ, he is truth. If one turns aside from him to go toward the truth, one will not go far before falling into his arms."[10] Justin Martyr in the early Church corroborates this when, drawing from his sense of the Christ-Logos as a seed in everyone, he says: "Whatever has been nobly spoken in any place is a part of Christian heritage."[11]

This reverses that sectarian Christian view which narrows the truth to explicitly Christian language and practice, cutting off the fuller transcendent truth revealed everywhere, truth symbolized by the covenant of God with all people through Noah. Such overly securing, triumphalist, and exclusive sectarianism serves only to further divide, blind, and alienate people in a time of desperate need for human interdependence and mutual learning. This rigid, dark side of Christianity betrays its great accountability for just reconciliation on earth and for humility before the awesome ways of God among us.

At the same time I believe there is a great wisdom to be shared out of Christian experience that, if true, is in some way a treasure for all people. Spiritual guidance out of a Christian tradition at its best is not meant to be a narrow "in-house" affair (though it often has been treated as such), but a personal bridge to the Ground of all human life, one holding a particular broad lineage of experience and interpretation of that Ground. Only on such a basis can Christianity claim to be a universal way and not a sect that closes off and divides the truth.

I will be raising up spiritual guidance in Christian tradition, then, not just as a contribution for committed Christians, but as an offering, a bridge, a "way in" to our shared holy Ground available for all people yearning to touch that Ground more firmly. Such spiritual guidance, like the Church at its broadest, is meant for every serious seeker. Its language must be careful and broad enough not to cut off people unnecessarily. Yet to the extent that language must be used and a particular lineage of experience shared, inevitably some people will be missed and will search elsewhere.

Our Common Condition

I am banking on our common human condition as the best basis for making sense to you in these pages, whatever special language or religious-philosophical tradition (or extradition) you may have. We all share at bottom a certain sense of being—an unstable, painful/joyful, free/compelled, yearning being that is in the mysterious process of becoming. Just what this means and how it is lived out are the oldest existential questions.[12]

Spiritual friendship at its broadest helps us with these questions. More specifically, it helps us when we sense a larger Source than our egos coursing through and around us. More specifically still, spiritual friendship helps us attend to a trusting, discerning response to this Wellspring, in the context of a particular deep tradition, and its whole way of life.[13]

Our focus will be Christian tradition informed at points by other traditions and by contemporary knowledge. We will stroll through the history and contemporary practice of that tradition looking for its contribution to current human existential guidance and its corroboration by and difference from certain contemporary approaches to human understanding and guidance. We then will look at concrete ways we can receive, offer, and learn such guidance today, revised and claimed for our time.

First, though, we will need to look at the sea in which we swim today, a sea whose turbulence is calling out the art and gift of spiritual friendship for renewed and expanded service.

Part I
BACKGROUND

1. The Spiritual Sea
in Which We Swim Today

"And what rough beast its hour come round at last slouches toward Bethlehem to be born?" (W. B. Yeats)[1]

Away, away we slink,
Away from that vile beast
Whose form is manifold,
And name is legion,
Whose presence rises any way we turn, outward and
    inward.
Who can face the beast
Without succumbing to madness?
Better to face away, around, beside;
Nurse your wounds
Weave your safety nets,
Be content with the surface of things, domestic woe
    and bliss.
Too great the beast beyond for us.

Yet in fear we writhe beneath
Till someone rises for us and slays the beast,
or beguiles it into submissive friendship, gives us the
    reins,
And leads us out of cowering sloth to rise up in hope
    for ourselves—and all.

(Tilden Edwards)

New versions of the old beast seem to rise from the murky, tempestuous sea of our time with relentless steadiness, with vast armaments, wars, famine, and disease, earthquake and flood, with political and social oppression, bad jobs and no jobs, unresponsive and entrenched bureaucracies, brutality and callousness, family and social disintegration, with environmental rape, with trivial, mind-numbing consumer diversion.

Inside us, driving, competing, confused desires and fears bounce us from fleeting pain to fleeting pleasure, making us ever restless, causing us to seek ever more and other there, rarely content with enough here. That is man becoming without being, adrift without compass, revolting in revolt, falling though in blindness calling it rising, or in darkness calling it damned.

Of course, there is the other side, the light side: steady caring for the dying and the living, happening through our neighbors and institutions; an endless stream of scientific breakthroughs in human service; many efforts to achieve justice; deeper spiritual search and direction; families that thrive and individuals who nourish human hearts; and humor, and soft rain.

Yet the beast ever lurks near; our hearts yearn for a fuller Home; the stability of inherited ways slips and slides ominously as quaking faults in the earth. Ours is a particularly shaky, even apocalyptic time. Our bloodshot eyes span the horizon for someone coming, someone, someway, that can save us from the many-headed beast.

And what do we see? Where do we turn?

Doctors. Doctors of medicine, law, history, psychology, sociology, the other sciences. Surely they can point the way with their command of old and new knowledge. We turn in our millions to them. Yet they speak in contradictory voices; we follow one, then another; disappointment follows enthusiasm; a little help for this and for that, yes; but one cure is succeeded by another disease, one healing by another brokenness, one fulfillment by another emptiness; and the doctors too are prey to the same disease, confusion, and corruption. Food they give, but the stomach is soon hungry again.

Social Action. Indeed, actors appear in every form who care for the undergirding justice without which no society can or should long endure. Our participation in that action is the base line of human citizenship. Yet no political system or company of leaders yet has established an enduring justice. Most are far, far from it, bastioned by fear, lethargy, and exhaustion among the people. And where justice has come closest on a societal scale, an undercurrent of restless boredom appears. Justice is the responsibility of all; yet it is a relative good; it is not the end; it is not enough to calm the beast. Justice fulfilled is in its specific content loving; this evades more than a tenuous beachhead in human life.

Highs. Perhaps if we can just "turn on" everything will fall in place and be all right. Many choices beckon to us from the wings. The shadowy choices of alcohol, drugs, and violence; the lighter ones of sports, sex, the "tube," and friendly family play—all promise respite, some dull the pain, some open new awareness. The lighter ones can be gifts of real joy. But no high endures, and most leave a complacent emptiness and a vague "low" haunted by fear that the high will not come back, or the fever of negligent drivenness through humdrum work/living, the mind riveted ahead for sight of another high, any high, down the road.

Religion. In fear and yearning perhaps we turn to our heritages of faith. If fear of losing what self seems to possess is deepest, we look for security there: a clear and rigid way; unquestioned rights and wrongs; high walls that keep out difference; fellowship that shares complicity in never speaking of what may disturb or transform us, only speaking of what will comfort and secure. This is domesticated spirituality. Prophecy rises in time to shock such dreamers into reality and courage; but if the beast of fear possesses a stranglehold, the prophet is exiled or killed, and the beast's sleepy spell drags on.

If yearning is deeper than fear, then we become suspicious of the emperor's alluring, securing clothes; we seek the nakedness of soul that is open in trust to the mysterious movement deep inside reality that points the way. When we are gifted with eyes that really see, life is turned around. What was hidden and constricted is now exposed as transcendent, leading, pervasive center. What was center before—a striving, ultimately protecting, possessive ego—now is *follower*, not leader; it is *cooperator*, not pretender to the throne; it is more *free* for the truth, less enslaved by the spinning of ego's protective delusions.

Such conversion of sight and heart is slow to pervade the many recesses of our being. Most of us remain an unstable see-saw of fear and yearning, and being lost and found. All of us, being human, need to see and touch the emperor's clothes for a foundation of security in facing the uncontrollable Mystery. We need to clothe the Mystery with form: words, ritual, sacrament, mutual support, a disciplined rhythm of life.

When our *fear* is deepest, we clutch these forms as the Mystery itself and worship idols that will fail us.

When our *yearning* is deepest, and the Mystery willing, we meet the Mysterious One obscurely *through* the forms, and we taste our wondrous coinherence.

Digestion of such fleeting awareness is crucial. The whole authentic history of spiritual discipline in the Church and in all deep religious traditions is to aid human digestion of the Holy, so that we do not 1) reject its nourishment 2) throw it up by not allowing room inside for it 3) mistake "artifical flavors" for the real thing 4) use its strength for building an ego empire, a head of the beast, rather than for sharing in myriad form for the good of others in appreciation of its giftedness.

Let's turn now more specifically to the situation of the Church today.

The Church Today

What is the potential and limitation of the Christian Church today as a disciplined vehicle for the Holy, and for helping to tame the beast, in our society?[2] That is a massive question, in response to which I will hold up a few selected areas to the light.

Polarization. The Church, made up of human beings, is subject to the same fear, yearning, suspicion, being lost and found spectrum seen in us all. In the West, and particularly in the United States, the Church is saddled with an inheritance of polarization that on balance has impoverished its potential gifts for our time. Yet, perhaps in growing awareness of its destructive fruits, there are indications that polarization is lessening.

The basic form of polarization is very old in human and Church experience. It is the attempt to reduce reality to less than it is by raising to dominance one mode of knowing only: intellect, affect, intuition, or volition. A further step such polarization can take is to freeze reality into one rigid "correct view" of each of these, mistaking opinions ("notions") for final truth. Then notions lose their value as tentative probes, symbols, and pointers, and become devouring self-centered heads of the beast.

The current form of this polarization can be traced to the late Middle Ages, particularly in the division of intellect and affect.[3] The impersonal, tightly logical, complex thought of the later Schoolmen more and more lacked an undergirding of valued personal affective and intuitive experience of the Holy.

This elaborate intellectual "distancing" from intimate surrender and participation in the Mystery as basic to appreciation of the Real, led to a broadside revolt. The name "Devotio Moderna" has been given to cover its main thrust: desire to make the spiritual life more accessible to everyone, through emphasis on individual conversion of heart, virtue, and a simple affective devotion to Christ. The place of the intellect, and of apophatic mystical intuition, was very small.

Thomas à Kempis's *Imitation of Christ* is the most enduring example of this early period. He and the "Devotio Moderna" as a whole have influenced both Protestant and Roman Catholic spiritual leaders right up to our time,[4] reinforced by such movements as Pietism and Evangelicalism. In fact, it is possible that the movement's subjective psychological focus on interior personal experiences themselves (rather than their objects and context in larger reality), which has been so dominant in American Christian religious life in the past century, is related to the rise and popularity of secular psychology in this country. The *locus* of concern remains the same.

The philosophical nominalism of the later Middle Ages, however, led in another direction. Here there was despair of human capacity to contact the Holy through any of our faculties. Such thinking helped pave the way for the Reformation's "justification by faith alone," and led to an ongoing strand of suspicion in recent Christian history of interior experience as a road to God.

In its place is scripturally informed faith, objective worship, and discipline, ever interpreted anew in rational theological language. Perhaps the great Swiss theologian Karl Barth is the most influential recent example of this historical strand.

Beside these two broad intellectual and affective "schools," there runs a third strand, the apophatic mystical. The first two schools share an emphasis on image and form, the kataphatic way;[5] the apophatic more emphatically relativizes any affirmation to the "Cloud of Unknowing," where sense, concept, and self-image are suspended, and the Holy is free as it wills to manifest as it is, rather than as we might project it.

Such weight on "direct seeing" as the ultimate goal of human awareness and realization, together with its compassionate fruits, is a recurrent theme of many early theological and Desert Fathers and Mothers of the Church. It finds special weight later in the fourteenth century German and English and sixteenth century Spanish mystics. Among Protestants, it is found most steadily in the Quaker tradition. It always has been a dominant theme of Eastern Orthodox spirituality, given its enduring central indebtedness to the influence of early Church theological, desert, and monastic traditions.

This mystical stream is the Western bridge to Far Eastern spirituality (and to that of Sufi Moslems and some Hasidic Jews in the West as well). The Zen warning not to confuse the pointing finger (the kataphatic form) for the moon to which it points is a saying that a Christian mystic easily understands. It is no accident that the most active frontier between Christian and Eastern religions today is between contemplative Christian monks and their Eastern equivalents. Some forms of Eastern meditation informally have been incorporated or adapted into the practice of many Christian monks, and increasingly by other Christians.[6]

This exchange, together with the more popular Eastern impact in the West through transcendental meditation, Hatha Yoga, the martial arts, and through many available courses on Eastern religions in universities, has aided a recent rediscovery of Christian apophatic mystical tradition, which has been subordinate to the other two "schools" in most Roman Catholic and Protestant practice for centuries.

Mixed with these three polarizing historic strands in the Church today is the whole stream of learned secularization, marked by a human or nature-centered view of reality, and bolstered by the empirical sciences whose methods leave moot and mute questions of immeasurable transcendent reality.

This secularizing stream is brought to full flood in a society whose law courts increasingly interpret separation of religion and the state to mean not equal access and exposure of religious views in school and other publicly supported places, but the right to be totally uninfluenced by any of them. This leaves the reality defined by modern empirical science as the dominant, shared currency of public learning, together with the images of reality proffered by the mass media: images that are highly seductive and largely secular, amoral/immoral or, where "religion" is involved, sentimental and sectarian.

The only "guide to living" allowed on the public payroll (except for military and institutional chaplaincies) is the counselor/therapist, trained in the technology of psychological processes, cut off for more than a century from its broader roots in philosophy/theology, and with these cut off from the whole context of explicitly and sustainedly exposing and weighing assumptions of philosophical/religious values inherent in any therapeutic approach.

This view of technician human guide has slipped into the internal polarizations and confusion of the Church through its broad influence in seminaries and pastoral counseling.

How are these historic and current strands polarized today in the Church? A seminary dean summarized the situation from his side in a very personal way recently when he lamented: "How can you be smart, in graduate school, and still pray and believe this is God's world?"

If you are smart, and especially if you are teaching one of the solid academic subjects in a theological graduate school, you will have years of conditioning in rational analysis, with more and more sophisticated awareness of the contingencies, relativities, and complexity of reality that present themselves to analytical consciousness.

Attachment (tight or loose) to certain evolving forms of this rational clarity will likely take place. Grasping for intellectual clarity will tend to take center stage. The given obscurities and simplicity of prayer and faith to many such intellectuals will smell somewhat regressive, naive, simplistic, and frustrating. Analytical consciousness conditions us to keep a judging stance. Faith and prayer require its suspension at some point.

Any *feelings* toward the Holy will seem doubly suspect, especially in a cultural religious climate that the intellectual sees easily confusing self-defined "spiritual feelings" with real transcendent contact. Some practical dealing with emotional processes and blocks in psychological study and therapy is all right, but this should not be confused with theological substance.

Another viewpoint belongs to the "practical" (pastoral theology) instructor. He or she sees the psychic, social and managerial crises of seminarians, laity, churches, and communities abounding. The instructor learns all he or she can from the applied behavioral sciences about how to approach these effectively. Theological/philosophical concerns, though peripherally present, operationally seem too abstract and general to be very helpful in real-life situations. Prayer and faith are seen especially as they are able to be useful instruments in particular practical situations. Coping with people and institutions are the valued focus. These take a lot of practical know-how.

The chaplain or spiritual-formation director on the faculty (if there is one), will tend toward another viewpoint: people need to be dealt with in their integrity as unique existential beings, not only as intellects to fill or egos to mature or roles to play. Each person is a mystery needing unique attention to his or her calling, moral development, and maturing in faith. Prayer reflects an end-in-itself relationship. Intellectual work is not a scholarly endeavor but an existential struggle for understanding; it is meant to be more "ecstatic" than "technical" knowledge.[7]

These overstereotyped faculty positions are a microcosm of the larger Church situation today. In a seminary setting, with everyone having to live together serving as something of a team for the preparation of religious leaders, differences are likely to cause more tension than polarization. However, these differences often enough are not struggled with openly over time, to everyone's loss. The net result can be a side-by-side living of views narrowed and impoverished by lack of sufficient peer challenge, and confused, fragmented students.

In the larger Church scene, less sustained by such a contained and sophisticated environment, these differences can explode into movements that sometimes freeze a position to the point of distortion or incompleteness, movements that are maintained in part by the continued existence of "opposite" positions they are reacting against.

The complex array of these groupings: charismatic, evangelical, confessional, liberationist, sacramental, scientific, devotional, psychic, tend to weight either intellect, volition, affect, or intuition to the neglect or contradiction of one another.[8]

It is as though these basic ways of knowing were projected out like a beam of pure white light through a prism, its unity split into many colors that freeze in the prism, forgetting their ultimate unity. Then the affective red unchecked by the others distorts into a sickly color, cloudy, sentimental, and subjective. The intellectual green becomes too bright with its own lustre, arrogant and sterile. Intuitive blue softens to the point of subjective fantasy or at least incommunicability. Volitional yellow exhausts itself in action that has become more blinding heat than clear light.

If the Church is to be true "religion," an integrating force in our society, then it must remember the unity of these ways of knowing. Each is a gift needed to forge a full human response to our shared Mystery. Each is a curse when isolated from the mutual edification of its companions. This is our "internal" community of resources, which together forge the lens for human guidance. Different personalities and groups, in different personal and historical moments, may be led to emphasize one avenue over another (usually in reaction to its neglect, or in response to the call of the living situation), but the price of denying the value of all together is inevitable distortion of the truth.[9]

Apophatic Contributions

The beginning recovery today of Christian apophatic mystical tradition perhaps has a special mission to perform in turning these resources from competitors to friends. A great strength of that broad school of knowledge is its capacity to encompass all of these resources in intimate relation to one another.[10] *Intellect* is given its due as interpreter, explorer, communicator, and check on the others. *Affect* is affirmed as energy for contacting different shades of life relationships inside and around us. *Intuition* at its most mature is recognized as a capacity for "direct seeing" of reality, unmediated by our normal senses. *Volition*, at its height, i.e., in compassion, is affirmed as the spontaneous fruit of intuition, checked, interpreted and assisted by intellect and affect.

Thus each resource for knowing is given its due, but relativized to one another and to the great Mystery of God. In terms of content, scripture, tradition,[11] and reason are accepted as informing, guiding gifts, but the goal is firsthand intuitive awareness of the truth; the end is to be "inside" the truth, "in" Christ, not forever outside guessing (even though the inevitability and humility of an "in-and-out" rhythm is recognized for this life).

Perhaps most valuable of all, this loose school maintains a clear-cut iconoclasm in its testing of whether or not we really are "in," or just think or feel we are. The rampant Western confusion of special good feelings with true and direct contact of the Holy is cut through. Feelings of any kind, good or bad, are "sat through," lest a person become fascinated and stuck with affective "highs" and "lows" as the end, confusing experience of creatures for the Creator, effects for their Source.[12]

At the same time, such experience is not critiqued only by "outsider" reason, the dominant means of iconoclasm in the Church. An "insider" discernment path of precognitive, intuitive attentiveness is affirmed. This path is aided by various "experiential" disciplines: including the classical ones of fasting, prayer, and a simple, caring, humble life-style.

Thought in both its conceptual and pictorial forms is affirmed, yet always with care not to fall into another prevalent Western trap: confusion of a concept or image with the reality to which it points or, more subtly, confusing the more precise exchange of one concept for another as being in more direct touch with the truth, rather than simply having a clearer idea about the truth, with the truth itself being qualitatively different than any perceived objective image of it.

This is the constant danger of the kataphatic path (when separated from the apophatic), where the affirmation of particular forms can freeze those forms into ultimacy, into idols that close them off from their infinitely dynamic Source. Then people are left with cognitive balls of ice disguised as rocks, which never are allowed to melt, remaining hard, brittle, unyielding, reified into more than the formed water they are, losing the fluidity of their natural state. When this happens theologically, the "handmaid, protector and interpreter of the Mystery" functions of theology usurp the throne of the Mystery itself and become a head of the beast, fomenter of demonic crusades and witch hunts.[13]

The way of apophatic mysticism can bridge the polarized gap widened since the late Middle Ages between experientially *relating* to the Holy and thinking critically *about* the Holy. The choice is not just between uncritical feeling and critical distance. This third way attends directly to feeling and intellect, but as arrows that can pierce just so far into the Mystery. It sees the Mystery itself seeping into us unawares, asking for ever looser reigns of feeling and intellect, for subtler appreciation of what lies hidden for our peace when we lighten and surrender all we would assert and form (yet without negation), into the Cloud of Unknowing.[14]

The apophatic path in Christian tradition often has borrowed Platonic concepts to describe the way. The weakness here is the dualism and hierarchy between matter and spirit, and with this, at least an implicit denigration of the body and of history.[15]

Our better understanding of Hebraic and scriptural Christian integration of matter and spirit today overcomes this dualism and allows Christians much more concern for historical process and for body-mind collaboration as sacramental, as ways of unfolding and calling out unique possibilities of co-creativity and sharing of the fruits of creation. Jesus Christ is seen not only as a savior from history, a way back Home, but as an affirmer of our place as creative stewards of history, forging a new home that eventually is caught up in our larger Home.

Thus "volition" takes on a new quality of historical concern. We are not on earth solely to find our way back to an original unity, but we are here also to carry forward a liberating process of unfolding toward that which has never been. The Garden of Eden is not the same as the Kingdom, the fully realized Reign of God.

The past "hook-up" of the apophatic mystical way with Platonic interpretation I believe is accidental. It happens to have been the primary available linguistic currency for interpreting an experiential awareness that could be expressed in many other ways, as more recent persons on this path have done (e.g., Thomas Merton, Douglas Steere, William MacNamara, Catherine Doherty). Many theologians in the twentieth century, especially Protestant ones, mistaking the inadequate interpretive words for the awareness, have thrown out the precious baby with the dirty bathwater, to the great loss of several generations of Protestant clergy and laity.[16]

A potential polarization is implied above between the historical and eternal, the visionary call to a new humanity and the vision of the inclusive All present in our midst. Is this an either-or choice?

The often tragic side of our Western theological/philosophical inheritance is seen where it forces choices that need never be made. If this is right, then that must be wrong. The truth, perhaps, often is more subtle (a constant discovery of the apophatic path). What is surface conflict, jagged peaks of icebergs facing off with each other, beneath may be joined when we have eyes to see. They appear in glorious/inglorious profusion, yet in whatever form, they grow from the same eternal Source always present.

The Reign of God is growing, and at the same time it is eternally present and full in our midst. The goal is at the same time both a return and advance to the fullness of this holy truth. God is equidistant from the beginning, the middle, and the end (as Augustine inferred), yet what unfolds is always fresh, unique form and possibility.

Conflict, if carried by an awareness of deeper unity, may serve to correct both sides and bring them closer to the truth.[17] "Sectarian" conflict tends to defend its peak blindly, at all costs. "Denominational dialogue," to use another ecclesial image, can listen as well as speak, and hope that everyone present will be enriched. Then a roomy "catholicity" of truth including different partial truths is affirmed, warping and woofing and blending into harmony, in the infinite Mystery.

Such capacity for expecting the "coincidence of opposites" in the Mystery of God[18] is particularly important in our pluralistic society and delicately interdependent planet today. One of the great strengths of American society has been its amazing capacity for religious pluralism along with

outbursts of polarization. That pluralism at its best acknowl-
edges a shared Transcendent Reality that catches up our differences into complementarity.

The current threat to this tenuous yet crucial bond
comes not only from continually revitalized sectarian trium-
phalism, but also from the powerful growth of atomistic individualism.

Such individualism's sad shriveling of valued reality to
individual ego gratification creates an atmosphere of indifference beyond self-concern. Where there is societal involvement, it takes the form of despairing conflict for personal or
subgroup rights (as in excluding low-income housing in a
neighborhood). This is *despairing* conflict because there is no
sense of transcendent unity that evokes responsibility and
identity with the *whole* as well as the parts. Religious institutions have particular opportunity and accountability for fostering this larger responsible identity in society.[19] Apophatic
mysticism can serve this end well, with its steady intuition
of coinherence.

Alongside such reinforcement of our larger identity lies
another potential contribution of the apophatic way, in this
case an antidote to yet another tendency in world societies
today toward authoritarianism and bland, herded collectiv-
ities of pacified people.[20]

Matthew Fox incisively describes the *via negativa*, the
"God is not this, not that" language often emphasized in apophatic tradition, as a profoundly political method, an "un"-
naming of God:

> In rejecting a culture's gods by rejecting language used
> to characterize them, a mystic implicitly rejects an entire
> symbol system, including the projection of that system
> into the culture's institutions. . . . The mystic rejects in
> order to explore new language for God and culture.[21]

After quoting Meister Eckhart's great illustrative line,
"I pray God to rid me of God," Fox goes on to criticize a theology of Word as inadequate pedagogy today:

> People are sick and suspicious of words. They want the
> nonword, unword, silence, touch, dance, music—i.e., a

new deeper word that the mystic who rejects society's language comes to utter.[22]

I would demur in accepting Fox's word, "reject" (language). Many Christian mystics have struggled to clothe the Mystery they touch with fresh words that describe as best they can what they consider indescribable. But in doing so they do not reject so much as *relativize any* language, including any new expressions they themselves may coin. Many Christian mystics in fact normally utilize very classical theological and scriptural language. Instead of changing the language, they use it to describe, guide, and corrolate with their own firsthand "experimental knowledge."

In any case, it is difficult to be "captured" by a particular political-cultural system, or an overly closed religious system for that matter, on the apophatic path. It asserts the Holy's radical transcendence of social structure, and thereby implicitly is a prophetic witness and threat to any system that absolutizes its assertions about reality.[23]

At the same time, the apophatic way complements such transcendence with immanence: person and Lord meet directly, though obscurely, in the Cloud of Unknowing. Orthodox Christian apophatics also share with kataphatics a sense of indirect presence, sacramentally, in every form. From *God's* side, all persons, all creation, are saturated with Holy Presence. In Christian faith this Presence is uniquely and redemptively (though not exclusively) manifest in Jesus Christ.

From the *human* side, however, we really hear, know, see nothing of the Holy, except by inference and trust. Yet we *can* know in obscure awareness, when we find ourselves caught up beyond our power to comprehend, yet apprehend.

Here we see the interwovenness of apophatic and kataphatic paths. Each contains the seeds of the other. Transcendence and immanence describe dimensions of one reality.[24]

The autobiographical records of obscure, intuitive apophatic awareness, and its many qualities, illusory forms, and fruits are the often neglected "clinical texts" of the historical Church. Though lacking in the breadth, vocabulary, and broader empiricism of contemporary psychology, these texts portray a depth of human awareness and development that is very rare indeed. The difficulty, just as with contemporary psychological texts, is that they were not meant to be prima-ry but supplementary guides for others. Primary guidance was meant to be in person (one-to-one and/or in groups) with a spiritual director over a period of time.[25]

Christian apophatic tradition suffers greatly from the loss of such a profound oral tradition. In interviews I have had with contemplative Christians, they corroborate my sense that, for a variety of historical reasons, we largely have lost a careful, subtle, sustained process of apophatic oral guidance. We are left with books of past masters, which pro-vide the rudiments, skeletons, and applications to particular other people of such guidance, but the cultivation of a close, profound "teacher-student" relationship, as once existed in desert, religious community, *poustinia*, and anchorhold situa-tions, is extremely rare today.

One modern contemplative, Abbot Thomas Keating,[26] once told me that he believes this is why many people turn to Eastern gurus now. They come with two questions, "What do I do?" and "How am I doing?" Eastern gurus are much more habituated to deal with such long-term questions of spiritual guidance, insofar as they have maintained em-phasis on an oral one-to-one teaching tradition much more carefully than we (albeit sometimes warped, to modern Westerners, by tyrannical authority). The Church is in the humbling situation of increasing demand for more adequate personal guidance that includes recognition of apophatic di-mensions, yet having lost, out of long neglect, fear, abuse, and misunderstanding, much of its oral-tradition resources for such guidance.

One intent of the program for spiritual directors de-scribed later in this book is to assist in some small way with a reincorporation of apophatic guidance along with kataphatic strengths in spiritual-direction practice.

Modern Psychology and the Church

One reason for the neglect of spiritual direction has been the meteoric rise of psychological schools of understanding and treatment of human development in this century. Largely cut off from their older roots in theological/ philosophical/ethical concern, they have become predominantly technical specialties for resolving emotional blocks to more free and full ego functioning. They have contributed enormously to the fund of human knowledge about psychological processes, and I have personally benefited from this knowledge a great deal. At the same time, lacking deep roots as a discipline in value theory, as well as in community (as opposed exclusively to intra-psychic) covenant, psychology is prone to certain blindspots that point to the need for the complementary art of spiritual direction. Kendra Smith, a psychologist herself, states a basic inadequacy:

> Western psychology, although it struggles to find a consensually acceptable model of health, has in everyday practice only a negative definition of health: freedom from gross pathological systems. Conceptually, the Western practitioner is almost blind to health. . . . Although the assessment of "ego strength" is given lip service, Western diagnostic procedures and tools are, like a surgeon's scalpel, designed to uncover only pathology.[27]

Undoubtedly this description would be unfair to some procedures (including contemporary psychoanalytic diagnosis), but apparently not to many. Some would go even further and state that the fault of many alternative methods prevalent today lies in their failure to uncover both pathology and strengths, because their concepts are insufficiently discriminating.[28]

Of course, implicit in every psychological approach and in every therapist's mind is some sense of health. The problem, as in the medical model so influential in most psychological theory, is that the implicitness is not exposed to explicit testing, thereby leaving the patient/client to trust the rarely stated personal values of the therapist and of his or her approach.

Since the values rarely are made explicit and open for deepening in the training of therapists, they may well be hidden even to him or her. This exposes therapist and patient alike to hidden values, and more than likely to unconscious cultural mirroring. Where values are not exposed and challenged, deeply and steadily, more than likely they will reflect those of the cultural or subcultural milieu of the therapist and those who trained him. When these subjective values do surface, they sometimes become confused with objective empirical knowledge.

Allopathic medicine and its mechanistic, amoral, aspiritual approach to human health, long virtually unquestioned and dominant in our society, is undergoing challenge today from those concerned with a different, "holistic" model of disease and health. Psychological theory has been undergoing the same challenge, with an increasing number of therapists concerned with a more integral physical-psychological-social environmental values-oriented model.

It is interesting to note that many of these recent challenges have been influenced by Eastern religions and cultures. Those who have studied Buddhism, for example, find a situation where psychological and spiritual development were not cut off from each other. Psychology (as once was true in the West) is seen as a way of understanding the mind so that it can be prepared for enlightenment, or as we might say in the West, for deeper conversion into the image of God. It is incorporated into a whole way of life: moral, physical, intellectual, liturgical, spiritual, preserved especially in intensive religious community.[29]

Why does it seem so rare that these health professionals turn to Western religions for such learning? It is not adequate to say that the pasture always looks greener and more romantic somewhere else, though this often is a factor.[30] More deeply, I think, is the loss in the West of an integral way of perceiving life. I will restrict my remarks to the Christian situation, since I know it best.

Earlier I mentioned the historic polarization between

mind, affect, and intuition in Christian history. In the competition rather than collaboration between these ways of knowing, the analytical mind (in benevolent or exploitative form) largely "won" in policy-making (as opposed often to popular) circles of most mainline Western Churches. This has meant the subjection of affect and intuition to analytical reason, and (perhaps less and less in our culturally dominated Churches) to the norms of scripture and tradition as determined by this faculty.

When narrowly interpreted, a priori rational theological beliefs concerning the truth dominated historically, the sciences were subject to theological inquisition. Reason itself was polarized between such a priori based inquiry and empiricism. Psychology (and other sciences) had no adequate breathing room in this milieu, and its rigid independence, once given a chance, was inevitable.

The price has been a tragic Western categorization of the truth into bits and pieces that never seem to weave a single cloth. In the mainline churches, for example, theologians offer broadscale analysis. Helping a person with the integral appropriation of the truth to which theology points, however, is left to "practical" people, especially pastoral clergy. Unable adequately to translate their theological training into the nitty-gritty of the personal crises and developmental help asked of them by people, and goaded by the lack of perceived spiritual concern on the part of many people coming for help ("Just help get me through this crisis and everything will be all right—I don't want to be converted"), they usually turn to the empirical sciences for assistance. In terms of practical human guidance, this has bred clinical pastoral education and the pastoral counselor.

This person theoretically brings a theological background and his or her own implicit faith to human situations. Potentially, therefore, the gap of the secular therapist is filled in terms of an explored, tested "value lineage" (which of course has the strengths and limitations of a particular value stance). However, the gap rarely seems adequately filled.

Many pastoral counselors in my own and others' experience have been disappointed in their religious backgrounds: by an emotional and/or rigid fundamentalism they have thrown off as false, or by an affectively bland and domesticated spirituality that seems dead, or by an intellectual theological education that just wasn't transferable in the midst of people's crises and development.

Empirical secular psychology came to them often as a theory and therapeutic method that had "conversion" power in their own lives, so much so that past religious dimensions paled by comparison. Often there is little personal motivation left to deal seriously with people's authentic spiritual yearnings, and if there is, few or no tools or ongoing personal spiritual discipline are at hand for help.[31]

One source of difficulty here is the lack of "spiritual theology" in theological education. This bridging discipline perhaps always has been an inadequately present (if present at all) part of theological education, especially since the historic polarizations earlier described. This is an area in which many seminaries, and the Church as a whole, have shown growing concern in recent years.[32]

"Spiritual theology" is the concrete application of theological/scriptural interpretation, and of the empirical ascetical/mystical experience of Christian spiritual proficients, to the unique interior development of a person or group.[33]

One result of neglecting this area has been to leave the religious leadership of the Church almost totally dependent on secular models for human growth.[34] The theoretical base of these models often implicitly denies any reality, value, or even awareness of classical Christian ascetical/mystical experience and goals.

Historically the Church always has utilized the current psychology of its culture. However, what it has borrowed, it has modified and transformed in the light of its own tradition.[35] But if there is no deep awareness of the experiential, developmental anthropology of the tradition, then there is no real mutation, just a whole-hog graft. If the graft takes, it tends to take over. Sooner or later then the Church loses its unique experiential wisdom for the society; it finds itself more and more absorbed as an expedient base for someone else's "revelation," unqualified by its own.

When the graft fails, there often is a fundamentalist reaction, a sense of an alien body to be thrown off, a rigid "sticking to the Bible" as all the guidance we need. Anything else is of the devil.

My plea is that we explore much more deeply the experiential tradition of the Church, lest we have no conscious unique inner heart left to offer, or just the very shrunken heart of the hard-shell fundamentalist or vague sentimentalist.

Much in that experiential tradition is *not* valuable for us today. But much is. In an a-historical, always "with the latest" American culture, we easily throw out too much too fast.

Theological interpretation is important, but it is no substitute for an awareness of the experiential tradition, and indeed even this awareness is not enough. An "inner" firsthand understanding is called for, personal, experiential exploration of selected practices of prayer, fasting, and other classical spiritual disciplines. If these avenues of knowledge are ignored, we have impoverished our ways of relating to the Holy and to our own deeper reality.

Psychology is accountable to the society as a unique empirical discipline. The Church, too, is accountable to the society, for drawing from its unique treasure what is needed by people today. That treasure can be melted down and reshaped in a myriad called-for ways. It can be a new alloy incorporating much that is good in contemporary society.

But the Church's discernment of just what is good and consonant in society will depend on its own "subcultural" integrity and deep appreciation of the tradition's experiential heart. Eastern religious groups, at least as they are perceived in this country, offer an integral way of life for people in a fragmented Western culture. It is crucial for the society that the Church be able to offer the same, avoiding in the process both the extremes of overaccommodation to the culture, and the rigid way of life found in growing sectarian fundamentalism. It is an open yet deeply rooted Christian way that is largely missing today, between these polarizing extremes.

A reappropriation of structures for personal spiritual guidance, including apophatic insight, is one way to aid this development. This reappropriation needs to take place in the context of the larger Church's life and history, and be cognizant of contemporary insight and social need. In this process, the Church might become a little less internally polarized, and a little more valuable as a unique, enriching, and challenging complement to psychological and other foci for human development in society.

What more specifically can we learn from Christian tradition that is valuable for personal human guidance today? Let us now turn to that history and see what treasures may surface.

2. Living Waters
of the Past

"Tradition is democracy of the dead, extending a vote to our ancestors, refusing to submit to the small and arrogant oligarchy of those who are walking about."[1]

Christian tradition is the lived and tested experience and reflection of a diverse body of people over time united by a commitment to approach the purpose and way of life through the lineage of Jesus Christ. That lineage has woven through countless cultures, personalities, and groupings over two thousand years and taken on infinite forms; dividing, reuniting, corrupting, renewing, killing, healing, narrowing to rigid definitions, widening to incorporate new insights born under another aegis. What can we learn from that tradition for human guidance today?

Several years ago I interviewed twenty nine respected spiritual leaders (mostly in the United States, and mostly Christian) concerning various issues.[2] One question probed whether or not there was anything inadequate in the understanding of spiritual guidance by Christian masters who lived before modern science and other recent learning.

Very few felt there has been anything *essentially* new learned for spiritual guidance, but most felt some new developments were *helpful*. These include a more careful understanding of psychological processes (e.g., anger, fear, and guilt); and a more cosmic, dynamic, developmental world view (e.g., awareness of the inadequacy of legalism, a sense of cosmic and planetary unfolding, democratization, and the

breaking open of our symbols and images which, as one leader said, "leads toward a cosmic Christianity where only God
is Catholic and Christian").

On the other hand, five leaders felt that our current culture is *less* hospitable to spiritual depth than in the past.
Comments pointed especially to the loss of what I have
termed the apophatic mystical: "Science has narrowed and
blurred our awareness of the way reality is." . . . "We have
been so absorbed in extracting nature's secrets and establishing psychological distance that there has been no felt need to
get in touch with deeper, more profound reality." . . . "We
have collected much information, but the genuine awareness
(of past masters) is much vaster than such knowledge. Unless
we learn to contact this deeper level, our attempts to im-
prove the world's external situation may only lead to further
imbalance, pollution, and general misfortune."

It is to signs of the living waters of "deep awareness" in
Christian tradition, as applicable to spiritual guidance for us
today, that we now turn.

Hebrew Scripture

"Now guide me with advice and in the end receive me
into glory" (Ps. 73:24).
"Your statutes are my counselors" (Ps. 119:24).

These verses perhaps summarize the abiding "deep
awareness" of Hebraic tradition: the direct guidance from
the sacred, from Yahweh, and from his revealed Torah (the
first five books of the Bible), lived out in a covenanted community. The role of spiritual/moral counselor (whether as
priest, prophet, wise person—later rabbi or priest), involves
expected obedience not to the guide bearing individual divine authority, but to his or her reasoned teachings and interpretations of the Law, or ecstatic prophetic calls back to
it.[3]

An apophatic mystical note seems present more powerfully in the response to Moses' request on Mount Sinai for
the Torah Giver's name (Exod. 3:14). The answer was an untranslatable sound that protects the Mystery from human

projection. Yet the Mystery has substance, guiding in cloud by day and fire by night. This ultimately unnamed yet trustworthy One, surrounding us by benevolent guidelines for a way of life in human/divine covenant, has remained the core of Jewish and the framework for Christian spirituality. It gradually replaced guidance by magic, oracle, and lots.

Though the Law usually is relativized to the trusted emerging New Age of God's Reign in Christian tradition, Don Browning has pointed out the crucial Christian inheritance of a system of practical rationality, with its publicly articulated reasons for moral action, including a regulated but positive view of impulses, and an openness to refinement. Without this context, Christianity degenerates into amorphous ambiguity and cultural chaos, unstable self-definition and personal/social commitment. When this moral/spiritual guidance is lacking, people turn elsewhere, such as to Eastern religions or fundamentalist sects, to find means of self-control, decision-making, and self-transcendence.[4]

The overrigidification of the Law as a means of guidance always is a danger, witnessed by the revolt of many Jews from Orthodoxy, and of Protestant and post-Vatican II Roman Catholics from particular Christian corruptions and ossifications of the Law as it was modified and syncretized with Graeco-Roman law in Christian history.

But, in the United States, our danger seems much more that of total secularization of moral guidance into a state legal system, inviting the frequent public attitude of getting away with whatever you can. Behind this attitude lies that head of the beast, unchecked private individualism, an increasing euphemism for socially corrupting, drifting narcissism.[5]

The Law also can be seen in more *mystical* terms, an emphasis that appears periodically at least from the time of Philo, the influential first century Alexandrian Jewish exegete. For him, the moral purification afforded by living in the Law is done by *God*, as a way of making room for his transcendent spirit to live in us.[6] Remembering that the Law is not "just" rational allows us to be open to its greater richness.

Christian Scripture

Jesus assumed the framework of Torah and covenant community, interpreting and relativizing them in the light of his sense of the growing Reign of God.

That Reign of the Wisely Loving One, as he conveyed it, involved a great human/divine intimacy: he spoke of God with the unusually familiar "abba," "dear father" or "daddy"; he saw himself *in* God, and he *in* his disciples, and they *in* him; he and light were one in the Transfiguration; and the powers of the Holy One flowed through him in the Gospel accounts: for healing, reconciliation, justice, and resurrection. Jesus promised the abiding bridging of the holy/divine chasm through the indwelling of God in all his followers as Holy Spirit.

In these ways Jesus raised to central focus that unmediated strand of direct guidance and intimacy found in Hebraic awareness, not thereby throwing out the guidance framework of Torah, but drawing out its inner meaning and context. As Moses' firsthand intimacy with the Transcendent One provided unmediated context for the gift to the people of mediated Law, for a holy "way" of life, so Jesus' firsthand awareness and vocation in the Holy One provided the unmediated context for the gifts of mediated acts of redemption, interpretation of the Law, and the promise of an eternally present inner Advocate welling up in us, the Holy Spirit, in a dawning New Age.

Thus in the Transfiguration Jesus was caught up in light, speaking with Moses, and with the other prime exemplar of such divine intimacy in Hebrew scripture: Elijah (who heard God in a still, small murmur and is the one person in that scripture said never to have died).

And yet there is no self-deification. The "untranslatable name" of the Transcendent One is preserved at the same time as the unique intimacy and gifts are manifest. Jesus knows his finitude as a man: he must suffer and die; he must struggle to communicate day by day, often unsuccessfully, with hard-hearted, fearful, and incomprehending people, in-

cluding his own followers. As seen in the Garden of Geth-
semane, he must struggle with his own will and the will of
God. He rebukes a man for calling him good, "No one is
good but God alone" (Mk. 10:18).

This then is the basic context for Jesus' guidance: the
paradoxical transcendence and intimacy of God, and the
fruits of Law, discernment, and empowered compassion.
Therein lies the source and marriage of both apophatic and
kataphatic paths: the unmediated intimate Mystery of the
former, the named and formed path of the latter.

Within this framework, how did Jesus provide guidance
for others?

Our problem in reading the Gospels whole is that they
contain a patchwork of different situations (most of which
we know too little about for certain interpretation), and in
each situation Jesus responds uniquely to the person and situation, with mind and heart-opening questions and comments, and with symbolic and healing acts.

Here he sets a pattern for the best of Christian awareness concerning human guidance: each of us needs a special
"saving" word or act at this moment in our lives. What I
need may be contradictory to what another needs. And yet
this is not simply subjective individualism; it is within the
framework of a shared covenant, i.e., an affirmation of the
trustworthiness of the Intimate, Reigning Unknown/
Known Force of Life, and the guidelines of the covenant
community's tested, evolving experience for living in the
reconciling intent of this trustworthiness.

In guiding groups as opposed to individuals, it is in this
large framework, evolved to special power and focus in himself, that Jesus spoke. He often used parables[7] because these
are concrete and open-ended compared to logically linear
statements. They mediate the ineffable loving Mystery to us
in different ways, as we are ready to hear, always leaving a
little mystery left over.

He chose, maintained, and cultivated an inner circle of
disciples for special guidance, preparing them to succeed
him. Their recorded imperfections maintain a sense of their

unpretentious humanness, a sign of hope for those who know their own sins and blindness, and would despair of divine attention.

Jesus suffered from his disciples' lack of comprehension, betrayals, laziness, and fights for power, but he did not throw them out (except Judas, who really threw himself out). He seemed to work patiently with them until the end. At one culminating point he is recorded as saying:

> No longer do I call you servants, for the servant does not know what his master is doing; but I have called you friends, for all that I have heard from my Father I have made known to you. You did not choose me, but I chose you and appointed you that you should go and bear fruit and that your fruit should abide; so that whatever you ask the Father in my name, he may give it to you. (John 15:15f)

And what qualifies them as "friends?" They must forgive and love one another (as God forgives and loves them), and be poor, joyful servants of all. They must pray,[8] fast, and understand and proclaim the inner meaning of Jesus' words, what they say about the way reality is: a gift, a mysterious, evolving, trustworthy Reign of Righteousness, a struggle with the "dark" side of reality in sin and evil forces, forces which ultimately cannot prevail.

Reality also is a call to a life of unanxious, confident, shared, just, bearing, empowered responsiveness to the Light revealed in Jesus, in Torah and the prophets, and in creation. It is a willingness to let go one's old life and follow Jesus' way without reservation, even to death.

Jesus did not restrict himself to this "inner circle." There was another ring of people he befriended and who responded with trust and repentance, a diverse assortment mostly of low status in the society (friendships for which sometimes he was criticized by established religious leaders): tax collectors, thieves, harlots and other sinners, children, housewives, foreigners, soldiers, the diseased and handicapped, as well as occasional religious leaders.

Beyond these were the anonymous crowds he addressed

with exhortations to let go their sinful separation from their calling, merciful Father. To such crowds he offered a vision of inner and outer *shalom*, a Reign of Righteousness, through and beyond the empowered struggle and waiting for its fullness.

Thus we see an outline of the content and method of Jesus' guidance. There was a rhythm of dealing with individuals, groups and crowds, saying and doing whatever would best reconcile them to their larger life with one another and in the Holy One.

There was one other dimension of this rhythm: solitude. Jesus' culminating preparation for his ministry was alone, in the wilderness, going through the dark, diverting, corrupting forces of evil, until they were faced down and their power shriveled. He emerged empowered, emboldened, with an indomitable sense of vocation.[9] After this time, he continued to go off alone to pray from time to time.

The records of Jesus' ministry marked the path of spiritual guidance taken throughout the Church's history. Through a great variety of forms, there have been these constants: a sense of serving and sharing with rather than "lording it over" another; a sense of confidence in human capacity and calling to be in contact with the Holy, and to mediate it to one another through word, sacrament, and deed; an integral relation of moral and spiritual development; a vision of bearing, struggling hope in the final reconciliation of all creation in its intimate Source; a willingness to work with all sorts and conditions of people, one to one, in groups, in crowds, near and far; a valuation of ritual/sacramental means of grace: bread and wine, water, hands, and words of reconciliation.

These "constants" for human guidance, I believe, are as much living waters for us today as two thousand years ago. Where they are lacking, people and societies suffer. Where they are present in intent, though, our wounded human nature leaves them spotty in realization, both in the guidance and in the response of the guided. G. K. Chesterton's old quip that the problem with Christianity is "that it never has been tried" is a half-truth that can be said of the followers of every profound tradition. Nevertheless, these constants are gifts stretching back through a long lineage, always waiting to be unwrapped and applied more responsively.

St. Paul

Paul of Tarsus, who had no human contact with Jesus but a profound inner one, is our other primary New Testament source for spiritual guidance.[10]

Paul took up the "constant" of spiritual guidance in his ministry, adapting them to the particular situations of the churches where he worked. Like Jesus he traveled frequently, setting up and visiting new centers of converts. He held a developmental view of human spirituality. He speaks of the *napioi,* the beginners who are ready to be fed only with milk, and the *teleoi,* the mature who can be fed solid food, those with spirit-filled knowledge (I Cor. 3:2; 2:13–n16; Eph. 4:13–15; Col. 1:10).

The *teleoi* have moved ever more decisively from the way of the "flesh," i.e., the way of enslavement to blind human destructive passions, to the way of the "spirit," where these passions have been transmuted into compassion, and law is transformed into an undergirding awareness of grace, of unmerited gift. *Teleoi* are hopeful for the full revelation of God, a hope that encourages patience in suffering. They are aware of being mystically "in Christ," a complementary, serving part of a corporate Body. Such are the fruits of those who have "died to sin" and "the old man," and live to God in the new humanity.

Paul bridged Jesus' way to the Gentile world, helping to shift the basis of relationship from physical Jewish descent to faith in Jesus as the Christ, and from synagogue and temple to Christian fellowships. Paul exhorted these struggling fellowships, lacking the common conditioning and guidance of Jewish tradition, to provide spiritual guidance and correction for one another, an emphasis passed down through the history of spiritual guidance as "mutual edification" and "fraternal correction."

Paul's apparent sense of the imminent end of history

and return of Christ in glory conditions his advice, leading to a very tenuous relation with social structures. In one sense this is the most obstructive advice for our time, with our desperate need for creative, historical stewardship of our social structures. If you are just waiting around for the end, you won't care very much about the reform of structures.

On the other hand, there is indirect value for us in this "end of time" eschatological framework. Though there is Jesus' warning that knowledge of death can lead you simply to "eat, drink, and be merry," and the social activists' warning that looking beyond this life can take you out of social struggle within it, there also is the opposite possibility: facing "life beyond" can give you perspective on this life. Instead of compulsively "storing up treasures where moth and rust corrupt," as though these preserved you from death, you can let these go (or never go after them), and share the wealth and stewardship of this mortal life.

Women as Spiritual Guides

Paul also leaves an ambivalent heritage for guidance in his view of women, reflecting too often the cultural attitudes of his time. His clarion call to equality in his declaration of there being neither "male nor female" in Christ, has been overshadowed in history by his call for women to keep silent in church, cover their heads as a sign of "second placeness" in creation, and be obedient to their husbands. This no doubt influenced the focus on men as primary spiritual guides in Christian history, and contributed to the later avoidance or persecution of women by men as temptresses and distractors.

Alongside this subordination, however, there rose from the early Church forward an increasing awareness of Mary as divine mother and guide, culminating in the recent Roman Catholic proclamation of her bodily assumption to heaven, together with theological speculation pointing to her as coredeemer with Christ.

There have been recorded Christian women spiritual guides from the early days of the Church onward. These included guides of men and mutual spiritual friendship with them (the most well known perhaps being the relationship of John of the Cross and Teresa of Avila).

There seems to be an unquenchable sexual equality and complementarity in spiritual wisdom that cannot be held down, even though oppressed. (This contrasts with the much more uniformly male dominance of speculative theology and doctrinal development.)[11]

Greek Contributions

Socrates used the Greek words for "healer of the soul" to represent his vision of guide (the same Greek syllables later recast to form "psychiatrist"). Perhaps his greatest contribution to contemporary guidance is his emphasis on free inquiry, a reverent, searching sense of life and of one's true place in it, as more important than mindless living and acting in the cultural womb. Here he is an oblique collaborator with the transcendent yet incarnate focus of Christian guidance.

His method of soul guidance involved reducing a person to perplexity and self-distrust, abandoning the security of the unexamined life. This process, as John McNeill has pointed out, is a counterpart to Judaeo-Christian "conviction of sin," pointing the way to virtue.[12]

Though his view of sin, as in most Greek thought, is much closer to *ignorance* than to the active human *hostility* toward God assumed in Judaeo-Christian thought,[13] his basic *method* brings the art of questioning another to great depth. We could benefit today from combining such an iconoclastic inquiry into personal assumptions with a framework of underlying shared faith. Such an approach could help save spiritual guidance from blind assumptions and too comfortable sentiment, while at the same time preserving an orientation to personal deepening in the truth as known in Christian tradition.

The Stoic philosopher Seneca expressed still-relevant, blunt opinion where he defended the office of "monitor" (a counselor who lays down precepts for inquirers) with the declaration, "amid the noise of city life we need a monitor to contradict the assumptions of worldlings" (Letter XCIV). He also asserts that God gives noble and upright counsel, and no man is good without this (Letter XII).

The Protestant Reformer Zwingli was sympathetic with the guidance of Seneca's letters. Other Christian spiritual leaders have been influenced by the many letters of "consolation" written by Greek philosophers.

Seneca and Pythagoras recommended a mental *examen* at the end of every day focused on virtues, a practice in modified form that later was recommended by various Christian spiritual leaders, one that many people practice with benefit today.[14]

Mutual Friendship

Perhaps the most important single contribution from this pre-Christian ancient European world comes from Cicero's dialogue *On Friendship*. Deep, loyal friendship rooted in love without corrupting expedient motives and its great potential for sustained human guidance is rare in our nomadic, restless, competitive culture. Cicero's work is one of particular relevance for us.

In terms of Christian guidance, it was rewritten by the great twelfth-century English Cistercian Abbot, Aelred of Rievaulx, and called *On Spiritual Friendship*, which holds closely to the form and much of the substance of its Roman inspirer.

Aelred believed that the love of friendship springs directly from God, coming closer to the love of the saints in heaven than most other loves. True friendship combines charity and good will, and is possible only between those who resist the sin and greed that would destroy it. It is "mutual harmony in affairs human and divine coupled with benevolence and charity." It is distinguished from carnal friendship that springs from mutual harmony in vice, and worldly friendship that is enkindled by the hope of gain.

Four qualities must be tested in a friend: loyalty, right intention, discretion, and patience. Aelred brilliantly elaborates each of these.

He quotes St. Ambrose's insights that friendships among the poor are generally more secure than those among the rich, since poverty takes away the hope of gain in such a way as not to decrease the love of friendship but rather to increase it. Ambrose also is quoted favorably in terms of correcting vice in a friend: "The wounds inflicted by a friend are more tolerable than the kisses of flatterers. Therefore correct the erring friend."[15]

Such intimate spiritual friendship in monastic settings rarely was advocated, given the dangers of factionalism, favoritism, and sexual expression. Experience with false, distorted friendships led monastic norms to stress an exclusive desire for God at the expense of loving friendship. But friendship had a certain flowering in the eleventh and twelfth centuries, especially through Anselm of Canterbury, Bernard of Clairvaux, and William of St. Thierry, along with Aelred. By the late Middle Ages and the Counter Reformation, however, friendships of any sort were banned from the cloister and the most ordinary of personal contacts were viewed with deep suspicion.[16]

This depersonalization was bolstered by an impersonal, abstract theology and moral legalism that was in power with Roman Catholics from the sixteenth century Council of Trent right up to the Second Vatican Council. Spiritual direction in this context often involved a "distancing" that was a far cry from Aelred's friendship. On the other hand, spiritual direction could involve a kind of compensatory and empowering intimacy, as the great sixteenth and seventeenth-century Roman Catholic schools of spirituality exemplify. Such direction seems especially important in an environment enforcing distance between people. It could be the only bridge of near intimacy with another in a person's life, along with the confessional.

Though today Roman Catholics have discarded this general distancing, there perhaps is a subtle positive lesson for us in understanding the importance of spiritual direction during such impersonal times. In nations where there is great totalitarian oppression, distancing and suspicion between people is enforced and friendship is more difficult and tense. The importance of the established secret intimacy of spiritual direction relationships in such oppressive climates could be particularly important for daily human sustenance and hope.

Married Friendship

The potential application of historic monastic spiritual friendship to *marriage* is an intriguing suggestion of Kenneth Russell.[17] In a time of frequently fragile, confused, and hedonistic relationships in marriage, as in other "friendships" today, this is worth exploring.

Russell notes that when the demands of marriage wear down the rough edges of egocentricity, a couple can evolve together in a friendship that grows more and more intense. He sees Aelred's view of friendship a helpful model here. Aelred understands true friendship as a mutual bond of love that does not seek personal advantage, but rather delights in the good of the other. Though charity goes out to all, this is a special bond. As Aelred puts it: "Only those do we call friends to whom we can fearlessly entrust our heart and all its secrets; those too, who in turn, are bound to us by the same law of faith and security."[18]

When friendship (marriage) is a rightly ordered relationship, i.e., a true sharing in the things that matter, it draws us out of ourselves toward the true good, toward God.[19] To Aelred, true friendship is a path of mutual equality and intimacy reaching toward God, and the unity it can create is a foretaste of the joys of heaven and even an image of the being of God.

Aelred's work is the more precious for us today, given the dearth of spiritual writing that presents a model for marriage integrating the classical summons to detached attentiveness to God with a couple's mutual attachment and sexual bond. The married person, as Russell puts it, "knows that s/he too is called to detachment from self and world—

yet knows that his/her path is different and goes through the
sacrament of marriage, a sign and cause of grace, to its very
Source."

I would add that the "detachment" Russell speaks of
does and should not exclude active stewardship for the world
and its needs. But this is more likely to be possible if a couple's energy is relatively detached from tight, protected, sustained, exhausting projects of insulated self-gratification, as
well as detached from identification with "the world" where
it fosters idolatry and injustice.

Such detachment in family life can aid its potential as a
training ground, a seedbed for the larger community's well-
being, and reduce its influence as a diverting barrier to that
larger good. This positive potential is not easy in a compulsively attached culture and wounded human condition. It
needs support, wherever it can be found, especially from the
subculture of the Church, and from a personal rhythm of life
that fosters it (a rhythm I will amplify in the next chapter).

Though marriage is an important and natural framework for spiritual friendship, there are realistic limitations.
Many roles and expectations are involved, and these lurk in
the background of more intimate moments. The children are
sick, budgets have to be agreed upon, Aunt Jane is coming
for a visit, the dog has made a mess, there are disturbing
things going on at work and we want to talk about them, we
argue over what to cook and who is to cook, and on and on.
Such situations, especially during child-raising years, raise a
whirl of mutual expectations that can crowd and distract the
"airwaves" between husband and wife, leaving little clear,
direct time for spiritual friendship.

In trying with a friend recently to name married cou-
ples who have had a deep spiritual friendship, we had a very
hard time (and those we did name usually had no children).
Not only is the marital relationship complicated by such
things as those just mentioned, but the partners' spiritual
growth often diverges: they move at different paces and in
different (though hopefully complementary) directions.

This means that it may well be best for the individual
partners not to expect their mates to be sufficient spiritual

friends, at least not all the time. Having someone outside the marriage, where spiritual development can be focused upon in a relatively "clean" relationship, undiverted by other dimensions of the relationship, may well be called for and be of benefit to the marriage itself (just as having a "clean" relationship with an outside therapist can be helpful at times).[20]

Such spiritual friendships outside of marriage are frequent in Christian history. It is no accident that the history of spirituality in all developed religious traditions includes a valuation of *celibacy*. In traditional Hindu culture, for example, the "householder" stage of life has been seen as bound by particular requirements of family, job, and community. The fullest opportunities for spiritual development are seen coming after children are grown, when an often celibate spiritual quest is taken up. There are some parallels in Christian tradition.

The other celibate path is vowed usually from youth. The particular freedoms of this state allow for a particularly intense experimental spiritual quest. It is not necessary for us to consider that a celibate state denigrates the married way as invalid (such denigration was condemned formally early in Church history). In fact, Linda Sabbath asserts that marriage has been seen as a sacrament only in those Christian traditions that respect celibacy. They are complementary spiritual states supporting each other.[21]

It is often to such celibates that married people have turned for spiritual counsel historically. Most of the publicly recognized great spiritual directors in Christian tradition have been celibate. In a historical time when there seems increasingly little respect or understanding for this state, it is important to raise it up as an option for living that has enormous cross-cultural historical weight.

Neither marriage *nor* celibacy is "natural," since both are vowed states of intentional fidelity that require transmutation of wandering erotic impulses. Both can be training grounds for letting go our slavery to those surface impulses that can hide, distract, and dissipate our responsive awareness to that deeper Ocean of loving truth where alone, as Augustine knew, we find our rest.

Genital sexual expression can serve as a bridge to that Ocean, too, within the disciplined confines of a loving relationship and covenant. Such a sacred intent for sexuality perhaps is brought to its historical height in Buddhist Tantric tradition where a male/female physical relationship is helped directly to serve a transcendent awareness.[22]

Let us turn now to some of the great celibate spiritual directors of Christian history, from whose awareness living waters still flow for us.

Desert Springs

I remember once driving several Europeans across the United States from the East Coast to the West. They were very chatty along the way, taking in the environment with unimpressed glances—until we came to the desert in the Southwest. Suddenly they became very silent. There was something unspeakably awesome about it. Europe contained no such open spaces, nor the Eastern United States. Its great silence could be met only with inner silence.

Words seem petty and narrow in such vastness. Each living thing takes on special preciousness amidst the paucity of life, standing out the more starkly in the sharp, clear sunlight. Each shattering call of a passing bird seems but to open the silence more deeply, as a rock thrown in the water probes its depths.

Such space invites us to attend the underlying fundamentals of life. The complex restless surface is stripped bare by the sweeping, gritty wind. You are exposed, vulnerable to the way reality is within and without; the still, small voice is not drowned out; the mysterious, obscure Heart of it all beats a soundless beat that pulses nakedly through everything, coaxing us to ever deeper stripping, confidence, participation.

By the end of the third century, and explosively in the fourth and fifth, Christians streamed to the deserts of Egypt, Palestine, and Syria. At its height, as many as twenty thousand people lived in the desert alone or in monastic groups, and countless others visited them for counsel.

The impelling forces were not so different from those that press people in our time to seek the desert or country, and set up some "counter-culture" that witnesses to the radical possibilities of human confrontation with reality through poverty and solitude.

Scripture encouraged the purgative value of such living beyond the force of prevailing social structure: the Hebraic wilderness experience, and those of John the Baptist, Jesus, and Paul. Jesus encouraged surrender of the worldly self and its ambition, status, complacency, and material wealth, seeking instead the Kingdom of God. Paul exhorted the Thessalonians to pray without ceasing (I Thess. 5:17).

Such advice became increasingly difficult to take seriously within the bounds of the Church, with its indiscriminate growth after "establishment" under the Emperor Constantine. The Church increasingly became domesticated, an external form containing everyone. The yearning for discovery of its full heart seemed to call people elsewhere, especially to the desert.

It is in the desert that spiritual direction was born as a full-fledged charism, a gift of especially profound personal experience and insight.

In the early Church before its establishment, individuals were formed and guided by participation in the strict life of the community. Such instruction as was needed was given first by bishops and presbyters, and then, through informal admonitions, by one's parents, spouse, friends, and fellow Christians.[23]

Once establishment of the Church took hold, the Church community became mixed with many formal, expedient Christians, and the forces of the secular Roman culture entered the Church's life in ways that watered down its intensity. Physical martyrdom no longer was called for. Spiritual martyrdom could replace it, but not normally in the tame town churches.

How could you "lose your life," really purify yourself, in such a situation? Desert solitude seemed to promise this: it gave fresh opportunity for radical commitment, for martyrdom of false self, and for spiritual combat. It brought to bear an "experimental" spiritual life more fully than it had been known in Christian practice (and perhaps as fully as it ever has been known since).

This new intensity had no community womb and lineage of living spiritual masters to hold it up in its inception. The first "abbas" (fathers) of the desert had to be courageous, tough, charismatic pioneers of the Spirit, breaking ground for others.

Though St. Antony of Egypt in the fourth century was not the first of these, he was one of the early pioneers, and one we know most about.[24] After he had spent many years in prayer, fasting, simple labor and solitude, other desert seekers demanded that he come out from his walled-in cell in an abandoned fort and guide them.

> When he emerged from the fort, his soul was pure: neither contracted by grief, dissipated by pleasure, nor pervaded by jollity or dejection. He was completely under control, guided by reason. . . . He performed healings, exorcism, comforting, reconciling. . . . To all he was a father and guide.[25]

There we see the birth of the Desert Father, and the search for him by those needing discernment in the midst of the arduous, dangerous, promising, tempting life of desert spiritual combat. Those who followed Antony and others like him formed an organic oral tradition of spiritual guidance.

The "spiritual father" (there are four recorded "spiritual mothers" as well) replaced the bishop and presbyter as representative of Christ, but charismatically, not hierarchically. His guidance was so personal that it often involved the disciple's living in the same cell, and learning from the abba's whole way of being, not just from his words.

Their lives reflect austerities that most today would consider unnecessary aberrations, but through their experience often came a profound intuitive awareness of reality, a firsthand awareness that informed the methods and substance of their guidance.[26]

Listen, for example, to the alleged questions and comments given by Antony to some visiting philosophers:

> Which is first, mind or letters? And which is the cause of which? . . . The mind is first, the inventor of letters; one who has a sound mind has no need of letters.

Abba Theodore, an apparent master of scriptural interpretation, reinforced this:

> One who has a pure heart, and as a result a clear mind, has all that is required for understanding the mysteries of scripture. . . . Those with active faith have no need of verbal arguments. It is not word craft which we have, but faith through love that works for Christ.

Abba Moses adds, "Your cell will teach you all things."[27]

Though these comments can be taken as anti-intellectual (just as Zen stories can be), I think instead they simply try to assert the primacy of firsthand spiritual awareness and humble, purifying loving in the spiritual life, for which no intellectual mastery can substitute. Many of the abbas and monks were simple Coptic Christians with little learning. However, the intellectual mastery of such abbas as Evagrius Ponticus,[28] together with the appeal of the abbas' sayings to many early intellectuals of the Church (epitomized in the adulation of Athanasius for Antony), points to the consonance of their ways with intellectual effort.

Antony provides extensive examples of other kinds of advice given by the abbas in various form that still can speak to us today (though we might need to shift the vocabulary a bit):

> Expect to die each day; then you will be poor, forgiving, sinless.

> Write down actions and impulses of your soul as though you were to report them to another.

> Flee conceit.

Pray continually. [The repetitive "Jesus Prayer" came to full flower in the desert.]

When you pray for healing, always give thanks, not boasting when heard, or complaining when not.

When a phantom appears [during meditation], be fearless, and ask "Who are you and from where do you come?" If the vision is good, you will be reassured. If not, your steadfast calm mind will weaken it.

If you keep thoughts on things of the Lord and let your soul rejoice in hope, you will see the trumperies of demons as so much smoke . . . demons are impotent to do anything except threaten.

Keep from a full stomach.

Sing psalms before sleeping and after.

Hark back to the deeds of saints.

Don't judge others, but have sympathy and bear one another's burdens.

If your soul is pure and in a natural state (i.e., as it came into being), it becomes clearsighted.

[We need to discern] the two sources of fear: cravenness of soul (which is turbulent), and awareness of the presence of higher beings. [This latter] vision is quiet, gentle, giving instant joy, gladness, courage.[29]

Though the abba's weight on *obedience* to himself by the disciple is beyond what most democratically conditioned people would accept, there is a dimension of value in voluntary temporary submission to a trusted, highly experienced guide that is corroborated in Eastern as well as later Western experience, a value that is neglected and misunderstood today.

The intent of the true abba is not blind enslavement, but a submission to the truth; a "sense of the truth of meeting the infinitely real in the center of one's nothingness/creative possibility."[30] The abba provided a kind of ego shock treatment to help the disciple slowly mutate from his false, illusory self, from belief in pretentious, idolatrous, protected self-image, into a larger, more free and "humbly confident" trust and realization.

This involved not just advice, but insistence that the disciple learn for himself, by staying in the "fiery furnace and pillar of cloud" of his cell (Antony), and in faith and prayer facing through the raw truth firsthand. Obedience and trust with a caring, experienced abba could help you "face through" all the way.[31]

A famous example is the story of the monk who was told to plant a dry stick in the sand and to water it daily.

> So distant was the spring from his cell that he had to leave in the evening to fetch the water and he only returned in the following morning. For three years he patiently fulfilled his abba's command. At the end of this period, the stick suddenly put forth leaves and bore fruit. The abba picked the fruit, took it to the church, and invited the monks to eat, saying, "Come and taste the fruit of obedience."[32]

Obedience implies a willingness to be a voluntary adult son or daughter in the intuition that such a relationship will help us relinquish those desires and ways that keep us ourselves from being mature spiritual fathers and mothers. Such an intuition is alien in a culture that increasingly appears to believe only in brothers and sisters. However, I sense that the loss of strong "parental" relationships often leaves us as childish brothers and sisters, with little sense of responsibility for "fathering and mothering" the world, only playing in it. Though we can remain dependent and never grow up with a parental guide, if the guide is true, he or she will help you take his or her place.

Perhaps today we need a fresh blending of parent and sibling relationships, and not fall into the trap of throwing out either inappropriately. If true "parents" are thrown out, human need for them invites totalitarian regimes and sects to fill the gap. If sibling equality is thrown out, we invite revolt and suppression of mutuality. The historical desert experience helps us remember such realities.

Inheritance of the Desert

Thousands of people sought out these abbas during their ascendency in the fourth and fifth centuries, not only permanent desert monks, but lay people from towns and villages throughout the Roman Empire. Each sought a unique "saving word" for himself. They were aware, as Merton points out, that "books, lectures, and written instructions of past masters are no substitute for direct contact with a living teacher, who knows your inmost thoughts."[33] The power of such "transparency of soul" that could emerge from the abba's solitary "spiritual combat" cultivated a still-living tradition of discernment of spirits, to which I will return shortly.

The desert tradition was continued in a more domesticated, structured way through both Eastern and Western Church monastic communities. The "abba" became the "abbot" or "abbess," drawing into himself or herself both the discernment function of the Desert Father/Mother and the organizational authority of a ruler.[34]

At the same time, the tradition of solitary charismatic living was maintained spottily throughout the Church's history. Its last great exemplars were the Russian *poustinikki* of the nineteenth and early twentieth centuries. Some are reputed still to be living in the forests of the Soviet Union.

These were drawn from all walks of life to poverty and solitude on behalf of others. They normally would move to a hut, a *poustinia* (desert) away from the village or city. Here he or she would live in solitude, but not isolation. The Russian word for solitude means "being with everybody." The *poustinik* lived in solitude, but with the people in intercessory prayer, often prayer without ceasing (the Jesus Prayer), counsel and service. By tradition, the latch was always off the door; the *poustinik's* priority at anytime was his neighbor's need (which might stretch beyond prayer and counsel to physical labor, as at harvest time). At times he or she would be expected to come out with a public "word from the Lord" for everyone.[35]

I always marvel at this *poustinik* tradition. It put together what the West has tended to divide or overinstitutionalize: a charismatic gift of spiritual counsel, solitude, and availability. Perhaps the closest Western parallel is the medieval English anchorite and anchoress, attached to village churches, living in contemplative solitude for life, yet usually available for counsel.

I believe this Russian tradition has important potential for the contemporary service of the Church to the community, a service different than that of the pastoral counselor, yet not devoid of contemporary psychological insight. Two different existing probes I know of that move in this direction include a woman Roman Catholic hermit in Appalachia, whose cottage is available for *poustinia* and counsel, and who is available for neighbors in need, as a nearby dying farmer's wife. She supports her simple life by coming out of the hermitage occasionally and working as a waitress.

The second probe is being made by two Roman Catholic Sisters in a house next door to a parish church in Michigan. They work in a very limited way in the parish's adult education program. Primarily, though, they live together for prayer, available for counsel and prayer with any who come. They function as a contemplative balance for the activist parish, a crucial complementarity I will return to in the next chapter.

Many other similar probes are being made, or are in the making—an instinctual attempt to expose the desert's permanent truth for our time.

Discernment of Spirits

The desert abbas and their successors, as we have seen, sought to "see through" to what a person needed for his or her spiritual nurture. This tradition, as applied to diagnosis of interior mental movements, came to be called "discernment (*diakrisis*) of spirits."

Contemporary psychological understanding adds greatly to our diagnostic and prescriptive knowledge. But its de facto standard severance from any assumptions concerning human connectedness to purpose in life beyond that defined by a frequently circular view of individual and societal conditioning and needs satisfaction leaves a gap for those whose trust and experience of reality involves that connectedness. From Christian tradition, discernment of spirits can contribute to filling this gap.

Classical Christian discernment involves certain underlying assumptions: human life is not accidental; it is a gift from a mysterious, loving Source. The purpose of this gift is twofold: an *end in itself,* loving/enjoying/creating, reflecting the nature of our Source: and a *directed* loving/bearing/creating, aimed at unfolding that essential lovingness wherever it is closed off in a wounded, partially blind, and hostile nature.

Hidden within and around us are the subtle energies of the loving Source, welling up in different, often surprising ways and times to guide us: as still small voice, as cataclysmic assurance, or as reasoned inference from the consolations and desolations of our lives. All this is seen within the general framework of scripture and tradition: the handed down collective experience of the Church.

These energies form good movements that do not compel us, but invite us. There is a dimension of cooperation required, but the intertwining of the gifted movement and free response can be so subtle as to call for a single word, like "attentiveness," or "allowing," to account for their integral unfolding.

Given our wounded creation, there are "closed spirits" within and around us that, though ultimately from the same loving Source, in Christian thinking have fallen from it, and now compete with the "opening" spirits. Today most Western people would see these closed-off spirits as competing ego distortions of reality (in individual or social structural form). Classical discernment tradition would include another source: alien, hostile spirits afloat in the world that are more than ego projections, and which work primarily through connivance with our ego distortions (such as forms of greed and distrust).

There is an elaborate history of this discernment process, stretching from many scriptural sources through the patristic, medieval, and modern periods of Church history.[36] A recurring theme is the focus on fruits of an inner movement. If it is good, the inner response and outer results will be good (though not necessarily painless)! St. Paul's list of the Spirit's fruits (Gal. 5:22f.) is central to the tradition. Authentic gifts for Paul are marked by light, peace, charity, and humility that spread to the community.

Elsewhere Paul sets up the standard of continuity with past normative experiences of the Church: authentic revelation harmonizes with or deepens a revelation already confided. Such a standard has helped guard a sense of human unity in knowledge, a standard that is valuable in countering over-subjective illuminations that leave people more vulnerable to Jonestowns and other self-styled religious cults. Of course, if "revelation already confided" is interpreted too narrowly, as it frequently has been, the opposite danger of enforced, sterile conformity is at hand. The First Epistle of John helps to counter this danger in its assertion that anointing of the Spirit gives certitude and light independent of any human teachings.[37]

Spiritual discernment took a new step in the sixteenth century with Ignatius of Loyola. He provided a practical method and interpretation that shifted the weight of discernment tradition from our attitudes, virtues, sins, and general state of life, to our *actions:* What we are called to *do,* not only be, that will orient our lives in concrete situations "to the glory and praise of God."

A highlight of Ignatius's many still viable contributions is his sense of the three good times for vocational decision-making:

1. When our will is moved to a point where no hesitation is possible.

2. When we find light and information through reflection on our experiences of desolation (darkness, turmoil, sloth, tepidness, etc.) and consolation (movements tending toward faith, hope, love, peace, etc.).

3. In a period of calm, when the soul is not agitated by diverse spirits and exercises its natural faculties freely and tranquilly.

Ignatius suggests ways of enhancing the validity of this third more rational decision-making process, e.g., by deciding as if you were at the moment of death, or by picturing an unknown person you would like to see practice perfection— what should he decide?[38]

The discernment and other spiritual practices of Ignatius were spread widely in the Roman Catholic world after his death. In many religious communities, they provided the basic form of personal spiritual practice. Since the Second Vatican Council they have undergone a renaissance of interest and modification. I doubt that any other single approach to spiritual direction has had so much written about it, in relation to countless contemporary situations, problems, needs, and psychological processes. In this sense, it is the most "tested" and ongoing experimental approach to Christian spiritual direction.[39]

However, this does not mean that it is the *only* possible approach. I do not think that it always suffices for a person attuned to a more simple and apophatic path, though it may aid that path to remain rooted in the concrete Christian mysteries. Particularly when interpreted through the many screens of Ignatius's successors, there frequently is an analytical, conceptual weight that simply has a very different flavor than the more direct, intuitive, charismatic, "shocking" style preserved from the desert, for example, in Eastern Orthodox writers.[40]

Perhaps we in the post-medieval West come closest to this simpler discernment style through the Society of Friends (Quakers). There is a disarming simplicity in the corporate and individual discernment practices of this seventeenth-century English movement. They reflect the gentle, stable domesticity of the best English spirituality, together with a subtle attunement to "the Light within," with much mutual edification from the movements of this Light arising in shared silence.[41]

Quakers offer us today an integral concern for contemplative intuition and socially valuable fruit that bridges the more powerfully contemplative Eastern Church and the more rational or affective and active Western. I fear that Quaker lineage is so "loose" and "thin" in many places today, though, reinforced by its rejection of such stabilizing and focused kataphatic elements as sacraments (Baptism, Communion, etc.) that it is in increasing danger of losing its depth to a more shallow eclecticism, a danger every subculture faces in our homogenizing, cafeteria culture.

Community Guidance

The mutual edification of Quakers developed on top of a long history of emphasis on the value of the *gathered community* as a source of spiritual guidance. The intensity of the pre-Constantinian Church's mutual edification was replaced by monastic communities of lay people. This life was viewed not so much as a new way, but in fact as continuous with the old way of the apostles, persevering together in prayer, community of goods, and breaking of bread (Acts 2:42), rejecting as inadequate the real novelty of the Constantinian established Church.[42]

There are lessons for us today from this long, complex communal history.

Commitment to a "Rule," a "way" of life in community can plow the ground of our souls over time to a pliable readiness for the growth of spiritual sight and fruit. Rules have varied, but there are some frequent constants.[43] These include special times of prayer alone and prayer together, labor for the maintenance of the community, undiscriminating charity toward those outside, poverty of personal possessions, submission to the decision-making process and larger good of the community.

The act of personal voluntary commitment to such a way involves an ego relativization that in itself can be a step toward the larger Reality of our lives. The rhythm and content of the Rule taken on carries its own implicit guidance day by day. Its stable repetitiveness can help us resist greedy grasping and flighty search for the Truth: we can relax a bit and let it unfold in the process of a lifetime, prodded by the steady plow of the Rule.

Such a stable, communal way, especially when respect has been maintained for individual differences and needs within the larger whole, presents an attractive picture in the midst of current Western culture. There was a time when the whole community in the West participated in certain rhythms of life, marked by Jewish or Christian liturgical calendars, concerns, penitence, mutual edification, and celebration.

These "larger" rhythms today are dictated more and more by commercial, educational and expedient political calendars and concerns, whose guidance often reverses the conditioning of religious communities: divesting of goods is replaced by stimulus for accumulation; education toward simple presence is replaced by education for complex ambition; time alone for being in deeper touch with underlying loving Truth is filled instead with lonely anxiety and surface diversion; time together for communal forgiveness, affirmation, mutual edification, and celebration of transcendent rootedness is replaced by expedient business, by entertainment, and by power plotting.

Communities living by religious Rule provide individuals with an alternative "structural guidance." They also are a visible witness and symbol in the society for another possibility than its dominant norms.

These community covenants have been developed for both celibate and family communities. History witnesses to the greater difficulty of the latter, given the complications of nuclear family subcommunities within these larger communes. These family communities seem to have endured best as loose congregations, though at the price of watering down the covenant sometimes, as in modern congregations/parishes, to a point where there is little operational guidance given by (or accepted from) the covenant. Nuclear families themselves, of course, often develop their own informal religious covenants within these larger bodies.

There also are negative learnings about the guidance of a religious, covenanted community. *It can be oppressive:* Individual uniqueness and need can be crushed; obedience can become an excuse for exploitative tyranny; adaptive creativity can be replaced by rigid, sterile conformity.

It can be too secure: The pioneering spirit of the desert abba is lost; the Rule substitutes for personal responsibility for your own soul; dull complacency (rather than attentive waiting) sets in. This particularly became a problem in the Middle Ages when formal religious community life was raised to a "state" of sufficient being, losing much of its earlier emphasis as a path, a means to deeper communion with the True One.[44] Such a "state" contributed (or reflected) a degree of attempted institutionalization and domestication of the Holy Spirit.

It can be false: Such historical developments point to how a covenant can guide persons to trust themselves in obedience to it as a magical and superior way of salvation, a security electric blanket that we can plug in and it will "make everything all right." No room is left for surprise, for individual discernment; the free Spirit of truth is smothered to death.

On balance, though, I believe we have more to learn than to fear concerning the positive guidance such covenant communities can provide us today. The more individualistic and erratic the conditions of our lives, the harder these communities can be to live within, yet that very conditioning can lead us the more to yearn for them.

They can save us, in trying to satisfy this yearning, from capitulation to the proferred "ordering" of life by totalitarian political figures. They can be bastions of small groups, subcultural voluntary ordered living, perhaps the only viable arenas for approximating full implementation of both Marxist and Christian ideals.[45]

For all their human weaknesses, such communities can be seedbeds that nourish not only their members for stabilized service to the larger society, but also nourish that larger circle of people who retreat with them temporarily, tasting the guidance of the community's way, providing new strength and perspective for both personal life and larger caring; such "temporaries" also might take with them a mod-

ified "Rule" for their lives, for which there are many historical precedents.

Individual Guidance

The practice of one-to-one guidance within the community's life was known from the earliest days, and a right and
responsibility often written into the Rules themselves. It
complemented various forms of group direction. In the "pre-
desert" Churches, and later in Protestant communities, this
one-to-one guidance apparently was more an informal, occasional meeting on a needs basis. In the desert, and in monastic communities, this counsel often takes on a more serious,
regular character, an opportunity to pour out your soul in
confession and description of inner movements, aimed at
seeing and relieving obstacles to progress toward whole-
ness/holiness.[46]

The context of this sustained personal guidance is an integral system of moral and spiritual assumptions, to which
both director and directee are committed as a basis for living
into the Truth. Their work together is but one part of a reinforcing way of life that is providing guidance all the time.
The up-front focus is the person's gradual transfiguration
into communion with the deepest Wellspring, and the overflow into spontaneous and vocational charity. This focus
touches every dimension of a person's life, so nothing traditionally is withheld from the director's sight.

Confession often was included (a function sometimes
separated from that of spiritual direction); the aim of this
confession, when authentic, was acceptance of accountability
for one's own life and a desire to let go whatever comes between one and the loving reality of God, neighbor and true
self. Its hoped-for result was recovery, healing, purification,
peace, a capacity for freshly innocent presence.

This relationship has obvious parallels with the openness of a modern therapeutic relationship. It differs from
modern therapy, though, in its integral context of values and
community life, and within this context, in the director's
knowledge of the person with great daily intimacy, often

over a lifetime.[47] This provides opportunity for dealing ho-
listically with the person, and at the best allows for the ever
more subtle process of deep oral transmission of the heart of
Christian realization of the mystery, giftedness, meaningful
agony, and end of life.

The spiritual guide could approach this transmission
with great versatility. Basil illustrates this when he says,
"Know that humility, authority, rebuke, exhortation, compassion, freedom of speech, kindness, severity, in a word everything has its own time."[48]

Prayer, of course, and exhortation to prayer are a standard dimension of this process. Being a long-term involvement, there often is a sense of rough stages of prayer and the
interior life emerging from the experience of the guide, most
frequently spoken of in terms of purgation, illumination,
and union (paralleling scriptural references to repentance,
sanctification, and union), each with nuances and special
needs that an advanced guide recognizes.[49]

The literature indicates an awareness of both unconscious and conscious motives long before Freud. Cassian, for
example, in the fifth century looked to dream imagery and
desires for evidence of unconscious maladies of the soul. But
the aim was not only their relief, but replacement by virtuous attitudes and deeds.

In unskilled hands this guidance process could turn into
moralism, legalism, and tyranny of soul, with inadequate diagnosis and prescription. In the hands of a true master, this
process could provide liberation and preparation of great human hearts and societal/spiritual leaders.[50]

Such recorded masters always seem to have been rare,
but their wisdom lives for our day in many ways. After all, if
someone has intuited and appropriated the inner truth of existence, it is the same truth for all and for all time, though its
particular form, expression, and fullness will vary with personality and circumstances, and accordingly always will re-
tain some inadequacy for us.

I have spoken of the Desert Fathers. Following them
and those closely related to these abbas in time (e.g., Basil,
Origen, Clement, Jerome, Cassian, and Benedict of Nursia)

there is a lineage that reaches high points (by inference from their writings more than we can be sure of in their practice) in such individuals as Maximus the Confessor, Dorotheus of Gaza, John Climacus,[51] Pseudo-Dionysius, Diadochus of Photike, St. Simeon the New Theologian, and Gregory of Sinai in the East; in the West Augustine, Gregory the Great, Bernard of Clairvaux, William of St. Thierry, Aelred of Rievaulx, Hugh and Richard of St. Victor, Francis of Assisi, Angela of Foligno, Catherine of Siena, and the thirteenth through the fifteenth century German and English mystics.

We can be a little more sure of the personal gifts of direction beginning in the sixteenth century with Teresa of Avila, John of the Cross, Ignatius Loyola, and perhaps Martin Luther. In the seventeenth and eighteenth centuries Francis de Sales and Augustine Baker seem to stand out. Examples of others whose writings indicate they may have been worthy guides include Nicholas Farrar, George Herbert, Jeremy Taylor, William Law, and Richard Baxter in England; Bérulle, Jane Frances de Chantal, S. J. Olin, Fénelon, and Vincent de Paul in France; and in Germany Jakob Spener and Johann Arndt. More recently, there are such persons as Cardinal Henry Newman, Seraphim of Sarov, and Theophan the Recluse, among many others.

Penetrating writers, and personally illumined people, are not necessarily able to transfer these gifts into personal spiritual guidance for others, so there is a certain amount of guesswork involved in this list, and it is a very incomplete and merely suggestive one. Nonetheless, the written words of such people preserve selected wisdom that still can feed us. Indeed, given the predominance of group rather than one-to-one spiritual direction in the history of the Church, especially before the Renaissance, their writings can be seen as one form of group direction.[52]

Baron Friedrich Von Hügel in the early twentieth century deserves singling out for special mention. His value, beyond his penetrating writings and gift for personal direction, includes his lay status, a sign of encouragement for laity today, who need to reclaim the early Church and Protestant impetus toward gifted lay spiritual companions. Most of the other names mentioned since the "desert" days are founders or members of religious communities, most of them clergy.

The dominance of men is another obvious reality. My suspicion is that there have been many more great women spiritual guides than the record shows, but who have remained in obscurity in the normative dominance of men in the positions of visible leadership. Hopefully, this "negative learning" from Church history will be corrected in our time. My own experience points to more potentially gifted women than men as spiritual companions.

The paucity of famous Protestant directors I think refers not to the lack of Protestant spiritual depth but to their focus on the priesthood of all believers, involving countless historically anonymous persons in mutual and informal guidance. Also, until very recently, there was little concern with long-term, one-to-one guidance with a single guide. A mainstay of Protestant guidance has been preaching and personal work with scripture and prayer. For reasons I have described in the last chapter, and will discuss in Chapter Four, there is growing interest among Protestants today in sustained one-to-one and small group guidance.

Conclusion

I have held up certain key contributions of Christian tradition that I think have particular value for spiritual guidance today. There are many others, particularly concerning *methods* of ascetical discipline, such as prayer, fasting, use of the arts, sacraments, and pilgrimage. In one sense everything in the Church that has ever been written, artistically expressed, and done can be seen in the light of its potential for spiritual guidance today (negatively or positively!). In Chapter Four I will say more about this "spread" of approaches, in terms of their availability for us in our time.

The stream of living water running by us now carries with it these sparkling gems of the past, but the nature of re-

demptive history purges much along the way, so that much
rightfully can be left behind; the moment calls us to fresh responsiveness.

One fantasy that keeps me from freezing any gem of the
past into nostalgic sufficiency for our time is this: I imagine
that a great spiritual guide from the past still is living, and
has continued to evolve his or her understanding and communion with the "Real" in our midst, in the context of each
passing generation and culture of the world. With that vastly
extended experience, what would that guide say about his
original legacy to us? He or she may still see a core of truth,
but he or she probably would find it unbelievable that we
would freeze what was written as ultimate knowledge. After
all, only physical death stopped what we saw as a dynamical-
ly evolving awareness in a given person. There was no real
"finishedness" to his sight—only a responsiveness in the limited time given.

We are one inclusive river together, but alone we belong
to a never-definitive generation, a bucket of water passing
by. In Christian faith, though, the Holy One is an undercurrent running throughout, welling up in us as the particular
love called for in the fullness of our gifted moment, our
kairos. This love is connected with all other loves, which are
transformed and reconciled slowly together, in the agony
and glory of the Holy One's loving exposed on the cross.

The holy undercurrent embracing all mysteriously carries us Home, through and beyond history. Spiritual guidance in its many groping ways, now and in the past, exists to
help us see, trust, and allow this hidden force in and around
us, and not in fear or pretense mistake some back eddy for it.

3. The Eternal Rhythm

Not long ago the religion instructor at a Christian high school decided to introduce silent meditation into one of his classes. He gave the students instructions simply to "be" during the silence: to be relaxed and awake, open to life as it is, with nothing to do but appreciate whatever comes. Week by week he slowly increased the amount of time to a maximum of ten minutes.

The student response was very revealing. One boy summarized a general feeling of the class: "It is the only time in my day when I am not expected to achieve something." The response of several irate parents was equally revealing: "It isn't Christian," said one. "I'm not paying all that tuition for my child to sit there and do nothing," proclaimed another.

How is it that ten minutes of silence can be so special and so threatening?

An answer to that question hopefully will lead us to appreciate a guiding rhythm in life that is essential for individual and societal well-being, and crucial for spiritual awareness. Spiritual guidance, as we shall see, can be an avenue for encouraging life to be lived out of this background rhythm ever more integrally.

The rhythm has countless names and is as old as creation.

In physical nature we see it in the ebb and flow of the tide, the contraction and expansion of our muscles, day and night, rest and activity of all kinds; we also see it in the shift from the unique beat of two cells in our hearts to their unison beat when they touch.

In human society the rhythm flows between collective work and festivity, hierarchy and equality, public roles and general crowds, diversity and unity, a collective sense of eternity and history.

With individuals the rhythm pulses between effort and relaxation, analysis and intuition, animus and anima, sexuality and androgyny, engagement and withdrawal, health and sickness, anticipation and presence, thrust and balance, activity and receptivity, manipulation and appreciation, doing and being, problem and mystery, action and contemplation.

These rhythms are buried deeply in us. In traditional societies they have been enshrined in custom and happen largely as a matter of course, not conscious choice.

In complex modern societies the power of custom, and its unconscious wisdom as well as inadequacy, increasingly is lost or tenuously held.

In its place is individual choice and a new innocent: born out of the womb of custom, ignorant of the treasures of human experience it upheld, now groping, grasping for a new way, a self-made way, with alternating arrogance and despair, and as little reference to history and respect for nature and the transcendent as possible.

Part of the "light" side of the Western 1970's was its pause in this headlong leap in order to look again at our connectedness with history, nature, and the transcendent, and see if we have thrown out some gold with the fool's gold, and perhaps with Esau have sold our birthright to this connectedness for a mess of ephemeral pottage.

On the other side of the 1970's was the exhaustion of social courage, the trivialization and conceit of concerns, and simplistic nostalgia for the secure past.

These sides of the 1970's are connected. If the ominous side is to become light in this decade of the 1980's, that positive "pause" must turn itself into fresh understanding of our situation and guidelines for our lives, lest we succumb to the ugly beast of dead-ended frustration, with its violence and lurking despair.

This rhythm is one for which the Church is peculiarly accountable. Indeed, along with other religious bodies it is the only institution in the society that can be expected both to understand it adequately and to provide leadership for its implementation. One group of behavioral scientists, as we shall see, goes so far as to say that assistance in the management of this rhythm is the Church's primary task in the society, and if it fails, the whole society, including those who have nothing to do with the Church directly, suffers greater division, sickness, illusion, and injustice.

To help us understand this rhythm and its relation to spiritual guidance, we will step back into Western religious history and its Near Eastern roots once again. Then we will return to the present and look at the rhythm as it is seen by an anthropologist and a group of behavioral scientists. Finally, we will look at the particular role personal spiritual guidance can play in its furtherance.

The Rhythm of Sabbath and Service

Last year I was privileged to spend most of a Sabbath day with a Hasidic rabbi in Philadelphia whom I greatly respect, Zalman Schachter. He had not invited me up from Washington just anytime, but specifically for "Shabbos" (Sabbath),[1] that day of days for the Jewish community, yet paradoxically, beyond its ethnic identity, the day when all people are meant to be together because it is a day of unity.

With a flurry of activity all necessary work was brought to a close by sundown on Friday (the beginning of Shabbat), work not to be resumed again until the sun sets on Saturday. The "Sabbath Queen," a traditional personification of the day, was welcomed by the small group of students present, with *yarmulkes* (skull caps always used during prayer as a sign of humility), special prayer, song, and with musical instruments distributed to everyone who wished to play them. Everyone is invited to participate, even the angels.

For the evening service the small group of us walked to the home of another rabbi, Arthur Green.[2] With babes in arms, children, and all generations beyond, the traditional greeting of "Shabbat Shalom" was exchanged. All then shared together in the read prayer service, which connects the redeeming ways of the Holy One in the past, present, and future.

We returned to Zalman's house for the traditional Shabbos meal, prepared before sunset. Hands were ritually cleansed for the meal. Zalman's wife was away, so another woman present lighted the traditional candles. A special blessing, the ancient kiddush, was proclaimed over wine and "challah" bread, the probable precedent for the Christian Eucharist.

The bread was cut with the special Sabbath "challah knife"—special because no weapon is allowed on the Sabbath, since it is a day of peace and equality, an anticipation of the full Reign of God. The fine meal lasted for several hours, laced with conversations about each other's lives, and a special written note that Zalman had composed for each of us concerning his unique hopes for our lives.

On Saturday morning we walked some distance to a synagogue. In orthodox tradition no machine can be used on the Sabbath because that is making something work for you, and everyone, everything has the right to rest on this day. In fact, in ancient biblical law it is a capital offense to make anyone, including any animal, work for you on the Sabbath. It is a *legal* right for all to be "left in peace" on the Sabbath; all of nature is to be allowed its natural, untampered-with presence.

We participated in the more informal of two services. Formal prayer, scriptures, and sermon were mixed with informal greetings, inquiries after people's well-being, and public discussion of the world's well-being.

About noon we returned home for a cold meal (no fire can be lighted on the Sabbath—that would be work) and friendly conversation. The afternoon, if I could have stayed, might be filled with reflection on life alone and together, with scripture and other spiritual reading, walks, rest, and in general anything else that would help mark off the day as different from the other six days of the week. Traditionally the day ends at sunset with another special prayer service.

Shabbot is celebrated differently in different observant Jewish families. But it is always marked by its difference from other days. Its origin stretches back to the command in Exodus 20:8–11:

> Remember the sabbath day, to keep it holy. Six days you shall labor, and do all your work; but the seventh day is a sabbath to the Lord your God; in it you shall not do any work, you, or your son, or your daughter, your manservant, or your maidservant, or your cattle, or the sojourner who is within your gates; for in six days the Lord made heaven and earth, the sea, and all that is in them, and rested the seventh day; therefore the Lord blessed the sabbath day and hallowed it.

In Deuteronomy 5:15 another purpose is given for the Sabbath, a redemptive memory: the delivery of the Hebrews from slavery in Egypt. Thus historical sensitivity and identity is linked with an end-in-itself day of rest and worship.

From Jeremiah onward its observance is stressed by the prophets as a delight, as part of the law of righteousness, and as a sign of covenant devotion; by it time is hallowed and the community and the land gain strength and refreshment.[3]

Legislation concerning Sabbath observance is found elsewhere in the Torah[4] and in rabbinical interpretive commentary through the centuries. In Jesus' day, legislation apparently was very strict. He did not deny the Sabbath's specialness in illegally healing and plucking corn on that day. Rather he connected it with the advent of the messianic order of wholeness, *shalom*, for which Sabbath is a sign brought toward fulfillment in Jesus' coming.[5]

This connection of the Sabbath with an incipient fulfillment in Jesus, reinforced by the experiences of the resurrected Jesus and the coming of the Holy Spirit on the first day of the week, gradually led the early Church to shift it to a special Christian observance, on what we now call Sunday.[6]

This sense of a "special day" of the week spread through Christian missionaries far and wide. Its observance through the centuries has varied greatly, but it always has included worship and rest.

Today, in the Protestant-dominated parts of the West especially, we are pulling away from the last vestiges of a well-intentioned but oppressively legalistic period of Christian Sabbath observance. Sunday legislation probably reached its height of narrow, rigid interpretation in the English Puritans' seventeenth-century legislative acts that prohibited any kind of recreation on Sunday, even going for a walk.[7]

With the gradual demise of the last related "Blue Laws" legislation in the United States, there is a general sigh of relief. On the other hand, with them one of the few remaining symbols of a meaningful basic rhythm of life has been abolished from public consciousness. As Harvey Cox says, though Sunday is a holiday, it increasingly is just another day whose emptiness is filled by leisure industries.[8] The Churches themselves increasingly are limited to a rushed hour of vestigial Sabbath gathering, with no sense of a whole day's different rhythm of life. Numerous nonobservant Jews ignore the Sabbath altogether. Liberal Jews can water it down to a glancing tip of the hat, along with a majority of Christians. For others in the culture, the Sabbath is simply unheard of.

What are we missing in ignoring the guidance of this different quality of time represented by the Sabbath? We are missing a profound human truth: our need for what the great Jewish scholar and mystic, Abraham Joshua Heschel, called "a sanctuary—a cathedral in time."[9]

Perhaps no one has evoked more poignantly the inner heart of this sanctuary than Heschel. Here are some of his insights that reveal the power of Sabbath time:

> Six days we wrestle with the world, wringing profit from the earth; on the Sabbath we especially care for the need of eternity planted in the soul. The world has our hands, but our soul belongs to Someone Else.[10]

> Six days we live under the tyranny of things of *space;* on the Sabbath we try to become attuned to holiness in *time,* a day on which we are called ... to turn from the *results* to the *mystery* of creation; from the world of creation to the creation of the world.[11]

Unlike Aristotle, the Sabbath is not for gaining strength for more efficient work—man is not a beast of burden. . . . Sabbath is the climax of living, not an interlude. . . . Rest as if all your work were done. . . . Sabbath is an example of the world to come (R. Akeiba).[12]

Labor is a craft, but perfect rest is an art—the result of accord in body, mind, and imagination.[13]

The Sabbath is a palace in time we build, made of soul, joy, and reticence (discipline and abstention). . . . How else express glory in the presence of eternity, if not by the silence of abstaining from noisy acts?[14]

Sabbath is a day of independence of external obligation, on which we stop worshiping the idols of technological civilization; we use no money; it is a day of armistice in the economic struggle with our fellow-men and forces of nature. It is not *renouncing* technological civilization, but gives some *independence* of it.[15]

When we celebrate the Sabbath, we adore precisely something we do not see. To name it queen, to call it bride is merely to allude to the fact that its spirit is a reality we meet rather than an empty span of time we choose to set aside for comfort or recuperation.[16]

Our constant problem is how to live with people and remain free, how to live with things and remain independent. . . . The Sabbath gives us this inner liberty, exempt from the domination of things and people.[17]

The Sabbath cannot survive in exile, a lonely stranger among days of profanity. . . . All days of the week must be spiritually consistent with the Day of Days. All our life should be a pilgrimage to the seventh day. Sabbath is the counterpoint of living, the melody sustained throughout all agitations and vicissitudes which menace our conscience; our awareness of God's presence in the world.[18]

These pictorial words of Heschel circle again and again around a paradoxical truth of human life: though we all yearn for the quality of Sabbath time as a taste of Home, and though we may strive to allow its "melody" to be sovereign in other times, the fact is that much of our life is spent in structures, situations, and inner perplexity that resist the fullness of Sabbath.

Those religious and political groups that have attempted to force all days to be like the Sabbath in intensity of equality, unity, and peace have found that this is impossible. Attempted enforcement of such a pure ideal historically has led only to tyranny and an eventual modus vivendi with the necessities of social structure and the human condition.[19]

The great realism of Sabbath tradition is that it recognizes both our human vision and condition, and allows a way for the vision to be maintained through all conditions.[20] Human beings are saved from reduction to mere animals of production, and at the same time saved from the temptation to permanent Sabbath withdrawal from the tension and conflict of human social structures and service.

Neither Marxist nor secularized Western democratic nations seem to understand how to maintain this balance. Perhaps it becomes impossible as a corporate, operational sense of trustworthy transcendence is lost in these societies. Without this sense, anxiety and paranoia reign. There can be no special time to appreciate the gift of life, because it is only a blind accident, utterly dependent on our works and their protection.

We fear collapse into nothingness without constant productive activity, for there is "nothing" apart from our activity. The only way out is real escape, flight from our terrorizing knowledge into the oblivion of drunkenness (of one kind or another). Life itself, activity and inactivity, takes on a quality of drunkenness, of crazed drivenness both to build and to escape a world and a self that do not exist, that have no meaning, except by ceaseless self-definition, toil, and fixing.

The rest of the truth, the Sabbath truth as posited by Judaeo-Christian experience, is that we can afford to rest and work with eyes steadily open, trusting that we are held even when we do not tightly hold. A more sane rhythm of life then is possible, one that oscillates and meshes Sabbath and ministry, rather than desperate achievement and escape. Now let's turn to look at the Church's place in fostering this rhythm.

The Church's Task

According to Bruce Reed, director of the Grubb Institute in London,[21] the Church's primary task is precisely guidance for people through and toward this basic rhythm of life.

The Institute's research with churches over a twenty-year span has convinced them that this is not only the normative, but the *operational* task of the Church as social institution, i.e., it is exactly what it *does* do for people, though the form and results may be far from ideal.[22]

Several years ago I attended a conference led by Institute staff on its theses concerning the Church's functioning and task. I have been struck by the way their interpretations have helped to confirm and clarify my own experience both before and since that conference. Though Grubb does not speak of "Sabbath and ministry" or "achievement and escape" time, their work I believe points in the same direction.

Bruce Reed, as Institute spokesman, proposes two alternating modes of experience in human life, each with its own validity and way of being. One is the mode of "intradependence," when we are being focused and analytical, seeking to master or adapt to our environment. Religious values basically are internalized and invisible in this mode.

However, Reed's thesis points to the inadequacy of this mode of being for human life. Adults never outgrow the oscillation seen in a child between intradependent play and return to the parent for a "checkup," which refreshes and encourages them to venture off again. Thus there is a second mode of being, "extradependence," marked by a positive regression toward a trusted source outside one's own ego, a regression that moves toward an unfocused, symbolic consciousness more characteristic of artistic and religious activities.[23]

This process is marked in an adult by search for someone or something on whom to depend; by the frequent fear of, and resistance to, disengagement and acknowledgment of helplessness; and by the emergence of new ideas and constructs of the self and world that take place during the period of disengagement.[24]

Individuals use the actual or imagined presence of another to provide a setting in which they can acknowledge their own weakness and vulnerability, and reorder their view of themselves and their world.

Such reversion can be understood not necessarily as return to the primitive mentality of the infant, but as opening to the unclouded vision of the child (both of which may be embarrassing to an adult).[25] Corporate worship is a prime example: in such acts our thoughts and feelings are engaged by narratives, images, and ideas which refer to a world, or a realm of experience, other than that of our working and social lives.[26] When worship is fully and undefensively experienced as a mode of extradependence, including a transforming sense of transcendent trustworthiness, people are able to shift to intradependence with greater capacity for risk-taking and change projects, and for exploring the unknown.[27]

Reed's experience points to the conclusion that those who engage in this personal oscillation between worship and work in the world actually do so on *behalf* of many others in the community. Some people subconsciously send others to worship *for* them, and in fact become anxious if no one goes. Others engage in *vicarious* oscillation: these do not identify with any individual worshiper, but it is important for them that church buildings are visible, that they hear church bells ringing, and that they see people going to church.[28]

Reed is speaking predominantly out of research in British culture. Such a thesis may be less true in the American scene where organized religious life formally is separated from the state, and thus is more removed from *public* consciousness and identity. However, even if it is less true here, it is a hypothesis with great implications. It means that worship in the churches may be serving the needed oscillation process of many more people than those who physically participate. This implies a social guidance function of the churches well beyond their active membership.

This function becomes particularly important in light of the growing privatization of the "extradependent" side of Western culture. Public worship encourages a broad identity with humanity, and indeed with all of creation, and provides a sense of its unity in a shared Source and trustworthy, hidden Guide. Such a sense of reality allows resistance to the temptation to reduce reality to the private ego and its desires. When this temptation becomes behavior, then extradependence time is not feeding a perspective and strengthening that moves one to be a creative and responsible member of the human family in "intradependent" time.

There are no guarantees that this process will be effective in worship. A person's psychological background may not permit adequate trust really to regress deeply enough for internalization and fresh strength and vision from the Holy; such a person leaves worship "stillborn," unable to be fully intradependent.

The way worship is done also may impede the process. If worship leaders are unaware that the quality of this time must be different from ordinary work time for deep positive regression and its transformative power to happen, they may refuse to allow people to let them be the "sacramental authorities" they need them to be. They also may hinder the structure and content of worship from guiding people through its needed phases.

These phases include owned responsibility for their lives and intended restitution where needed (confession); forgiveness; experience of dependent, trustworthy relatedness to the Other; a sense of worshiping *with* others, on *behalf* of others; an awareness of symbols that point to Mystery beyond themselves (thus avoiding fundamentalism), and that contain values transcending those of the unmodified culture (thus avoiding folk religion). Further, the phases include crossing the threshhold from feelings of separation from power, goodness, and wholeness to *union* with these, leading to an increasing orientation to the day-to-day world with an attitude of power, wholeness, and love (this point is reached ritually in digesting the Holy in bread and wine).

Finally, there is a transformation to intradependence, when the world is seen differently. This difference may be exciting, threatening, or saddening (e.g., in mourning the loss of a clear, whole, vision and response in face of the "intractable otherness" of the material/social world); changes in intradependent attitude and behavior may be seen as called for over time.[29]

Reed summarizes the primary social task of the local church in his interpreted experience in these words:

> To monitor the oscillation process by containing or rendering manageable anxieties associated with the activities of the profane world so that individuals and institutions are able to carry out the tasks on which the survival and well-being of their social group depends.[30]

This task is carried out through corporate worship, the annual rhythm of the liturgical year, and pastoral functioning that allows extradependence leading toward intradependence.[31]

Reed believes that in theology the Church is accountable for dealing with all issues of life. God is seen as active both in the Church and in the world; only the form of relatedness is different. But in its pastoral work with people, the Church is responsible primarily for helping them go through a positive regression process that connects them with corporate as well as individual reality, and allows them to come back to daily life with renewed energy for caring and awareness. As he puts it, "The Church should manage the dependent aspect of corporate life in order to free the community as a whole to cope with other aspects of human existence."[32]

If the Church does this job well, its fruits will be seen in community life marked by greater energy for justice, realistic coping, and cohesion, *even if* the Church has no *direct* role in these specific community tasks.[33]

Reed thus combines his broad psychological-organiza-

tional-scientific background with his sensitivity to the
Church to portray for us a process of human and societal oscillation and Church function that provides clarification and
reinforcement for the inherited Judaeo-Christian rhythm of
Sabbath-ministry time. His more flat but precise language I
believe leaves him a bedfellow with the more exalted, sweeping, and specific sense of Sabbath seen in Heschel.

Heschel, though, does go further in giving an end-in-itself value to Sabbath time that is not apparent in Reed's
strictly "functional" approach.

Also, Heschel's metaphorical language retains a subtlety that seems more appropriate to religious experience.
"Extradependence" as a description of human relationship
to the Holy loses the paradoxical immanence-transcendence
of God in Judaeo-Christian experience. "Intradependence"
inadequately accounts for interdependence, the Mystical
Body. Reed's focus on the term "regression" loses the many
connotations of "childlikeness," as well as being a word with
so many popular negative connotations that I am not sure it
is functional beyond a very limited professional audience.

Psychological language just is no substitute for metaphorical and theological language. However, Reed is not trying to substitute for these forms of expression. He is trying
to describe strictly the social-psychological process involved.

Besides providing us with an illuminating sense of the
Church's primary social function, Reed helpfully distinguishes the unprophetic function of adaptive folk religion
from what he calls "apostolic religion," i.e., the real depth of
Christian experience and symbols that aim at risk-taking
transformation of life through an oscillation process, focused
on an integral trust in the transcendent Source of life.[34]

His view of life as alternating between two different
modes of experience I think needs complementing, though,
if it is to be fully apostolic, by a transcendent trust that this
oscillation has a goal, a direction—that it is part of a corporate and cosmic spiritual journey that is moving toward fulfillment.

This fulfillment for some very gifted people is foreshadowed now in lives where the oscillation is very slight, a foreground and background so integral that being and doing, regression and coping, appear to exist simultaneously.

Such folk are rare, however, and for most of us, Reed's view of oscillation seems realistic and helpful in understanding human need for guidance in this process.

I will return to the implications of this broad spiritual-guidance process for specific personal spiritual direction shortly. Before that, though, I would like to present one more recent source of empirical support and clarification for this proposed universal rhythm of human life so basic to an understanding of spiritual guidance.

Communitas and Social Structure

The American anthropologist Victor Turner describes a universal dialectical process for both individuals and groups between what he calls "communitas" and "social structure," akin to the rhythm of Sabbath and work, and extradependence and intradependence, but with added insight, and including a special focus on social relationships.[35]

"Communitas" is marked by spontaneity, immediacy, equality, lack of status, comradeship, passivity, sacredness. It has an existential quality: a whole person relating to another whole person. It represents the "quick of human interrelatedness," and the "emptiness at the center" of Lao-tzu's chariot wheel, which is nevertheless indispensable to the functioning of the wheel.

Communitas breaks through the *interstices* of structure in liminality (ambiguous threshold experiences, as in rites of passage). It also appears at the *edges* of social structure, in *marginality*, and from *beneath* the structure, in *inferiority*. It is a holy relational time that dissolves and transgresses social norms, provides experiences of great potency, and models that incite persons to reclassification of reality and relationships and to action. Liturgy at its best involves relationships of communitas. Communitas can burn out or wash away the accumulated sins and sunderings of social structure.

It is a product of "[persons] in their wholeness wholly

attending," "I-Thou" relationships.[36] People can go crazy because of communitas-repression; sometimes people become obsessively structured as a defense mechanism against their urgent need of communitas.[37]

Social structure, on the other hand, is marked by roles, status, and differences of all kinds necessary for a society's functioning, or which have been accumulated over time. It is rooted in the past and extends into the future through language, law, and custom. It has a cognitive quality for ordering public life and thinking about culture and nature. Whole individuals are only ambiguously grasped behind their segmentalized positions, offices, statuses, and roles.[38]

History shows that exaggeration and distortion of *structure* leads to a pathological communitas outside or against the law (today, for example, urban riots, drugs, and campus rites of spring).[39]

Exaggeration of *communitas,* on the other hand, is followed by despotism, overbureaucratization, or other rigidities, in its attempt to suppress all tendencies toward structuring or toward alternative structure (as in religious or Marxist states "after the revolution").

Either exaggeration sets up an unstable oscillation in a society and in the lives of its affected individuals.[40]

Historical wisdom, Turner believes, "is to find a right relationship between structure and communitas under the *given* circumstances of time and place, to accept each modality when it is paramount without rejecting the other, and not to cling to one when its present impetus is spent. . . . Communitas and structure are married to one another; they are in dialogue; together they make up one stream of life."[41]

The major religions (as opposed to sects, at least in their beginnings) have always taken account of this bipolarity, Turner recognizes, and have tried to maintain these social dimensions in balanced relationship. In the course of time, they learned how to incorporate enclaves of communitas within their institutionalized structures—just as tribal religions do with their rites of passage—and to "oxygenate" the Mystical Body by making provision for those wanting to live in communitas and poverty all their lives.[42]

Turner speaks of the ideal dialectic in terms that echo Heschel's vision of the penetration of Sabbath "melody" into daily living, or Reed's "internalization" of extradependent perspective:

> The ultimate desideratum is to act in terms of communi-
> tas values even while playing structural roles, where
> what one culturally does is conceived of as merely instru-
> mental to the aim of attaining and maintaining commun-
> itas.[43]

We could continue to build evidence for the importance of this basic human rhythm of life.[44] Perhaps, though, enough has been said to demonstrate that any kind of personal spiritual guidance will be affected by this rhythm. I will turn now to look at some of its implications for such guidance.

Implications for Guidance

When someone comes to you and asks for help in his relation to God, that person already has stepped to the threshold between the sacred and profane, and you are needed to represent the sacred. Thus you do not seek to be a "pal" or a therapist; you accept the responsibility of your symbolic position.

One dimension of the spiritual companion's task is to assist that person's positive regression to extradependence. This means, first of all, resisting your own or the other person's temptation to turn the situation into problem-solving. Problem-solving requires intradependence: a work-assignment, a task to do, a situation to figure out.[45]

As Reed points out, many people don't know how to regress to extradependence. "Any symbols they knew which could have assisted in the transition from intradependence may have been drained of their power through intellectualizing, or due to a bad experience years before so that the thought of dependence may now be humiliating."[46]

The companion can be aware of these background difficulties and help the person face them at some appropriate point. Besides this, the companion can directly help the person's "childlike" (as opposed to childish) openness by offering an early opportunity for guided silence and prayer. The quality of such experiences at their best ebbs toward exposure of underlying desires, fears, and guilt that can be lightened, and hopes that can be nourished. Such shared experience also can encourage a nonpossessive intimacy that lets the guide be more trusted and trustworthy as a transparency (not a replacement) for the loving God of Truth.[47]

The relationship seeks to bridge the sacred and profane: to realize the quality of the former, and to discern its vocational inner direction in the latter. The companion thus can be key to checking and assisting a person's authentic rhythm between the integration of the two basic modes of human life.

The awesome, beckoning sacred dimension can be encouraged not only through experiences of prayer and silence within a meeting, but also through reflection together on how this dimension is tasted and disciplined outside the relationship. Does he or she allow real "Sabbath time": mini-Sabbaths daily, weekly special time, vacation/retreat time? Does the quality of this time invite both an end-in-itself appreciative presence and a transformative, energizing perspective for daily living?

Does daily living express an active involvement with the needs of interpersonal and community "love and justice," and acceptance of the forbearance and turmoil these can involve, or does he or she tend to escape into a limbo between true Sabbath and true ministry time?

Such a relationship can be a crucial complement to corporate worship, which I believe Bruce Reed overidealizes in terms of its capacity to carry so much of the load of extradependence. I think more *time* is needed than an hour's service really to be effectively distanced from routine ways (which is the wisdom of taking a Sabbath *day*), and personal *help* is needed in seeing *how* this time can be taken in a production-oriented culture where the art of "attentive rest" is alien.

A *sustained* companion relationship becomes important

when we see the disorientation and threats that come with "transformed" perspectives on life that can rise in Sabbath times. What are the implications for my daily life? Where am I being led in my relationships and work? Where is illusion and where is truth in what is happening? What is the relevant experience of others in Christian traditon? The companion can be a crucial ongoing support, giving a person room to develop responsive courage and direction for his or her life, lest it be swallowed up in fear, lethargy, and counter-pressures from the culture.

If clergy and lay spiritual directors are to have opportunity for their own regression, they in particular can benefit from the presence of a spiritual friend. The pressures under which they live as representatives of the Holy and as foils for others' regression leave them with crucial need for such a relationship.

They need it for their own soul's health, especially given the "aloneness" of their position. They need it also for the sake of those who come to them, not only for the firsthand experience it provides, but also as a check against mistaking people's respect for their authoritative *position* with any extra specialness of their *personhood*. Such a confusion can tempt clergy and lay directors toward one of two dangers: arrogance and authoritarianism based on a bloated self-image; or the reverse: self-deprecation and overpleasing based on a sense of personal worthlessness compared to the sacred public position.

The first danger represents an overweaning sense of *positive* specialness, the second of *negative* specialness. Both miss the simplicity of being an open channel of grace, in which one's own complicated self-efforts to "make things happen" need to be checked and attention paid rather to "letting" things happen, as the situation is blessed. In this way spiritual directors themselves participate in a dimension of childlikeness: they sit with the person, listening and responding to movements of truth that come from beyond their management and possession.

For clergy, awareness of this spiritual function can help them resist the frequent pressures to focus on social relationships and therapeutic problem-solving with people, tasks which can eat up their *unique* offering as representative of realities that transcend and give crucial strengthening context and perspective for self-defined problems.

This does not infer *ignoring* presenting problems, but it does speak to the spiritual task related to them: not how to "solve" problems, but how the mystery of grace is happening through them. This focus can invite an *appreciative* response. Then the "problem" is not just a private ego struggle, but part of a larger caring frame, allowing a larger response: moving toward participation with one's gifts in the stewardship and celebration of life.

Where such a response is heavily blocked, as when resentment or fear keeps a person self-enclosed, then a special therapist may be needed to help a person let go the accumulated psychic barriers that clog his awareness and responsiveness. This is an ego task not normally suitable to the guidance of a spiritual companion, though its effects are recognized in that relationship.[48]

Turner speaks of communitas and social structure as "immortal antagonists," even though both are essential. A spiritual friendship can help these antagonists in each of us understand and enrich rather than ignore or dominate each other.

In the larger societal scene, the spiritual guidance offered by public worship and preaching can assist these social as well as personal dimensions of our lives to be aware friends. Then the equality and transcendent perspective of communitas can be allowed to leaven and loosen the rigidities and idolatries of social structure. In turn, the roles, law, and other structures in the society can be respected as necessary in some form.

Conclusion

Such an understanding of this bifocal setting of human life can be a particularly valuable gift for our time. American culture, including its religious institutions, has tended to weight social structure to a destructive degree, inviting pathological frenzy in our substitutes for authentic Sabbath and work time. Thomas Merton points out the violent results that mark even the socially concerned idealist:

> There is a pervasive form of contemporary violence to which the idealist fighting for peace by non-violent methods most easily succumbs: activism and overwork. The rush and pressure of modern life are a form, perhaps the most common form, of its innate violence. To allow oneself to be carried away by a multitude of conflicting concerns, to surrender to too many demands, to commit oneself to too many projects, to want to help everyone in everything is to succumb to violence. The frenzy of the activist neutralizes his work for peace. It destroys the fruitfulness of his own work, because it kills the root of inner wisdom which makes work fruitful.[49]

The Church, by inheritance and by mission, needs to be aware of its particular institutional responsibility and opportunity for fostering an authentic and corporate rhythm of life that nourishes this "root of inner wisdom" and help it connect with compassionate action. At this root of wisdom is a trust that life is a gift before it is a work; that besides a task, life is given an end-in-itself love by its Lover, a Gospel-Good News that frees us to *allow* dependent/nourishment/appreciation time, without fear that we will collapse into nothingness when we no longer "produce" our own identity and the world's.

With such trust, we can afford to "rest" in appreciation of the mysterious *givenness* of our most basic identity ("I have called you by name, you are mine." Isa. 43:1).

This gifted rhythm of life can be described in different ways: as modes of time or relationship, as foreground and background of a gestalt, as "empty" center and spokes of a wheel, as being "in" but not "of" the world, as left vs. right brain activity, as floating and swimming, as seamless and parceled Presence. Whatever imagery is used, the underlying reality is a crucial container for offering and receiving spiritual guidance.

One of the earliest theologians of the Church, Gregory

of Nyssa, describes this container as the very nature of God: Stability and Movement, Being Love and Doing Love.[50]

It is this intrinsic nature of reality that was sensed by those students in the simple rhythm of appreciative silence and work in that high-school room where I began this chapter. It is the misunderstanding and ego threat of this rhythm in our time that angered those parents.

4. The Many Colored Coat of Spiritual Guidance

As a child I remember being fascinated with those fairy tales that centered around a lost throne.

They followed a basic pattern: A boy or girl is raised in poverty in some obscure place. However, the child really was born in the royal household; some wicked relative who wanted the throne for himself saw to it that at birth the real prince was banished to a distant place.

When the child grows up, he stumbles onto his true heritage at a particularly graced time, through sudden revelation with someone who knows the truth. Scales fall from the newly discovered one's eyes; a new dignity and purpose are born.

Finally, there is a period of struggle with the entrenched forces of evil (within and without); after much suffering and loss, the royal inheritor ascends his rightful throne, and rules with compassion, equity, and wisdom.

These stories reflect the intuition and experience of many people. They can be interpreted on many levels. Spiritually, for me, they express that basic insight found scattered throughout Christian literature that each of us is a child of royal lineage. Royal means a status that cannot be earned, only given. It is a gifted right and responsibility from the beginning, not a goal that is earned at the end, though there is struggle along the way to *realize* the full truth.

Those who would grasp for their own kingdom, however, are ignorant of the gift, or hostile toward recognition of

90

its royal Source beyond themselves and its broad responsibilities. Such people forcefully spread their blindness and isolating self-importance. The gift is hidden from view. Yet it cannot be destroyed; it shows itself as an inner gnawing, a yearning that cannot be satisfied by our confused and willful efforts—until the time is ripe, and the giftedness is revealed, for those who have eyes to see.

There, in broadstroke Christian terms, is the human condition. Christian spiritual guidance in all its forms exists to reveal this condition in us and encourage our reconciliation with transforming power to our royal Source, whose hidden Realm is one of connectedness and compassion. That reconciliation, to Christian faith, is unfolded in the mystery of God's gift of a royal son, Jesus Christ, through whom we inherit the Kingdom.

What is the range of guidance available to us today? If it is *spiritual* guidance, then it is guidance that is trusted to be, however veiled, from a dynamic source transcending our construction, which in Christian terms is called the Holy Spirit: a very free Force. "The wind blows where it wills, and you hear the sound of it, but you do not know where it comes from or where it is going. That is how it is with all who are born of the Spirit" (Jn. 3:7–8).

Thus we are dealing with an uncontrollable mystery. We cannot domesticate it through a neat system of guidance and progress. The Spirit is too free and subtle for that. It resists every label and cage. If the Spirit is willing and our spirit (unbeknownst to us) is ready, then, as an old Zen saying has it, we can look at a stone and be enlightened. Anything and everything can be our spiritual teacher .

On the other hand, if we consciously undertake every form of visible guidance year after year, nothing is guaranteed. No technique, no method, no adviser, no effort can build a bridge from the human side alone. Only the Spirit knows when we truly are ready for the truth, and we will not be given more than we can bear.

Where does that leave us? With lots of listening and experimental waiting room! We cannot make anything authentically spiritual be realized. That is a gift—a grace—for which we can only be attentive and trust. Such an assumption underlies all orthodox Christian views of reality. However, "how" we can be attentive and nourish trust, and "where" we look for guidance, show great variety in different Christian traditions.

In most Protestant traditions forms of guidance are limited to corporate worship (including preaching), scriptural study, sometimes theology, pastoral counseling for crises and rites of passage, private active prayer, and whatever indirectly may come through active involvement with others. Roman and Anglo-Catholic and Eastern Orthodox usually include these forms today also, with Protestants having been influential (especially with Roman Catholics) in their recent fresh weight on preaching, scripture, and free individual discovery in community.

Catholic and Orthodox traditions include other forms of guidance that recently have had influence with many Protestants. Such forms include greater appreciation of the guidance of liturgical forms, the Church calendar of seasons and saints, private confession (the rite of reconciliation), retreats, silent meditation, and spiritual direction. These forms have grown in influence with Protestants especially in the years since the Second Vatican Council, as their old corruptions have been purged and as Protestants began to see that they perhaps had thrown out a lot of valuable gems at the Reformation because they had become tarnished beyond recognition.[1]

Thus today we have the felicitous situation of different Christian traditions' active openness to one another's gifts. In fact, there is a certain irony in the way many Roman Catholics appear to have thrown off with a sense of good riddance many of those tarnished gems of guidance after the Second Vatican Council, and now are being drawn to the sparkle of those traditional Protestant gems mentioned above. At the same time, many Protestants now sense the unnecessary limitation of their own forms, and seek to recover some of those lost at the Reformation.

Both groups now often look with awe at the mystical depths preserved in Eastern Orthodox traditions. The Orthodox, in their turn (at least in North America), seem influenced by the other groups' attempt to transcend ethnic boundaries and offer guidance more broadly and in the common tongue of the country.

All three groups, but especially Roman Catholics and Protestants, are at least tacitly influenced by the focus of guidance offered in the larger secular society. Since the Spirit blows where it wills, there is, for example, openness to looking beneath contemporary forms of psychological, political, and educational guidance for signs of the Spirit's fruit.[2]

At the same time, there is suspicion and required discernment born of the Christian tradition's sense of deceptive blindness and willful self-centeredness in the world (in and out of the Church).

The openness has led to an enormous influence in the Church of these modern guides. Where there is little positive sense or valuation of the Church's own tradition, methods, and ways of discernment, this openness can take the form of indiscriminate vulnerability to anything offered up by the latest political, educational, therapeutic, or human potential populist.

On the other hand, where suspicion reigns, there can be a fundamentalist, sectarian reaction that restricts guidance to scripture and/or tradition, refusing to accept anything as of the Spirit unless born of explicit past Christian piety.

I would propose that our time calls for a "middle way," born of a renewed appreciation of neglected wisdom in Christian tradition and practice, yet, with this deep foundation, open to learning from contemporary knowledge as this can further reveal the "truth that makes us free."

The authentic history of the Church is one of constant struggle to carry on a received Truth about reality, interpreted, purged, and enhanced by whatever ways the same ultimately invisible Truth continues to clothe itself in individual and corporate human experience. Where the Church fails to discern accurately the places of continuity and discontinuity with this Truth in a given time, it falls either into one of two pits inferred above.

On the one side is overaccommodation to the culture. Then, though it has people, the Church loses its unique capacity to guide out of its own culturally transcendent resources. It can only reflect the values of the culture, and thus succumb to folk religion, becoming an indiscriminate tool of cultural affirmation.

On the other side is sectarian irrelevance. Then, though the Church has a unique sense of self as guide, it tries to be one by containing the uncontainable truth in rigidly and narrowly interpreted words and forms. The unity of truth is lost. It is imperiously reserved to the container, cut off from its fullness. People then are likely to be attracted to it not because it offers a way into the Truth, but a way into security from the Truth's ambiguities and vastness in human life.

As I earlier have implied, American Christian history appears to have seen more of these two pits than of the middle way of "open tradition." The guidance function of the Church has suffered both loss and distortion accordingly. As the dominant religious influence in the nation, society thus has suffered too. Our oversecularization is the sad fallout on one side; our national aggressive self-righteousness is fed on the other.

However, despite such crippling, the Church every day provides forms of authentic guidance that affect many millions of people, toward their own and the society's well-being. Let's look a little closer at some of these forms available to people today.

The rite of reconciliation, whether corporately in a liturgy, or more personally and often more effectively in private or small group confession, is one of the oldest forms of guidance. It can encourage a sense of personal accountability for and awareness of personal actions and their consequences, purge guilt, and empower a sense of reconciliation and caring with self, God, and neighbor.

Today increasingly such confession takes account of social as well as personal sins, and of psychological limitations. In the new, more informal, personal, and less legalistic Roman Catholic practice, counsel with the person after confession can involve a form of spiritual direction more uniquely focused on the person's situation than was likely in the past. This can stimulate a person to seek direction in its fuller form (i.e., unfocused specifically on penance) apart from the rite.[3]

Baptism and godparents can empower a sense of unique personal belonging, calling, and being cared for beyond blood family and the state. Knowledge of Baptism (and Confirmation, where it is offered) is a guiding knowledge of unearned "royal lineage" that can save you from succumbing to the anxiety of having to "make a name for yourself," with its frequently accompanying idolatry of works and expedient use of people. On the other side, such knowledge can save you from the lethargy and indolence that comes from lacking any sense of purpose, of calling, of "response-ibility" in life.

In the last chapter I spoke of the guidance inherent in authentic *corporate worship* (including preaching). Such participation can provide renewal of transcendent *corporate* identity beyond our isolated egos. It also allows us to sink into a different quality of consciousness that can feed our awareness of transforming connectedness with the Real. The words and acts of liturgies serve these ends, reincorporating worshipers into the gist of the Christian experience of God. Such worship, especially in the form of Eucharist, is particularly central to the guidance of Catholic, Anglican, Lutheran, and Orthodox traditions, and is important to all Christian traditions. Our perspective and energy for caring and coping are then renewed.

Guided retreats and quiet days can extend corporate worship and its Sabbath quality into corporate solitude. Such times can provide a different perspective on community, and encourage both intimate relaxation and struggle with the Real One welling up in and around us. They can offer protected respites from the breathless driveness of culture and ego. The structure of such times in itself can become a form of guidance as well as any human leadership.

The *arts:* religious drama, poetry, novels, music, painting, sculpture, movement, stained glass, and architecture have a long history of service in the Church. When these are truly inspired, they can become sacraments through which our intuitive gifts can sense the Holy and its transforming power.

Reading and studying scripture can help us "listen" more deeply, if it is approached as a guide to the deepest truth. Our minds then are more innocently present, more vulnerable to the truth we may not hear when we are aggressively culling through "just another book." We sometimes are drawn through the surface sounds to a steady Voice that beckons us to its wellspring. We are not put off as quickly by what our egos normally would reject. This guidance sometimes can be aided by letting ourselves image particular scenes and identify, perhaps dialogue, with particular scriptural people.

Other spiritual reading can lead us in the same direction, if it is not exploitative of desires for sentiment and oversecurity that hide us from the Truth. These same desires in us can lead to abuse of scripture as a securing vault rather than an opening window.[4]

Laying on of hands and anointing with oil, with prayer for healing, guides toward reception of the wondrous gifts of physical, mental, and spiritual wholeness. Coming forward for such an act reinforces personal desire and initiative in asking for healing so valuable for its success. Mediation of others helps connect the person concretely with the larger resource of human community and that healing transcendent power so manifest through Jesus Christ. Its misuse is greatest when healing and grace are confused. Grace—the living, gifted, truth-evoking force of God—always is present in orthodox Christian understanding, with or without such specific healings.

The tacit guidance available in small *prayer, faith, and discernment groups* is another Christian resource. Today these take a great variety of forms (including charismatic tongues and prophecy). At their best, they provide an arena for corporate openness to the Spirit's way, personal support, the perspective of others' views, and opportunities for sharing pain, anxiety, thanksgiving, prayer for others, and surrender to God in faith. At their worst, they can provide mutual complicity in avoiding the deeper and harder truths of spiritual life, or worse, they can damage an unconfident person's integrity and authentic direction by insisting on a particular spiritual path or interpretation.

The *prophet* also provides guidance. This is too uncomfortable and upsetting a guide to ever become "institutionalized," yet Christian tradition is clear about the importance of prophecy and its normal availability when called for.

The prophet helps reveal our corporate complicity in evading the covenant call to sharing and caring for the resources and people of the earth and for faithful relation with their Giver. He or she points to the dire consequences of this complicity, and to forgiveness and renewed life if we will repent.

The judgmental, ringing, redemptive shock of the prophet's action can wake us up to responsive, spontaneous action of our own (if out of resentment we don't turn on the prophet). The self-forgetfulness of authentic prophetic action can inspire the clearing of many cobwebs from lethargic lives, and serve a deeper sense of spiritual calling and truth-telling. All other forms of spiritual guidance can be affected and cleansed by this impelled mediator of the Holy One, the One who for the sake of human well-being will not allow truth to be buried for long.

The *calendar of saints* gives opportunity for a range of heroes to be held before us as signs of grace and "ways in" to the Holy. It is too bad that more of these are not lay and married people; this would make identity with them and hope for these states of life easier. It is also sad that so many of their biographies often are missing or prettied up. Even so, they provide the guidance of a living chain of whole human beings that are infinitely more inspiring and instructive to the average person than abstract theological ideas cut off from their human incarnations. They are complemented by the living influence of the more holy people experienced alive in Church and society today.

The seasons of the Church year guide people through a valuable rhythm of examination and celebration, fasting and feasting. They recycle the deep mysteries of Christian experience corporately and individually. They provide bonding and transcendent focus for the body of the Church, and indirectly for a society, aiding resistance to the temptation to fragment and focus around petty things. Sometimes the seasons seem artificial and don't "fit" our personal rhythms. Yet they always remind us of and catch us up in a larger rhythm than our own.

Guidance also is available through *teaching:* learning the experience of the Church as it is summarized and interpreted in doctrine, theology, ethics, scripture, history, and forms of prayer and discipline. Where these are connected positively with the lives and integrity of those being taught, they can provide cognitive bridges that aid an understanding of a whole, integral approach to human life. Where they are not so connected, the teachings can be stillborn, misunderstood, intimidating, or alienating.

Guidance can come in numerous ways through the everyday *relationships of members of the Church.* The Mystical Body of Christ, the priesthood of all believers, involves countless mutual gifts of transparency to the Spirit at needed times. This is most sustained in *families,* where parents have special guidance opportunities, and where over a lifetime mutual guidance is provided.

Pastoral counseling and sustaining by pastors and other specially designated people normally involve dealing with particular problem-centered situations in a person's life. The forefront of concern is coping with or bearing the problem and getting on with life (e.g., getting through or bearing marriage and family difficulties, job loss, or illness). Psychological understanding today often is centrally brought to bear. Faith resources can be included and often are very important. However, the pressing weight of the problem (and often the training of the counselor) encourages focus on specific ego coping.

This contrasts with a more relaxed, up-front, usually long-term focus on the way grace is happening, being resisted, and being responded to in prayer and action, a description of *spiritual direction.*[5] As we can see from these last few pages, that direction is one color on a many colored coat of resources. It is meant to be part of a whole way of life, not an isolated resource. Its full helpfulness depends on a person's willingness to use it in conjunction with other mutually reinforcing and mutually correcting resources.

In this way it differs significantly from secular counseling, which cannot expect a client to share seriousness and participation in a whole approach to reality represented by Christian faith (or any other faith).

On the other hand, in its authenticity spiritual direction is not a "propagandistic" resource, seeking to mold a person into conformity with some mechanical external model. There was a more authoritarian time in Christian history when this was a real danger.

Today, however, the director dominantly functions as someone sensitive to the subtle "movements of the Spirit" in the unique circumstances of a particular person's life. These movements connect with scripture, tradition, and faith, but in a unique way discerned through the person's full current existential integrity. The director imposes nothing but seeks to listen for and evoke the unfolding image of God, the fullest, called-out humanity of the person.

Reasons for the Renewed Importance
of Spiritual Friendship

The re-emergence today of spiritual companionship as an important resource for a wide spectrum of people reflects a number of current human needs emerging from recent history. Four of these I believe are particularly significant.

The *first* is the need for personal help in the growing collapse of a shared world-view within the Church, and cultural support without, for a Christian "way of life." Everyone is on his own now to choose between the myriad, sometimes contradictory visible options the Church and society offer for a way of life.

This is true in a self-conscious way even in Roman Catholic seminaries, once bastions of an enforced way. In the bulletins of two Roman Catholic seminaries in the Washington area I have read what once was an exclusively liberal

Protestant position, words which in effect say: "You are personally responsible for the development of your own formation process" (within certain broad guidelines).

In this widespread situation, it can become lonely. We need someone who can help us sort out the many options and to discern the subtle threads being woven by the mysteriously moving Spirit in our lives. Such structured opportunities and resources are particularly rare in Protestant situations, though concern is growing. In terms of congregations, Clebsch and Jaekle have remarked that "there is no place in [their] structure and rhythm where a serious discussion concerning the state of one's soul is expected."[6]

A *second* need calling for more weight on personal spiritual guidance today emerges from the sense of limitation in educational and professional therapeutic relationships.

Public and private education increasingly seems dominated by technical knowledge, and both ignorance and studied neglect of basic religious-philosophical questions and structures for long-term exploration of them. This leaves many hungry people, teachers and students alike, for whom a simple Sunday worship service and educational hour just don't suffice.

Many therapists along with their clients seem increasingly to sense the need for something more transcendently rooted for themselves than Western psychology normally has permitted. The increasing interest among therapists in transpersonal and Jungian therapies and in Eastern (and to some extent Western) mystical traditions attests to this hunger. Though the quest often is veiled in psychological language, and usually is limited to intrapsychic investigation, I sense in many of them a yearning for a transcendently rooted way of life.

Alienation of Western psychology from its religious-philosophical heritage, as previously described, together with the strong individualism of psychology and of the middle class from which most psychologists come, makes it extra difficult for many of them to bridge fully into the Christian communal-historical way of life. Psychologically aware spiritual direction is a potentially invaluable resource for such people, as well as a complementary form of guidance for their clients or ex-clients.

A *third* need calling out such guidance comes from the starved half of the social activist. In the sixties most social activists (except those rising out of the black Church) were deeply suspicious of any kind of interior focus beyond confession of social sin. The personal self was to be sacrificed to the social self. In the seventies there was a clear shift with many such people. Something proved inadequate and empty about a totally exteriorized and communalized life. Something more interior and uniquely attentive to their personal situation was called for. It was not therapy they sought. It was their soul.

Some turned for help to Eastern groups, others to Western, and many still drift. Spiritual direction, with its capacity to take seriously an integral and meaningful social-personal way of life, is coaxed further to life by such people.

Finally, spiritual direction is receiving special attention in the face of our reawakening to the neglect of a careful oral tradition of spiritual guidance in the Church. Today we are almost totally dependent on books and scholarship for reminding us of the depths and nuances of human interior development that have been known in the light and path of Christian experience. We have been largely missing the careful, chastened, long-term, faith-grounded, tested, and intuitive person-to-person conveyance of the heart of Christian awareness. Perhaps certain parents, faithful in their child-rearing practices, especially mothers, came closest to this earlier in the twentieth century. However, little of this faith nurture seems left in the frenzied, confused, everybody-working, emotionally and materially distracted and often broken family settings that increasingly dominate our culture.

Such a situation cries out for a spiritual friend who can be with us not only through crisis, but through the more mundane times of spiritual attentiveness in our lives. Proliferation of such friendships perhaps can help shape, deepen, and stabilize the shallow spiritual infrastructure of the Church, aiding its renewal and unique service to society. As we shall see in Chapter Six, such friendships do not require spiritual masters, just attentive faithful companions.

The remainder of this book will focus on particular resources for carrying out authentic Christian spiritual friendship today. As we do so, it is important to keep in mind the broader context of resources described in this chapter, the long and varied history of spiritual guidance in the Church, and its rhythmic frame of Sabbath and ministry. All these together provide a foundation for reawakening to our royal lineage, and living out its confidence and sharing of gifts.

Part II
FOREGROUND

5. Seeking a Spiritual Friend

If you have sought a spiritual companion before, you know the ambivalence it can involve. Whom can I really trust with this most intimate dimension of my being? Will he or she be able to understand me? Dare I really bare my soul with someone else?

At one time we might have seen our sexual lives as the most intimate and difficult to reveal. Today that has become almost a casual subject for many people. Our Victorianism now is more likely to show itself in avoidance and embarrassment concerning our relation to God.[1]

Indeed, my spiritual life is a delicate subject. If I really open it up with someone over time, who knows what might happen? My tacit modus vivendi with God and my soul might be shaken. I might be led to change my way of seeing and behaving.

There is something in us that stubbornly resists this possibility (just as we resist psychological change). Why not let corporate worship, personal prayer, and my own discernment be sufficient?[2] And yet now these somehow leave me on the surface. I sense some small murmur inside drawing me deeper. There is a yearning that presses me to look freshly at my purpose in the light of Christian faith, my involvement in the "Really Real," my inmost being. I need someone with whom to share, understand, and listen with me for the ways I am called to respond authentically to this yearning. The need is greater than my fear. I'm ready for a spiritual companion.[3]

Mutual vs. One-way Direction

Should I seek someone for whom I also will be companion, or someone with whom the focus primarily will be on me?

All direction in some sense is mutual. The director can be opened to his or her own cooperation and resistance to grace in listening with another.

However, I believe that most relationships need a primary focus on one person or the other, lest they become a give-and-take of spiritual conversation that, though perhaps valuable, loses the intensity and depth of focus needed in full spiritual direction.

This "one-way" focus, however, *can* take place *within* a mutual-direction relationship. That is, one person can be the focus in a given hour, and another in a second hour or at a separate time.

It may be, though, that a person whom you want as a spiritual companion already is in a direction relationship with someone else. Or the person may be right for you as director, but you would not be right for him (or vice versa).

I have been in a mutual-direction relationship for some years now, and it has proven a great mutual blessing. However, I think the "just rightness" of two people for each other as spiritual friends is fairly rare. Most relationships I know of focus primarily on one person. If you do happen to find someone with whom a mutual relation seems right, then from my experience I would suggest that you be sure to give each other separate time periods. If you want mutual spiritual conversation time, that can take place before or after the "one-way" focus period.

For the depths to which such friendships can aspire, I refer you back to the section on "Friendship" in Chapter

Two. Also, you might find Dorothy Dever's *Faithful Friend-ship* helpful.[4]

Areas for Consideration

Whom you should see or respond to will depend on many things, including your age, sex, experience, personality, spiritual path, faith tradition, situation, and opportunity. Let's look at each of these in turn.

Age

Normally I believe it is best to choose someone in the second half of life: roughly thirty-five or older.

Carl Jung believed that every person who came to him over thirty-five essentially brought a spiritual concern, regardless of the presenting problem.[5] There is something new that usually begins to happen in mid-life: a sense of finitude, a sorting out of what is and isn't important in life, a fresh spiritual search or appreciation.

Before this age illusions of infinitude, ambition for a proper niche in the human community, and trust in salvation by techniques (everything will be fine with just a little more education, therapy, money, intimacy, etc.) tend to lurk behind attitudes and behavior.

By mid-life these often become at least partially burned out or relativized. An awareness of limits, unsolvable mystery, and related compassion become more real to us. Without this awareness, spiritual direction can fall prey to the Pelagianism (works-righteousness) so common in our youth. Then the necessary patience and trust in the Spirit's own timing are lost.

Of course, there are exceptions. Such maturing can happen much earlier. And maturing can happen much later, especially in American culture where youthful drivenness can continue until death.

In any case, especially if you yourself are in the second

half of life, you should choose someone who is likely to be over the hurdle of mid-life realization.[6]

Sex

What difference does it make whether you choose someone of the same or opposite sex for a spiritual companion?

Over the past seven years some of us in Shalem have paid particular attention to this question.[7] There is not one answer for all people in all situations. However, where there is a choice between two good people of different sexes, with each of whom you are equally comfortable, in *most* situations I think it is best to choose a person of the *opposite* sex.

In Church history it is revealing to note how, despite the frequent oppression and belittling of women, some great male-female spiritual friendships developed.[8] Today in our more sexually enlightened time it is increasingly common to see women directing men, as well as the reverse, in Roman Catholic seminaries and communities. Such opposite-sex spiritual friendships I believe are increasingly common among Protestants as well.

What can such cross-sex friendship add to spiritual direction?

Psychologically, if we accept Carl Jung's sense of the process for internal integration of anima and animus ("feminine" and "masculine" psychic dimensions), such a relationship can be valuable. Through transference, images of femininity from my inner world are projected onto the spiritual director (reverse for a woman), who "returns" them to me, to be integrated within my personality.

In the spiritual order, we might say that qualities of the Divine lacking in my own consciousness are projected, returned, and integrated.[9] Genesis 1:27 implies that the very image of God is male and female. Scriptural imagery also reflects masculine and feminine associated qualities of God interacting with their opposites in people.[10]

The sexual other can reflect more of the mystery and otherness of God, and yet the intimacy of that relationship.

There is more likely to be complementarity in the relationship and less likely to be subtle competition.[11]

Thus we see much special potential in a male-female friendship. There are situations, however, when it will not be as good or any better than a relationship with a person of the same sex.

Anthony Storr remarks that this kind of transference involving the animus/anima is appropriate only to persons in the second half of life who have worked through relationships to the point of discovering that sexual intercourse is not the most important experience in life. For such people salvation lies elsewhere: in art, science, or religion.[12] This implies the easy deflection that sexual, genitally directed attraction can bring to the task of spiritual direction. This reinforces my earlier view about the age of the director. It also infers that directees in the first half of life may have any advantages of a contra-sexual friendship offset by sexual feelings that cannot or will not be redirected.

It is interesting to note the strong themes of celibacy in male-female spiritual friendships in both East and West (all those mentioned earlier were celibate). The redirection of erotic energy toward heart and mind, from passion to wise compassion, is considered crucial for spiritual progress. This is difficult to conceive in a culture that has come virtually to the worship of genital sexuality.

In a conference Shalem once held on this subject we paired laymen and women over a number of hours and days to work on certain dimensions of spiritual friendship. I recall a woman saying with wonder that it was her first intimate male-female relationship that was not dominated blatantly or subtly by genital sexuality (and related dominating male behavior). She found fresh insight and relief in sensing the possibility of intimacy with a man that was not overshadowed by a drive toward genital expression. Some other dimension of humanity and spiritual sight became available.

Eros ("self"-fulfilling love) was transmuted perhaps a little closer to agape ("self"-emptied love), which in Christian tradition is God's love for the world, reflected through humans when they are most open. This love, "emptied" of self-grasping, paradoxically becomes fulfilling of our deepest self in God. In our super-sex-conscious culture, however, such an approach to a person of the opposite sex is particularly difficult.

On the other side of this attraction/transmutation in male-female relationships is the dammed-up energy of fear or warped expressions of anger. The differences of men and women, mothers and sons, fathers and daughters, involve tensions and histories that can make intimacy cross-sexually very difficult. In cases of blocking fear or anger, it may be best to cultivate a same-sex friendship, lest too much energy is drained into "keeping a distance," just as a same-sex friendship is best for a genitally very driven person.

NB

Finally, for persons very mature spiritually and emotionally, my sense is that it makes little difference whether the spiritual friend is male or female. These dimensions in self and God have become so integrated and transcended that anyone can serve as a transparency for the Holy.

God after all is not only male and female in Christian symbolism, but infinitely beyond male and femaleness, just as St. Paul speaks of being "in Christ" as a quality that is *neither* male nor female. It therefore would be misleading to speak of any *essentially* crippling or guaranteeing quality either in an intra or intersexual spiritual friendship. Moreover, the *primary* relationship in spiritual friendship is between God and the friend, not between the friends themselves. However, it is a potentially valuable consideration in selecting someone.

One parting note on this subject: In Chapter Two I mentioned the difficulty of a marriage partner in spiritual friendship. The many expectations and emotional dynamics inherent in such a relationship can make it as difficult for that person to be your spiritual director as to be your therapist. This does not mean that a quality of caring, listening, advising, and spiritual attentiveness is not possible in a marriage; it is necessary for a full one. However, it is a relationship that often needs complementing by someone with whom you can have a more easily focused and simple spiritual friendship.

Experience

If you have never been in a serious spiritual friendship before, and your own sense of spiritual life and experience seems thin, then you probably have little spiritual self-confidence and much vulnerability in approaching such a relationship.

In such circumstance I think it is important to seek out someone who is confident in experience yet humble in it. The confidence will free you to relax and be vulnerable. The humility will give you room for letting your own confidence rise; you won't be so intimidated by your sense of spiritual distance. On the other hand, such humility will mean your friend will be less likely subtly, probably unconsciously, to exploit your "newness" by lording it over you with superior sounding, overconfident advice which you mistake for wisdom. Your friend will listen, gently evoking from you the light of the Spirit within.

If you have much experience in spiritual practices and reflection, then perhaps you can bear someone whose style may be more varied and abrupt. You know enough to sort out what is valuable and what isn't in the relationship.

If your interior experience has reached particularly delicate points, such as a "dark night" of the soul, then you need someone who can understand enough of the subtlety of your experience not to misguide you. Such a person does not have to be more "advanced" than you to be helpful (though of course this would be ideal), but sensitive and learned enough to provide you with patient, prayerful support through the experience. The more subtle and incommunicable your experience, the more intuitively perceptive and empathetic I think your friend needs to be.

You also need to pay attention to the influence of exterior experience. For example, how important in your development is your experience of race or a particular cultural group? If these are very significant, then you will want to insure that your spiritual friend is capable of understanding such influences in your way of approaching God, neighbor, and self.

Personality

If we can trust the work of Carl Jung in personality typing and development, then you might find it valuable to look for complementarity. If you are very analytical, seek someone more of a "feeling" type; if you are a feeler, seek more of a thinker; if you are more intuitive, seek a more concrete, detail-conscious, sensate person; if you are more sensate, seek an intuitive friend.[13] However, be cautious of a person who is so *extremely* contrasting in personality type that he or she simply is not likely to be able to be in rapport with you.

Such complementarity isn't necessary, but it can be helpful in bringing out the fullest possibilities of awareness, and help you attend to blind spots in your way of seeing reality.

A personality is a unique constellation of experience and tendencies. Just how yours will "mesh" with someone else's is an issue beyond complementary types. You may find that there is an inherent way you grate on one another, for whatever reason, that indicates the relationship just should not be, no matter how "right" individual factors may seem to be. The opposite also could be true: other indicators don't point to a likely valuable spiritual friendship, but something so "right" is there in the way your personalities meet that other factors are outweighed.

Spiritual Path

Be aware of your dominant spiritual *path* now, a path influenced by your personality. It is important that your friend have some experience and sympathy with your path, even though he or she may not be traveling on it as centrally as you. In fact, someone with sympathetic yet critical experience of different paths is best of all: such a friend can help attune you to different possibilities you may be ready for, and call attention to possible deceptions.

Spiritual paths can be spoken of in many ways. However er described, each is but a different passageway into the same Truth.

Here is one way of looking at the highpoints of a continuum of paths, using descriptions that overlap particular Greek, Judaeo-Christian, and Hindu or Buddhist traditions. The spiral in the center symbolizes the way our lives can spiral through these paths over a lifetime.

The *devotional* path is marked by a very personal, intimate sense of God. An affective relationship predominates. God is caring Father, Mother, Bridegroom, Lover. Prayer on this path gives special weight to praise, petition, and thanksgiving. Beauty in God's creation may be greatly appreciated; this may involve special appreciation of the arts and nature. Charismatic tongue-speaking, prophecy, and healing may be encouraged.

Ernest Becker uses the evocative image of existentially "giving ourselves over" to different values in life.[14] On the devotional path, we give ourselves over to God as ultrapersonal Lover, with affective overflow and witness to those around us.

At its best, this path opens and channels our deep spiritual yearning toward the One beyond us, evoking self-forgetful appreciation and strong, intimate, caring participation in life, transmuting negative emotions in ourselves and others.

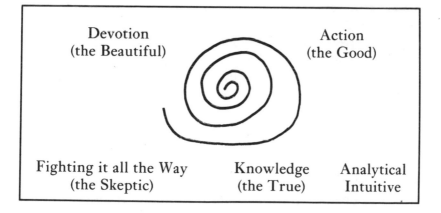

At its worst, the devotional path can become sentimental, unself-critical, privatistic, narrow, and cloudy, evading hard truths and actions in life. Also, it can seek and focus on feelings toward God that mistake the gifts of the Creator for the Creator, leaving us short of real communion.

The path of *action* focuses on moral concerns: the "good" in ourselves, our neighbors, and society. God is Redeeming Judge, calling us to personal virtue, mutual correction, covenant faithfulness, social justice, and ecological stewardship. Our vocation is righteous indignation, moral teaching, disciplined action. We are ever vigilant for corruption, apathy, callous behavior, and oppression of the powerless. The charismatic gift of exorcism (in the broadest sense) would be the closest of those classical gifts focused upon, together with prophecy in the sense of calls to repentance.

On the action path we especially give ourselves over to our neighbor (human and in nature), whose need mediates God's presence and calling for us.

At its best, this path channels our spiritual yearning into self-forgetful, risk-taking, community-building human concern and action.

At its worst, it can become self-righteous, imperious over other paths, and closed-mindedly intimidating rather than listening and collaborative with others in seeking an understanding and way to human moral goals.

The path of *knowledge* centers on wisdom. God is the Wise, Knowing, Seeing One; the image of God in us is revealed especially in conscious cultivation of and reflection on such gnosis (knowledge).

This path forks into two approaches. The first is centered on *analytical* knowledge: what we can grasp cognitively, conceptually of "the really Real." Theology, philosophy, and the sciences discipline such thinking.

The second fork moves toward *intuitive* knowledge: that which comes not through conceptually trying to "figure out" something, but from a subtle awareness of the truth that seems to be there without mediation of our intellects. Contemplation, Zen "koans" (riddles), the arts, parables, and psychic powers express or aim for this path. It moves toward the apophatic, the "direct seeing," imageless way of knowing. Analytical knowledge moves more fully through the kataphatic, the imaged way (though these can and do overlap without contradiction, as I elaborate in the first chapter).

In the first of these branches, the analytical, we give ourselves over to reason. In the second, we give ourselves to intuitive awareness.

At its best, the way of reason channels our spiritual yearning into a balanced, self-critical search for precise cognitive symbols of the Holy in relation to human life, symbols that are mutually connected, corrected, and communicable, providing people with chastened bonds of understanding and motivation.

The way of reason at its worst confuses the symbol with the reality, cognitive precision with direct and adequate intouchness with the Holy, and imperializes other spiritual ways.

The way of intuitive awareness at its best channels spiritual yearning into subtle, shared loving presence, into a quality of "direct seeing" through that human faculty of knowing that does not seem connected to our "normal" physical senses, except by later "translation." Such sight allows a quality of firsthand awareness from "within" reality as it is, with fruits of a quiet confidence and wise, insightful compassion.

At its worst this path either: 1) mistakes subtle ego desires and fears motivating intuition for direct, innocent contact with the Holy, or 2) allows its unpossessable "pure awareness" to be "attached" to ego, creating a sense of pride and proprietary power that is used to lord it over others.

Finally there is the path of *fighting it all the way*. This is the path of greatest iconoclasm—idol-smashing. Every word about the Holy is suspected of masking some wishful fantasy. We would rather be spiritually sterile than false. We approach the holy kicking, screaming, and dragging our feet all the way. It is to freedom from falsehood that we give ourselves.

At its best, this skeptical path lives out the First Commandment: "You shall love no gods except me," guarding the mystery of the Holy One's innermost name, "I am who I am" (Exod. 3:14). Clearing the path of false gods can eventually, without conscious intention but with the hidden action of the Spirit, reveal the obscure radiance of the Real One.

The trust present at the beginning for a person on the apophatic, intuitive-awareness path comes at the end for one on the skeptical path; but both paths share a lack of fascination with seeming signposts along the way.

At its worst, this pathless path turns cynical and bitter or fearful. Openness is lost completely. The disguised energy of spiritual yearning reveals itself only as a vague emptiness channelled into sensual drive and work, or lapsing into indolence. A blind, accidental universe is final—the last despairing meaningless meaning of it all.

All of these paths belong to the human potential of each of us. Probably we walk along each at some point in our lives. For some, there may be flashes of each one daily! For most of us, I think, one path will be dominant in our lives at any one time, sometimes for a lifetime.

Our personalities will have much to say about this. If our personality is highly intuitive, then we are likely to gravitate toward the path of intuitive awareness; if we are strong thinkers, toward the path of reason or "fighting it"; if strong feelers, toward devotion and/or action. As different facets of our personalities unfold, different paths take on fresh possibilities.

A spiritual companion needs to be someone who is aware of these paths in relation to our inner unfolding and calling. He or she can help us move appropriately, and not make us feel guilty if the path called for is different from that of the spiritual friend or others close to us.

No path is *necessarily* better than another in *itself*, though for *us* emphasis of one or another probably *will* be more *right* at any given time. Each path can be used to hide from the truth or to freeze its dynamic quality. Each is corrected and given perspective by the other paths. Each can be preparation for seeing and a way of integrating grace in our own lives. Each can be a "way home."

Faith Tradition

Particular Christian faith traditions as expressed in a given place tend to emphasize certain paths more than others, sometimes explicitly *over* others. If your tradition weights a particular path, that is fine, as long as it truly is your path.

If it is not, and there is little room or understanding of the path you seem to be called to walk now, then you may have to find a spiritual companion from a more sympathetic tradition, or someone who shares your "minority views" within your own.

In the last chapter I spoke of the great exchange currently in progress between many Protestant, Roman Catholic, and Eastern Orthodox traditions, a process that is stretching even beyond these to other deep historical religious faiths. One fruit of such exchange is the way it is opening up in some traditions a sense of validity to paths that once would have been considered invalid. Where such fruit is evidenced in your tradition, it is easier to trust that a companion can be chosen who will be more open to your path, even though it does not "fit" with that tradition's recent history.

Many Protestants, for example, who have been led toward a contemplative path have veered toward friendships with Roman Catholics, Anglicans, or Orthodox for whom this path at least has a place, if not always understanding. However, this path slowly appears to be becoming acceptable, if still not very available, within certain Protestant traditions. Spiritual friendships for this "minority path" can be found within them, a possibility that is likely to increase in the future as all traditions (except consciously restrictive sects) become more inclusive in our high-interchange culture.

Situation

Here is a sampling of life situations that point to the importance of giving them attention in selecting a spiritual friend.

You are a *seminarian*. Built into the seminary structure may be a spiritual formation director or spiritual/devotional life instructor. If the weight of that relationship is cultivating your life-style and spiritual practices in ways that "form" you in a particular spiritual tradition, then you are receiving formation and instruction, but not necessarily spiritual direction.

Direction involves unique attentiveness to your naked soul; it is not aimed at professionally forming you in some particular role or tradition, though this may be a by-product. The up-front focus is you, your total existential relation to the Holy, and its overflow into vocation and compassion.

Direction is open-ended in a way that may lead you in a completely different path than you are going. Besides this "directional" focus, it involves an awareness of "communitas," of the Sabbath, wherein social structure and your involvement in it is cut through by sheer appreciation of life as gift and not just task; life as intimacy and groundedness beyond role and function.

Thus you need to seek someone who is not going to see you primarily or exclusively as "seminarian." You need someone you can trust to see you beneath that label. And you need someone to whom you can expose your inmost soul without fear of its exposure becoming part of your "evaluation" for graduation or ordination. Such a possibility inevitably will tempt you to hold back your sinful, doubting, confused side.

Someone on the seminary staff, especially if he is on the fringe or out of the formal evaluative structure such as a chaplain in a Protestant situation, may allow you such a relationship. You may, though, need to find someone outside the seminary community completely in order to feel free in your own mind from any trace of evaluative functionalism.

If you are a *parish priest/minister*, or on the *staff* of a theological school or other religious center, you probably need to find someone who is "outside" your immediate institutional context, both to allow you the freedoms mentioned above, and also to save you from temptations to evade the delicacy of soul-focus by falling into "shop talk," theological or otherwise.

If you are a *layperson* in a parish, your pastor may or may not be right for you. Spiritual direction is a special gift and requires special time, neither of which may belong to the pastor.[15] However, he may be a good person with whom to meet and to help you sense who *might* be appropriate.

I have already spoken of *marital relationships* as very complicated and not necessarily right for spiritual direction. If you do not lay such high expectations on your partner, the relationship probably will be the better for it. You perhaps will be free to share helpfully prayer and informal spiritual *conversation*, without expecting the specificity of *direction*.

If you are someone on the *fringe* or *outside* the *institutional or parish church*, you will need someone who can respect your difficulties with the institution, and allow you to touch the deep awareness of the tradition for which the institution often is a frail vehicle. Perhaps it is someone who can gently help you bridge to the best values of the institution through some specialized community or ministry with which you feel compatible. College and other institutional chaplaincies, and monasteries and other intentional Christian communities, are examples.

You also may need to look for someone who can bridge the "language problem" with you. The contemporary theologian Bernard Lonergan makes a helpful distinction between "faith" and "belief."[16] *Faith*, he says, is a knowledge born of religious love, the love of God flooding our hearts. It involves discernment and judgments of value of a person in love that bring forth new energy and efficacy in all goodness. It is different from factual knowledge received by experiencing, understanding, verifying.

Belief is faith discerning the value of accepting the judgments of fact and value of religion. It is response to gift, the *outer* word of religious tradition, communities with varying expressions, but united by the eye of religious love.

You may have responded to your inner spiritual movements with a strong sense of transcendent "faith," but you are struggling with "belief," with the "superstructure" of particular historical forms and symbols that allow faith to be incarnate, nourished, shared, and passed on. National polls show over 90 percent of Americans have "faith in God." However, the proportion who have been able to bridge well into a committed "belief" structure is considerably lower, and even lower for commitment within a particular active institutional framework.

Spiritual yearning and experience is universal, but helpful, deepening, discerning forms of *response* often are difficult and call for a sensitive spiritual friend.

Opportunity

There is chronic complaint today that good spiritual directors are hard to find (a complaint not unknown in other periods of Church history). This is both true and false.

It is true that very few highly advanced guides are visible and available in the Christian Church today. The neglect of a carefully disciplined, tested, and sustained one-to-one oral transmission of Christian awareness has left us shortchanged in this regard.[17]

However, I believe it is false that "good spiritual directors" are unavailable. There may not be many people who are formally trained and experienced, but there are many who have the *potential* to be a good spiritual director for you, people who reflect the basic qualities of a good director discussed in the next chapter. The key on your part is to let your suspicions and fears loosen enough so that you can take a leap of faith with someone. When that "readiness" point is reached, my hunch is that someone will appear who is right for you.[18]

Finding a person near you is of course ideal, especially if you are beginning. You then can see him more frequently, which can be particularly valuable in your first few months.

If, however, the "right" person lives at a distance, you will need to plan regular times to meet, and perhaps exchange correspondence (or tapes) occasionally in between (and perhaps phone calls, if you can afford it).

Spiritual direction by mail is an ancient practice, but it is not an adequate substitute for meeting in person. By the time a director receives and responds to your letter you may already be in a different interior place. All the helpfulness and nuance of face-to-face interchange is lost.

Nonetheless, the discipline of attentively writing about the state of your soul to someone who cares in itself can be valuable. And the response you receive back, though perhaps not right on target for you at that point, is likely to be read with special inner listening to whatever you need to hear between the lines, just because it is written especially for you.

Exploration

You need not commit yourself to a friendship with the first person you consider. Your first meeting needs to be mutually exploratory, both in terms of your understandings of spiritual direction and your own sense of need—of just what you are (and are not) looking for. If you do not know each other, you also will be sensing whether or not there is a personality "fit." You need to intuit that the director is someone with whom you feel free to unlock your heart and trust, and who will be able to help you focus from where you are on your spiritual journey.

If you have any doubts, then it might be best to pray about and sleep on it before making any further commitment. Your initial tension may be due either to your own intrinsic fearfulness, to the "wrongness" of the other person for you, or to a combination of both.

Unless you come to a fairly clear sense that the person is wrong for you, then I would suggest a trial period of a few months with the person to give you time to "relax into" the relationship. This will help sort out how much of your ambivalence is due simply to the inner resistance you would have with anyone, given the nature of the task, and how much is inherent in the relationship.

After all, there is an inevitable sense of threat to our ego control and habits in "facing in" to our deepest purpose and ego-transcendent openness in life. That is just the reason we sometimes need a spiritual director, to encourage our freedom, as grace is given, for facing in to what otherwise we might evade.

Covenant

Once you have decided to continue with someone, you can help pave the way for a good spiritual companionship by clarifying together what really is important for you in the relationship. Your agreement about such things can form a "covenant" that helps to keep the relationship on track, and provides a basis for evaluation.[19]

Here are some areas for consideration in such a covenant:

1. *Meetings:* How often will you meet? For how long? If you are just beginning, especially if it is with someone you do not know, greater frequency is advisable: as often as weekly, no less than monthly. Planning specific, regular times ahead will help insure priority in your calendars.

Such planning also saves you from the temptation of scheduling times just when you have a special problem or crisis. You are attending to your ongoing total life of faith, prayer, vocation, charity, and discipline in spiritual direction. You are not primarily there to focus on "special problems." These can eclipse awareness of your whole self-surrendering to and resisting the Truth of your unfolding gifted self in the image of God. There are times where such problems can *reveal* this larger process, but it is that larger process, not the problem, that is the focus of direction.

Meeting times normally last about an hour.

2. *Focus:* Discuss together what is important within the sessions. Do you want to begin and/or end with prayer? With *shared* prayer, or led by you or the director? Silent and/or spoken prayer?

What do you want from the director? How does the director see himself or herself? Primarily as a listener? Adviser? Supporter? Confronter? Theologizer? Pray-er? Counselor? Teacher? Parent? Friend?

Your honesty here is very important. You need to be clear for yourself as well as for the director about your *desires* for what is *not* appropriate, as well as your sense of what is.[20] You need special awareness of your temptations to deflect attention into tangents that lose the *unique* potential of this relationship. You need to agree on the parameters for focus, and give each other permission to "call" the other on deflections from the focus.[21]

You can expect that your ego controls and habits will resist surrender to any focus that exposes them to unknown and extradependent territory that can only be *trusted* ahead of time. You will be tempted to stay on the surface and circle round and round the "one thing needful," letting your normal ego focus be relativized to your "larger Self." That Self is your more obscure, subtle wellspring in the image of God with its aware compassion and its unpossessive participation in the Real—your Christ-self.

You need to anticipate together this resistance, and the insistent yearning that shrinks resistance, and covenant together to feed the yearned-for larger Christ-Self.

What you decide upon for focus during sessions in effect will define your areas of accountability with the director. Such accountability ultimately is for your responsiveness to the grace revealed within and around you.

3. *Outside commitments:* You may want to know that your director is praying for you between meetings. Knowing that can be a powerful influence on your sense of "soul care" and belonging beyond yourself.[22]

You also might want to be accountable to the director for certain disciplines and actions that you agree together are important at a given time, such as times and forms of prayer, or some particular act of reconciliation or charity.[23]

Knowing that someone else knows and cares about whether you do what you agree is needed can be a powerful stimulant to follow-through that is missing when we just "decide on our own" to do something. Also, in the context of direction such disciplines and acts can be kept in perspective and not allowed to slip unnoticed into self-justifying and compulsive ends in themselves.

4. *Evaluation:* You will find it helpful to build in provision for periodical assessment of your relationship and its covenant, perhaps every three months or so (depending on how often you meet). Such times can give you opportunity to discuss together your sense of the positive and hindering dimensions of your time. You then can renegotiate your covenant, or perhaps determine that it is time to stop—either because the relationship has too many hindrances, or because you feel that you are so well in touch with your larger Self that you do not need a spiritual friend on the outside at the moment.

A caution is needed here: you need to consider very carefully before cutting off the relationship if your motive is to make "faster progress" with someone else. This may indeed be possible and right, but spiritual awareness (like much therapy) normally is a very slow, patient process that goes against the grain of a fast-paced, quick-fix culture. Your growth can be very obscure and hidden, yet very real. You are given as much as you are ready for; acceptance of that giveness as "enough for now," without trying to "push" it, in the long run may prove to be the tortoise attitude that beats the hare.[24]

6. Being a Spiritual Friend

In Chapter Four I spoke of that fabled lost throne, the awakening to our divine royal lineage, and our hard struggle for the fullness of that rightful heritage and calling.

Why is it a struggle? Perhaps no tradition adequately has explained that. Christian tradition at least accounts for a lot of repeated human experience when it speaks (one way or another) of our wounded nature that leaves us with partial sight, our freedom to attend toward or away from our royal heritage, and the forces within and around us that guide toward our whole/healed nature, or toward deeper separation from the Real.

Being a spiritual friend is being the physician of a wounded soul. And what does a physician do when someone comes with a bleeding wound?

Three things: He or she cleanses the wound, aligns the sundered parts, and gives it rest. That's all. The physician does *not* heal.[1] He or she provides an *environment* for the dominant natural process of healing to take its course. The physician really is midwife rather than healer.

The physician of souls explicity is a midwife, providing an environment for the birthing and nourishing of a whole soul. Always in the forefront of consciousness there is clarity that a three-way process is going on: between the midwife, the person struggling/allowing new life to come and take hold, and the Royal One whose loving/healing/driving Spirit we would serve, reflect, and enflesh.

125

Such a midwife of the Holy can function through all those forms of guidance mentioned in Chapter Four. Person-to-person spiritual friendship over a period of time is one form, involving certain gifts and skills.

Before turning to these, though, it is important to remember the freedom of that Royal Spirit. Though other people's gifts and talents are likely to be regular channels of grace for a person, there are no guarantees. When a person is very vulnerable and ready for regeneration, anyone may function as midwife, completely unconsciously. In a time of readiness, the veil separating us from the Holy is very thin, and we suddenly might see through it in any work or word of creation.

Everything that exists after all reflects the same *ultimate* Source and Healing, Driving Energy in orthodox Christian reflection on experience, no matter how distorted the surface of some things may have become. Anything is capable of mediating that ultimate truth to us, however obscurely.

Qualities of a Good Spiritual Friend

Within this framework, let's turn now to look at the gifts and talents that seem best to provide an environment for free spiritual struggle and receptivity.

In the last chapter I spoke of certain important variables that are involved in allowing for a good relationship: age, sex, personality, spiritual path, experience, and situation. Besides these variables, there are certain underlying "perennials" that nourish spiritual friendship.

A few years ago I interviewed twenty-nine spiritual leaders, most of them experienced directors, most of them Christian, concerning the most important qualifications for a spiritual companion. There was basic agreement around these qualities:

Personal spiritual commitment, experience, knowledge, and humility, and an active discipline of prayer/meditation.

The capacity to be caring, sensitive, open, and flexible with another person, not projecting one's own needs or fostering long-term dependency.[2]

Here are a few individual comments that bring out special dimensions not obvious above:[3]

Have experienced a movement from despair to grace: trust in the healingness of the universe, and delight in the freedom of others. (James Forbes)

Have gotten through your Messianism (about any particular spiritual path), i.e., that everybody needs this. (James Fowler)

Have no expectation or anticipation of where a person should go—not my will but thine be done; the bee keeper is the most spiritual, least assuming. (Hans Hofmann)

Have the capacity to step aside and let the Spirit of Christ do the direction—[realize that] skill development is secondary to this. (Peter and Linda Sabbath)

Be in full communion with the whole of your own humanity—not airy-fairy; be in the body of some tradition where there can be external validation of your experience. (Graham Pulkingham)

Be capable of noticing the movement of the Spirit, and of providing an environment out of which the person can pay attention and allow this intuitive noticing to become an important part of his/her life. (William Sheehan)

Apropos of this last quotation, John Cassian in the fourth century quotes an alleged saying of Jesus that speaks of the importance of such discernment: "Become wise money-changers, able to distinguish gold from brass, and to accept only genuine coin."[4]

In the canonical texts, Jesus implies qualities of humble service, love, empowered relation to himself, to the Father, to the indwelling, discerning Spirit, and to the community of faith. Given the many weaknesses of the disciples, he certainly did not imply moral and spiritual perfection as a qualification.

Paul continues Jesus' emphasis (e.g., Phil. 1:9–10, I Cor. 1:18–25), spelling out fruits of the Spirit that by implication should mark the spiritual friend (Gal. 5:22–23), a holy integration of body, mind, and spirit (I Thess. 5:23), and a willingness to test everything (I Thess. 5:21).

For the Desert Fathers, a steady personal qualification was *compunction,* a sign of valid repentance, metanoia, conversion—"a sense of the *truth* of meeting the infinitely real in the center of one's nothingness,"[5] and the fruit of tranquility *(hesychia),* purity of heart.

John of the Cross adds a qualification that varies with the relationship. Directors should be able not merely to aim at guiding souls according to their own way, but should determine if they can see the way "by which God is leading the soul, and if they know it not, let them leave the soul in peace and not disturb it."[6]

Teresa of Avila saw a good director as pious (a person of prayer and experience), learned (especially in ascetical theology—though *no* learning is better than a *little*), and kind (interested, trusting, consoling).[7]

Francis de Sales in the seventeenth century said a spiritual guide must be "full of charity, knowledge, and prudence."[8] He should be a faithful friend, who is able to help a person *follow* and not outrun grace.[9]

More recently, Vilma Seelaus speaks of six complementary "animus" and "anima" qualities: strength and gentleness, clarity and intuition, objectivity and receptivity.[10]

Jean La Place adds simplicity, "not focused on your own self-discovery and importance," and "the peace of God." He also recommends that the director be "strong enough to calm the nervous tension and hurry that is preventing [a person's] surrender to God."[11]

Norbert Brockman mentions the importance of being able to discern your own gratifications in offering direction, the humility of being able to learn with and through the person, and prudence with holding confidences.[12]

Adrian Van Kaam speaks of the director as one who can aspire only to be a facilitator, an awakener of what already is there; one who takes seriously the Hebrew meaning of Jesus' name: "Yeshuah": opening up, liberating, making space, setting free, taking away confinement and limitation.[13]

Thomas Merton speaks of the effective director as one

who knows that his or her first duty is "to see to his own interior life and take time for prayer and meditation, since you never will be able to give to others what you do not possess yourself."[14]

Perhaps this last "qualification" of the director best expresses the most important undercurrent in Christian tradition. It is not a matter of accumulated skills that is central, but rather facing into the call toward self-stripping of illusion and sin that frees us to be ever more transparent and truly present with someone.

If we do care most deeply about facing into the Real One, and notice when we are not, then we are more likely spontaneously to encourage and notice such basic things in our spiritual friend. It will not be a matter of trying to remember what some book said to do, and continuing a contrived "helpful" response. More and more you simply will be with the person as they need you to be with them. Your own experience in touching and glancing away from the same Reality with which your friend struggles gives you a common bond and sympathetic perception.

It is important at this point to specify in more detail than I have the differences between psychotherapy, pastoral counseling, and spiritual direction, as another way of clarifying the distinctive ministry of spiritual direction.

Gerald May recently has provided the most clear and on-target distinctions between these three that I have seen, though any outline of distinctions is bound to overcategorize approaches that in fact can fade into one another at times.[15]

Dr. May uses the example of depression or anxiety to illustrate these differences:

If you wonder what you can do to get out of depression or anxiety, you're being your own psychotherapist.

If you think God has given it to you to learn from for your own growth, you are being your own pastoral counselor.

If your concern simply is to give yourself to God, then you are being your own spiritual guide.

These further descriptions of the normal differences between therapy/counseling on the one side, and spiritual di-

	Psychotherapy	Pastoral Counseling	Spiritual Direction
SUBJECT	Disordered patient wanting cure	Disordered (troubled) client wanting help.	A soul searching for God; not a disorder but a sacred situation.
GOAL	Resolution of psychic conflict and adjustment to society. (Medical Model.)	Healing, sustaining, reconciling, and guiding. (More holistic model.)	Being and becoming in God.
METHOD	Techniques employed on client for desired results	Helping acts resulting in benefit to client.	Allowing self and relationship to be a vehicle of grace, of the will of God. Primary method: surrender; letting go whatever is in God's Way.
ATTITUDE OF HELPER	Responsible for cure of patient. *My* will be done.	Client or the relationship is responsible. *Our* will be done.	Only God is responsible for whatever healing/growth occurs. *Thy* will be done.

rection on the other, emerged in a dialogue with Dr. May in a seminar of the Shalem spiritual directors program (some of these points came from participants). Again, it is important to remember the likely overlaps, since both are different focal settings on the *same* ultimately indivisible human reality.

Determining Your Vocation

Your own awareness and experience, no matter how profound, does not automatically qualify you as a spiritual director. Some people simply are not gifted or motivated in one-to-one spiritual presence and communication. Their awareness instead may be shared helpfully in preaching, writing, group direction, counseling, or other forms of guidance.

Therapy/Counseling	Spiritual Direction
1. Solid self-definition.	Self-definition relativized and transcended.
2. Integration, adjustment.	Love that pours beyond self.
3. Ground of intra-psychic/interpersonal relations.	Ground of faith; human-divine relations.
4. Individual problem-solving, comprehension.	Sanctification; apprehension; personal calling in helping the larger community's growth; open mystery.
5. Mind-talk.	God-talk (different vocabulary).
6. Mechanic to help fix your Porsche; paid professionalism.	Someone to appreciate your Porsche with you; dealing with whole self in whole human/divine community; more charismatic than professional relationship.
7. Focus on *contents* of conscious and unconscious self; how feeling, thinking, remembering.	More focus on the *nature* and universal quality of consciousness/unconsciousness. What is the quality of your consciousness? What is the specialness of your being?
8. Mystical experience usually seen as pathological, or (in transpersonal psychology) something to be sought.	Mystical experience seen as sometimes delusional, but sometimes as gifted liberation. It is liberating if we don't fearfully try to hold on to ego boundaries (i.e., our sense of identity, self-importance), and really allow a death and rebirth experience. This involves a transcendent trust that one's self-*existence* is not lost in losing self-*definition*.
9. Psychological needs satisfaction.	Ongoing conversion; letting go or lightening whatever is held onto or identified with that blocks deeper open identity and loving evoked by the Spirit of God in Christ.

The primary ways of determining whether or not spiritual direction is a gift and calling of yours include:

1. Prayer for guidance about your calling, beginning with as "indifferent" a mind as possible about being a spiritual companion for others. That is, let yourself be open to what is meant to be for you, that is consonant with the gifts

and situation given. This will help you discern at a deeper and more authentic level than simply whether or not you like the idea of giving spiritual direction. If you do it just because you "feel good" about it, such grounds may reflect an ego trip, a motivation guaranteed to cultivate shallow, subtly self-centered, "fair-weather" guidance.

2. A second helpful determining factor is noticing whether or not others spontaneously come to you for help with the spiritual dimension of their lives over a period of time. Such evidence is an important confirmation of your calling. Be sure to distinguish between such people and those who might come to you for help in ego-coping, problem-solving situations. Gifts and calling for such psychological counseling situations are not necessarily the same as those for spiritual direction.

However, in our problem-solving oriented culture, it is possible that people are coming to you with spiritual concerns veiled beneath some presenting problem, simply because specific issue problem-solving is all they ever have been exposed to. If this is the case, perhaps they do vaguely sense that you can offer them another dimension for which they yet may not have a name.

3. A third determining factor is what emerges in reflecting on all this with your own spiritual director. Such a prior relationship and indirect "apprenticeship" with a spiritual companion, preferably over years, as well as conversation with him or her about your vocation, I think both are prerequisites before determining your own possible calling. In many Protestant situations, where spiritual direction has less place, this relationship may have been more informal and sporadic. Yet such experience of some kind is very important. Spiritual direction at its best is a handed-down oral tradition, a "lineage" of experience in which you have been nourished.

Skills

For those who do seem gifted and motivated as directors and who do give priority to their own interior nakedness in

God, the raw gift and experience I think *can* be shaped to a finer edge for meeting others. This shaping is not always necessary, but for most gifted people I think it can be helpful. This "shaping" involves knowledge derived from psychological as well as spiritual disciplines.[16]

In the next chapter I will describe a program designed for such sharpening assistance. For the remainder of this one, let me take you through the specific dimensions of a spiritual-direction relationship that provide the midwifing environment for cleansing, aligning, and resting. Please keep in mind that these are suggestions from a human perspective, and we need to remain open to the possibility that, if the Spirit so wills, good spiritual direction can happen in the worst seeming environment.

The Healing Process[17]

I. Cleansing

When someone arrives for a spiritual direction session with you, their first need likely will be for cleansing away the accretions of anxiety, crowded mind, and bodily tension that cloud clear presence. You can provide a helpful environment for this cleansing in a number of ways.

Physical Environment. Providing a "clean" *physical* environment is one way. If the place where you meet is cluttered by noise, probable interruptions of people (in person or on the phone), glaring lights, and a desk piled with debris between you and the person, that can reinforce a cluttered mind. Providing a badly contoured chair that either gives discomfort or too sleepy comfort also can get in the way.

The simpler, quieter, and aesthetically warmer the room, the more your space will invite a simpler, quieter, more secure presence. A simple, small, rugged chapel or prayer room could be helpful, though this might be too intimidating and awesome for some people.

Bodily "Confession." You can provide ways to help a person be still and let the churning mind and body calm down, if this seems needed. If the person is open to it, you can suggest that they close their eyes and take a few long, slow deep breaths, with particularly long exhalations. This will have the double effect of calming and slowing their minds and bodies, and giving them a certain "open energy" that serves attentiveness.

More involved physical movements can be suggested if the person is particularly agitated and breathing isn't enough. One possibility is to ask the person to stand up, bend over very slowly, slowly rise, bend back with arms raised and chin into the chest, open his mouth slightly and do some deep breathing for about a minute. This last act will allow a lot of anxious tension to flow out.

Ignoring the part our bodies play in keeping our minds "impacted" is to ignore a basic reality of our humanness. We need to pay attention to the value of letting our bodies "confess" and be cleansed of their accumulated garbage. Then perhaps our *minds* will be able to do so a little more freely.[18]

Confession of Faith and Opening Presence. The directee can be helped to confess his or her faith and hope. In some situations this may best be done vicariously by you as director. In others, it may be an open moment of spontaneous prayer open to both of you. It need not be elaborate. Just naming the Lord of life, and your hope for openness to the Loving One's presence and direction.

Where spontaneous prayer is difficult, a more formal prayer, such as the Lord's Prayer, can be said alone or together. Along with or in place of such vocal prayer you can suggest *silence*.

Five minutes of silence at the beginning of a session can be invaluable. You can suggest that the person just watch thoughts or images passing by without grabbing them. These often are surface reverberations of our ego desires and fears, "noiseclutter" the mind needs to confess, to let go. Then the mind is free to be more permeable to its deeper desire for the Holy One, and more open to that connectedness.

Another possibility is suggesting that the silence have a focus. This can be an interior one of the person's own choosing, such as imaging a cross, a body full of light, or a particular word of scripture or prayer.

It also can be an exterior focus, such as a cross, candle,

flowers, water, or ikon you have in the room or scripture you read. The instructions can be the same as in "open" silence: not trying to "do" anything, except relaxing into the open Presence.

Such silent time can help a person make the transition spoken of in Chapter Three from intra to extradependence, from work to Sabbath time. Emergence from the silence, marked perhaps by a quiet clap or word from you, will likely find the directee more calm, less compulsively controlling, less self-conscious, more spontaneously in touch with what needs to be shared.

Short silent times also can be helpful in the middle of a session. These can be helpful to the directee who has become too crowded or paralyzed with "trying too hard" and seems to be just beating around the bush.

They can be helpful as spontaneous silences in just the opposite situation: when a profound sense of Presence or discernment strikes, and the person just needs to let it sink in without "distancing" by any further interpretation for the moment.

Such silences can be as important, or more so, than words in a direction session. Your presence as director can help secure the person to listen with you in silence. It is, after all, a three-way "conversation" in classic Christian direction. Both director and directee are listening together for a more obscure "Voice." Or together in silence they simply are appreciating the Presence, letting it do its own obscure cleansing work.

So we need not fear silence as "dead" time to fill quickly with words. One of the great contributions of apophatic spirituality[19] is its appreciation of the power of a listening silence. This is an awareness that a true Word comes from profound Silence, and a profound Silence follows a true Word. Both are made of the same substance. They are not different "realities," but different forms of one reality, forever feeding one another.

When we realize this "unity in diversity" of Word and Silence, perhaps we are a little more free to realize that larger Unity in Diversity that, in Christian experience, describes

Reality as it is. We sense ourselves living *within* a mysteriously compassionate, dynamic Real One, yet living as many unique, communing forms that give us a sense of "outsideness" as well as withinness. In words this is a paradox. In experience it is whole.[20]

The closer you and the directee are to realizing this truth of faith, the closer I think you will be to the foundation of authentic Christian spiritual direction. Your time then will not be spent seeing life as pieces and categories that you must struggle to relate, but as one already-connected, gifted reality for you to *realize*. Our analytical minds in order to understand and function must divide this reality into pieces. Direction, though, at its best, weds analytical and intuitive mind to help us appreciate the gifted unity *through* the pieces, and the unique calling of our particular personal diversity within that whole.

Confession of Sins. One more form of "mind cleansing" can reinforce such perception. That is formal or informal *confession of sins.* In Chapter Four I spoke of the value of the rite of reconciliation, perhaps the most consistent single form of guidance in Christian tradition if we include the corporate confession in Protestant practice. Often in the tradition it has been included in the spiritual-direction relationship, at least as an option.

One value of allowing such confession for inclusion in the relationship is the way it helps connect moral and spiritual development. Focus on confession of sins in isolation from its larger ascetical context can tempt a person to identify confession exclusively with being good or bad. Much of spirituality in American practice seems to be in danger of such an identification, turning life into a heavy way of moralism, if not outright legalism.

Confession of sins, indeed, has a central moral dimension. In our freedom we do have a part in what happens. We sometimes are capable of other behavior. The very act of confession can strengthen this sense of freedom for accountability and our desire for letting go our hurtful ways.

Proclamation of forgiveness can free us from noncompulsive guilt and leave us reconciled with God, self, and neighbor.

This practice also has the *ascetical* function of freeing our energy to participate in that larger Presence threading through our lives. If we are focused on our own ongoing guilt, resentment, vindictiveness, negligence, etc., these not only hurt others and ourselves, they *deflect* us from our deeper purposes and presence in Christ, in the image of God.

The ultimate goal of confession I think is not to free us to be "good," but to let that "goodness," that inwardly reconciled and outwardly constructive activity, free us to realize more and more fully our "wholeness." Our *goodness* is energy for caring. Our *wholeness* is that deeper sense of context wherein all that we are and do, and all that the cosmos presents, ultimately is held together in the Loving One. Such sense of wholeness frees our goodness to arise more and more spontaneously out of confident appreciation of such giftedness, and less and less contrivedly out of subtly anxious attempts to merit that giftedness by our works.

Confession within a spiritual direction relationship has another potential value: it can save the relationship from temptations to evade moral responsibility. Just as in therapy there is the danger of subtly or blatantly reinforcing a sense of "sickness" as an excuse for irresponsible moral abandon, so in spiritual direction there is danger of focusing on some ethereal relation to God or of interior experience in ways that evade accountability for one's behavior both for things done and undone.[21] That perhaps is why Baron von Hügel asked Evelyn Underhill to work in a soup kitchen once a week.

In the history of Christian spirituality moral and spiritual development have always been connected (albeit with various tensions), reflecting consistent scriptural exhortation. Cultivation of the "virtues" often was considered prerequisite for higher spiritual development.[22] Much ego-forgetfulness and discipline of appetites can be the fruit of a virtuous life, which prepare a person for deeper attentiveness and surrender to the ultimate Truth of their lives.

Today, of course, we have a much better understanding of the complexity and psychological/social roots of human behavior, so that we can help a person distinguish between such things as free and compelled acts, sin and sickness, confident humility and fearful humiliation, as well as deal with these in the full context of a person's unique unfolding rather than as isolated attitudes and acts.

Within a direction relationship you simply can mention to a person that you are open to confession if and when that becomes appropriate, with no sense of pressure for it. If you are a lay person and in a tradition where the rite of reconciliation is restricted to the ordained, you can still hear a person reflect repentantly on his or her sense of sinfulness, and you are free to remind the person of God's promised forgiveness.[23] In many situations, expecially among Protestants, such a more informal approach to sin and forgiveness may be more appropriate, in any case.

So there we see some ways of allowing our wounded nature to be cleansed and prepared for attention to "alignment" in a direction session. Let's turn now to this second dimension of the process.

II. Alignment

Cleansing can allow spontaneous alignment. When the "lense of our perception" is clear, when the "eye of the body" is whole, the torn edges of our soul are likely to move together. We begin to see together what before were separated fragments. This perspective gives us clues as to how our lives are graced, and how we are called to unfold.

There are two dimensions to this sight: our interior awareness and our vocation.

Interior awareness. There are many questions you may want to ask about interior awareness, or have in the back of your mind as the person talks. Each question aims at fuller alignment of the person's fragments. Here are some examples.

What is the person's *image of God*? Directees may not be conscious of this, but it is affecting their whole orientation, whatever it is. The names of God in scripture reflect all kinds of images, such as Judge, Lover, Comforter, Redeemer, Father, Mother, Husband, Creator, Faithful, Lawgiver, Almighty, All Knowing, Holy, Provider, Ever Present, Merciful, Sufferer, Liberator, Spirit, and the name beyond our comprehension: Yahweh, "I am who I am."

Perhaps each of us images God in all of these ways at some time or another. At any given time, though, we likely relate more to some of these than others. Because they all express some dimension of that Ultimate Reality whose Presence we sense, it is important that a person sense their ultimate alignment. Even though one dimension may have more value at a given point, the others correct and fill out the image. One alone can become distorting and destructive. For example, if a person relates to God only as Judge, Lawgiver, Almighty, it can create a sense of distance, guilt, and drive to justification by works that is oppressive, dry, and rigid (even if some sense of thankfulness for the Law mitigates these). Such a person needs to align this "objective" sense of God with such qualities as Lover, Sufferer, and Liberator.

Some people image God very personally. Others sense the Transcendent more abstractly and impersonally. If a person's path is more devotional, it is likely to be the former. If it is more the path of knowledge, it is likely to be the latter. Respect for these different senses is important. At the same time, you may need to test how much the impersonal sense hides a fear of personal intimacy, and how much the personal sense hides the more awesome awareness beyond our secure intimate feelings.

Are particular Persons of the Trinity more alive than others for them? They may need help in unblocking their sense of the others for an undistorted, unified sense of God both within and without, incarnate and invisible, simple and subtle.[24] They may also need to be able to relate to God's image both through and beyond its "maleness and femaleness," the "image" of God reflected in Genesis 1:27.

Related to their image of God is their *image of themselves.* The goal here, I believe, is a sense of self as unique, unfolding giftedness mixed with both willful and blind resistance, and a self that is interdependent and intermingled with the rest of reality and its positive and negative impingements, as well as with the Sustaining Source of it all, closer than our breath, yet infinitely beyond our imagining.

In this image of self there is a permeability between God and the person, so much so that there is a sense of relative self, of unique, gifted/warped personality that has an open, everywhere-connected underside of Big Self in God; thus self is seen as being foreground and background of a coinherent gestalt.

Some of the resistances to such spiritually mature views of self and God arising from our wounded nature of which you need to be aware are:[25]

1. A fear of losing self-identity, of being consumed by God.

2. A sense of faith as a burden rather than liberation—a series of laws that limit freedom.

3. A sense of Christ as so much awesomely "other" than we that we lose the point of the Incarnation: the intimate and redeeming dwelling of God in all our humanity.

4. Psychological barriers, such as a low-grade chronic hostility, distrust, fear of intimacy, an insecurity leading to a need to control everything possible.

5. Seeking to please our own or other people's surface egos more than desire to listen and follow the inner light of the Spirit.

6. An inattentive laziness, indifference.

What is the *history* of these images of God and self? Early on in your relationship it can be helpful to suggest that you both need to be in touch with the person's spiritual journey thus far. You can do this very simply by just letting them free-associate with their spiritual journey. Or you can provide more focused opportunities.

For example, you can suggest some "homework" after one of the early sessions. Ask them to take an hour or two at home to write down what seem to be the "footsteps of God" in their lives: particular events, relationships, experiences, etc. What are the patterns noticed? What are the fruits in increasing conversion of the whole person into God's way: morally, intellectually, aesthetically, emotionally, intuitively?

Do the footsteps appear primarily alone, with others, or in nature? In a "religious," work, or recreational situation? Do they come as surprises or as consciously prepared for times? What was the place of any spiritual discipline, such as prayer and fasting, in this biography? What was the place of spiritual friends? How have their images of God and themselves changed through all this?

The "homework" can end with silence, allowing some image, some simile to rise for where they are now in their spiritual journey, completing the sentence: "My spiritual journey now is like ..."

If you want to ask them to do more, you might consider an adaptation of Ira Progoff's dialogue process. Ask them to close their eyes and image their spiritual journey as a "person" separate from themselves. Then write a dialogue, a script with the journey very rapidly (I say ... my spiritual journey says ...), until it comes to a natural pause.[26]

Such "homework" can give your directee and you a helpful perspective on his or her spiritual life, giving you many clues about the person's development. It also can be the beginning or continuance of a discipline of journal keeping.

Another important question related to interior awareness has to do with the person's *prayer*. Just what happens when they pray and meditate? How much is it "telling" God things, and how much is it listening? How much is "censored" (e.g., anger at God)?

Everything should be free to enter conversation in prayer. At the same time, it can be difficult for people to get beyond conversation in prayer: complaining, asking, thanking, etc., and just let the relationship subtly "be." That involves letting ego controls relax (as in the transitional silence suggested earlier), and listening ever more deeply, without expectation but with energetic attentiveness.

Such "quiet" prayer is difficult in our society, yet all the more important because of our aggressive activism (I will return to this subject in the next section).

Prayer is a mode of consciousness and relationship that is extremely important in spiritual development. Neither spiritual conversation and analytical discernment with a friend, nor active works, can substitute for it.

Prayer is a quality of participation in reality that belongs to our full humanity. Without authentic prayer we are more prone to ego attachments and self-centeredness that impair our unfolding, and probably our neighbor's as well. With it, we can tune in to our deepest Home and broadest Horizon.

Prayer like anything else, of course, can be distorted. Every spiritual practice can have a way of securing us against the really Real as well as preparing us more fully for participation. Prayer can be a weapon to call defeat down on an enemy, or a compulsive blanket we wrap around us everytime we get close to something we fear seeing for what it is. Prayer also can be a self-righteous way of seeming superior, or of building a ladder to heaven.

The director needs to attend to the many devious ways prayer might be used, or evaded, by the person.

Prayer at its best invokes appropriate humility, confidence in the obscurity of faith, openness to the loving truth from whatever direction and however painfully it may come, and an overflow of compassion. These are the fruits to look for.

These fruits are the test as well for any interior phenomena that may appear: voices, visions, tongues, smells, raptures, dreams, etc. There is some difference of opinion in Christian tradition concerning the spiritual value of such phenomena. If there is a rule of thumb in Christian apophatic tradition, beyond attention to the fruits over time, it might be that the more subtle, obscure, unifying, and "unspecial' the phenomenon, the closer the person is likely to be with the really Real. If it makes the person feel more rather than less important and self-concerned, it is likely not to be of God.

There can be great confusion between the precognitive awareness behind such experience, and its "translation" into a recognizable experience, i.e., into interpretive feelings and into image and word symbols.

There is a qualitative difference in apophatic tradition between such comprehensible interpreted experience and the subtle awareness itself. The awareness, if fully "of God," involves a suspension of our normal senses. Translation into these senses colors and narrows the awareness in accordance with the personally meaningful and recognizable symbols, and usually the ego desires and fears, our senses and hidden motives understand.

Words of prophecy in voice or automatic writing, for example, are mediators of an inspiration; that mediation can "pollute" the message. The more holy the life of the person, however, the more of a "clear channel" they are likely to be.

In Christian apophatic tradition, such phenomena tend to be treated as experiences along the way not to become fascinated with, lest our egos become possessively attached to them, and we confuse the experiences, the gifts of the Giver, with the Giver Himself. When this happens, we lose sight of the goal of pure surrender and communion, and the simple, unspecial, insightfully compassionate life that normally seems to follow.

If the experiences are of God, as John of the Cross sees it, then they will do their work in us without our having to do anything. If they are not of God, then we don't want to pay attention anyway. In either case, just attentively seeing and letting be, letting go, is enough. Such a view echoes Far Eastern apophatic religious traditions' approaches to such phenomena as well, as seen perhaps most extremely in Zen Buddhist practice.

In kataphatic tradition these phenomena are likely to be seen as inspired messages and graces to be taken seriously in their interpreted as well as precognitive form. Currently this is most obvious in the "charismatic" movement.

My own sense is that the apophatic is a helpfully iconoclastic tradition that we have ignored in relation to interior phenomena at the price of often naive and ultimately side-tracking acceptance of any personally interpreted inspiration, or that of another person.[27]

There certainly may be times when something of importance is "coming through" our interpretive channels that we or others do need to pay attention to, for which scripture gives many precedents. If we keep an apophatic "lightness" and even-mindedness through the experience, and a confidence in God *beyond* our experience, we are more likely to be able to sort out what is worth special attention, and what is but a happy dance of our egos (still ultimately a gift from God, but not directly inspired), and what perhaps is even of destructive demonic influence.

Does a director need to have experienced such phenomena to be of value to the person who has? The ideal I think would be someone who has not only experienced such phenomena, but who has *gone through* them to their other side, and from that more calm place can provide the person with his or her sense of confidence and perspective.

However, I would stand with many in the tradition who do not think such experience is necessary (for the director *or* the directee!). What is necessary is your calm trust in grace winding its opening way through the directee's life no matter *what* the interior or exterior phenomena, and enough knowledge of the way phenomena have been treated by Christian masters to give you some perspective and sense of options.[28]

β   *Vocation.* The second dimension of "alignment" takes us from interior awareness in God and self-images, prayer, and special phenomena, to the person's sense of "calling" emerging from this awareness and from daily life experience.

"Calling" is a much abused word today. In the Church it can be little more than a pious euphemism for doing what we feel like doing. Such abuse is brought to celebration in the secular culture, when doing what we feel like doing, attained by any way we can manipulate it, seems often to be what lies behind "career development."

Authentic sacred calling and secular career development at its best do meet at one crucial point: attention to our personal resources and situation. The difference is that vocation infers more riskiness and uncertainty about these. While you won't be given "more than you can bear," you will be led by "a way you do not know" to become a channel for grace in ways you cannot adequately predict.

This was Abraham and Sarah's journey in responsive faith, and that of all their authentic spiritual descendants. Jesus' vocation, too, is portrayed as unfolding throughout his life. As the Harvard theologian Arthur McGill once said, Jesus lived out of "ecstatic identity with God as His origin and continually operative cause ... He always was *receiving* his "self" from God. [For each of us], 'I am' is a constant receiving from beyond myself as a gift."[29]

Our identity in Christian tradition therefore is not some hard "possession" to find and clutch. It is a continually unique gift that by its very nature is unpossessible, only sharable. Our "called out" identity is an always freshly known and shared joy or pain that William Blake would kiss as it passes. It is never really a pickled, jarred, static specimen, or some elusive butterfly we would kill and mount, except as our wayward freedom would try to make it so.

When then a person comes to us in direction for assistance in discerning vocation, this is the setting for understanding: a sense of organically unfolding calling, our wayward resistance to its dynamic and risky character, and an influential secular culture that conditions us to deny or distort the first and ignore the second.

More specifically, we can look at four levels of vocation with a person: *foundational covenant, human covenant state, form of ministry,* and *immediate callings.*

Foundational Covenant Vocation. The first level is that of undergirding covenant. Though our identity always is being given afresh, this is not meant to invite a chaotic, totally unpredictable and unreliable flip-flopping around. It is an *organic* development, unfolding out of what is given in trusting continuity with the faithful Name Giver: "I have called you by name, you are mine" (Isa. 43:1).

The first level of vocation in Christian understanding therefore is the calling to live within this mutually trusting,

culturally and ego-self/transcendent covenant. This means
the steady acceptance of life in general, along with our particular life, as gifted and meaningful, not cursed and blindly
accidental. This is the greatest leap of faith, or nonfaith,
from which all else follows.

This covenant does not imply steady positive *feelings*
about it. The Psalms reveal every possible feeling about the
covenant, from anger to joy to flashes of despair. Yet beneath
our fickle feelings some obscure trust can remain steady.

It is this foundational level of vocation that you as director need to be aware of between the lines of the person's
comments. Does the directee confuse his feelings about life
with this foundational trust? Does he or she make the covenant's reality dependent on mood? Or dependent on the
institutional Church or particular spiritual leaders' purity or
corruption as mediators? Is there rather clarity that such
faith exists and points to Reality deeper than any frail mediation of feeling, institution, or person?

Focus on the mediation of Jesus Christ at its best in
Christian tradition empowers this discernment. To faith, his
death carried away with it all idolatry of structures, feelings,
or persons as sufficient vehicles of the covenant. His resurrection lifts the covenant to a plane of intimate, mysterious,
and obscure trust that relativizes any mediational vehicles.

Dependence on Christ then is independence of confused
idolatry, freedom for that deeper covenant of naked trust. If
this dependence in the directee's mind instead turns the
Christ into one more idol to please or disappoint, then I
think he or she has missed the deeper covenant to which Jesus links us: covenant with the intimately obscure "Abba" of
our souls, who calls us to a covenant so deep that on the surface of life we are liberated from much confusion and enslav-
ing idolatry, liberated for more authentic discernment and
community.

There is no magic in these words. The empowering
truth behind them is "in and out" with us; our wounded nature leaves us faint and dizzy, easily swayed by fantasies. We
need great forbearance with this inevitable human state,

both in ourselves and in our directees. "Telling" them such words indiscriminately, as though they will have some automatic power, is useless. The director's job is to help *evoke* such liberating awareness, as grace for it nears the surface in your mutual discernment.

This task of evocation continues through discernment together at the other levels of vocation.

Before looking at each of these other levels, we need to be clear about our own and our directee's assumptions about particular callings within the underlying basic call to gifted meaningful life. A guiding question for us here is, "Does God have a plan for our lives?" How we and our directee answer this will help determine how together we will see and go about discerning vocations.

Two extremes help to clarify the possibilities for answering this question. At one end, there is the view that God wound up the universe and let it go. At best we have that ultimate covenant of gifted life, but within history and day-to-day living most everything is in the hands of human freedom, conditioning, or coincidence. Life then is what we make it. There are no specific divine movements that call us.

At the other extreme, God is guiding almost every detail of human life. Human freedom and purpose involve careful discernment and awareness of this guidance.

Liberal Protestants tend toward the former end of the continuum. Fundamentalist Protestants, and operationally I think many devout Roman Catholics (modified by Church teaching), tend toward the latter. Christian tradition as a whole I think would be more toward the latter, but the strong tendency and influence of secular culture today *beyond* the former end toward *total* arbitrary human independence I think has been edging much of the Church increasingly in this direction (though certainly short of the secular extreme).[30]

An intermediate view of God's "plan" would focus on the way of life revealed in scripture. We are given guidelines for attitudes and behavior there that are central to God's plan for us. But "how" we express these at a given time is relative to the situation and our rational/intuitive discernment. God is not *directly* guiding us, but *in*directly through these guidelines.

Perhaps Ignatius Loyola most popularly integrated a range of views and experiences related to discernment of vocation by speaking of three different appropriate times for decision-making. These times he saw guided respectively by *reason* where God is "indifferent" to what we do (except the criterion of faithful loving), by *evaluation* of inner movements of desolation and consolation over time, and by *direct guidance* of God (as when Paul was knocked from his horse on the road to Damascus).[31]

Ignatius and his Jesuit descendants have been enormously influential in the vocational discernment dimensions of spiritual direction in Roman Catholic tradition, and there are signs of increasing influence among Protestants today as well. You might find a good deal of help as a director in reading some of the many articles available on Ignatian discernment in current periodicals.[32]

Sometimes directees need help in seeing such a range of possibilities for the way God might be operating in their lives, as well as help with specific applications of a discernment process to vocational decisions. Let's turn now briefly to the three *specific* levels of vocation that might arise in a direction situation.

Human Covenant State. There normally is a level of our lives that seeks to reflect the foundational covenant. Here we seek long-term commitments that provide a general framework for our living and caring.

Is the person called as an adult to commitment in marriage, or in celibate community? (The community being either a formally religious one with vows, or an informal commitment within the context of a particular ministry, which may include married people.) Or is the person called to that form of community with God and the world found in solitude, as a hermit or hermitess?

The experience of the Church assumes most people's call will be to marriage and family, fewer to the single life in informal community, still fewer to formal celibate community, and very few to solitude.

The transient state of Western culture and the Church at this point historically and operationally has shifted many people from *lifetime* to *long-term* commitments in one of these frameworks. There are fewer sanctions against and greater opportunities for shifting what once were lifetime vows. This situation increasingly has destabilized both societal and individual life. It has the positive fallout of more easily freeing people to move to more truly called covenants. Its negative fallout may be the way it more easily tempts us to evade responsible commitments and too easily obey a restless impulse to look for a more perfect covenant and relationship.

Perhaps the most stable covenant state remaining for the directee is the one into which he or she was born: the blood family. Even though it may be fragmented by divorce, there nonetheless still usually is an enduring sense of identity and commitment (however loose) within this covenant. It may be the only *enduring* communal identity the directee knows, and thus a valuable reference point in speaking of covenants.

Another dimension of covenant state is whether or not the person is called to *ordained* or *lay* status. How each state is understood will vary according to tradition. A general trend in the West today is to bring lay status back to the more complementary and respected place it once held. This change is seen especially among Roman Catholics (though not yet so *juridically* respected among them). It always has been important among Protestants.

A directee sometimes needs help in not confusing a call to serious Christian vocation with a call to ordained leadership, which involves particular gifts and work that may not fit the directee's particular gifts and form of ministry.

For persons just approaching the institutional Church, or reapproaching it after a long lapse, there may be need to help them assess the rightness for their establishment of an active covenant relationship with a particular ecclesial expression of the Church. This may involve consideration of

Baptism or Confirmation, or active relationship to a particular parish or other formal community.

Spiritual yearning is a universal human pressure for Home. The infrastructure of faith, as I earlier mentioned, Bernard Lonergan helpfully distinguishes from the superstructure of belief. Faith relates to that "first level" of foundational covenant. How this is "earthed" and communicated in a responsible *community* of faith inevitably moves into many questions concerning the emphases and structures of particular Christian (and other) faith traditions. Accepting the fallibility of particular traditions is very difficult for many people, the more so if compounded by a nonacceptance of their own failings, or a fear of commitment, or a nonunderstanding of or disagreement with particular Christian beliefs and practices as set forth in a faith tradition.

Compounding this further can be the lack of adequate attention that a particular faith community gives to the serious spiritual development of its people. Sometimes we have to bear the pain and irony of a directee seeming to be at a point of greater openness to the reality of the Holy than a congregation or its leaders can bear or foster. At such points it can be helpful to suggest visits or relationshps with "specialized" communities, such as retreat and educational centers and monastaries (an increasing practice even for Protestants who do not have these in their tradition).

The spiritual direction relationship can help sustain such persons through this search for an "incarnate" spiritual home. For those already committed within one, direction can complement its resources and sometimes help a directee sort out what is and is not important in that relationship.

Two other dimensions of covenant need brief mention here. One involves geographical *place*. The mobility of our times has slowed on the American continent in recent years, and a slowly growing valuation of place has been returning. How does the person see commitment to a particular geographical community and its relationships, responsibilities, joys, and pains? Is this the *place* wherein ministry for that person is meant to take place over an extended period of time? "Primitive" Benedictines still take a special view of "stability," vowing to remain in one *place* for a lifetime. This is an extreme answer to a basic question of geographical covenant.

The other dimension involves *social citizenship*. Church and state in American tradition often have been subtly confused, despite their legal separation. Folk religion uses the Church to affirm rather than transform the values of society. The strength of this confused overaffirmation should not deflect from an awareness of the call to transformation and care for the social fabric.

Each of us is incarnate in a particular society and called in some way to covenant with it, as leaven for social justice and for sharing its burdens and joys. (Even the hermit is called to it at least in intercessory prayer.) This is a particularly important relationship in a time when social structures are so fragile and more and more people become parasitic on the labors and concern of a few for the social good. The history of Israel is a prime example of the value of this covenant.[33]

The particular *form* of our participation leads us to the next level of vocation: our medium for ministry.

Form of Ministry. What are the person's particular *gifts* for ministry? How has the person used these? What is the person's current *situation*, and what opportunities and limitations does that impose (e.g., "human covenant" commitments, financial situation, age, health, and education)? What is the situation of need in the human community relative to the person's gifts and personal situation? How is he or she called to use these gifts now, in light of the situation?

Such questions could be asked orally. But if the person is facing a major discernment at this level, you might want to suggest that he or she do some reflection and writing at home. If you do, you can suggest that they pause after describing their personal and societal situations and write a spontaneous dialogue with their "ministry," treating it as a separate "person" (as suggested earlier related to the spiritual journey as a whole). This may help clarify what is important at a deeper-than-conscious level.

After this step you can suggest that they pause for some

minutes or hours for prayer. Such prayer can ask for guidance, for "Your will be done," and assume a lengthy, listening, open attitude. The person in this time might want to notice their own personal desires in the discernment process, if these have not yet been examined carefully. How much desire is related to fear of change and discomfort, and how much to hope for the real unfolding of ministry for which they are called and ready at this point?

It may be appropriate during such time for the person to look back over the past months or years and sense where have been the times of deep consolation—of a sense of rightness and peace in what he or she is doing, and where have been the times of desolation—of dis-ease and turmoil, of "distance" from the Holy One. What do these tell the person about the pattern of the Spirit's movement in his life?[34] In looking at this pattern, how does it reflect the person's unique participation in the classic pattern of the Christian Paschal Mystery: dying and rising, loss and renewal, weakness and the faithfulness of God?

Ignatius's helpful "indicator" of right discernment focuses on a deep sense of peace and joy in us, even though the decision might involve a sense of disruption, turmoil, and sacrifice at the surface ego level.[35] This is a particularly useful guide in a commercial cultural milieu that tends to foster the reverse: attention to surface ego comfort and ignorance of a deeper sense of "rightness."

This is an inevitable reversal, I think, wherever there is no sense of any given deeper purpose in life than sensual gratification. One sad result often is people basking in the sun in surface comfort, but empty and restless on the inside because they have missed, resisted, or repressed a deeper vocation.

In spiritual direction it is important to pay attention to this called-out "depth" of ministry. Though it may involve cost and risk at the "surface" level, that surface comfort never will give peace. If that deep peace, that sense of "rightness" is there, surface discomfort is more lightly bearable, and the times of true comfort and joy are more easily sensed and appreciated.

This process of discernment I believe is valuable not only for those who look for direct divine guidance in their lives, but also for those who sense more God-given human freedom for decision-making. These latter folk may believe that any number of directions in their lives would be equally "right" in God's sight, as long as they had loving purpose. Such persons still need to sort through the questions raised in this section, even though they sense more latitude for which directions will bring "peace."

Ignatius and others in the tradition would hold that both possibilities may be true: In some situations there may be a sense of direct guidance; in others, there may be no indicators of this, and we are free to move in a number of possible ministerial directions, as we judge best.

One final question concerning discernment you may need to attend to is this: Who (besides you) will help support the person in following through with the discernment? Particularly if it involves disruptive change, there will be temptations to give it up, or to go through it at unnecessarily great mental and physical price. Such persons may need to develop a support group of people who can help them go through the various steps called for in shifting directions. If God's direct guidance is trusted, then there will be confidence that such supportive people will be given, if they pay attention. Those sensing more indifferent human "space" will be moved to set out consciously to find such friends.

It is quite possible that a discernment process related to the form of ministry may simply confirm what a person already is doing or supplement rather than substitute for it. For example, a parent, involved in the human covenant of marriage and family, will sense the rightness of the particular ministry involved in this covenant of raising children and caring for the spouse. Yet there is some other ministry he or she may be called to undertake at this point as well.

Often people feel compelled because of economic or personal necessity to seek work or a situation that they may not feel is right for them. This can be an agonizing time, sensing that life is slipping away and true vocation is being missed. The only consolation of such a time perhaps is the negative one of purgation, purging ego of doing what it wants to do, perhaps conditioning it to live with difference and turmoil that it did not choose.

At its best, such obedience to necessity proves strengthening. If an unjust social structure is involved, this strength can be brought to bear in resistance and organizing for envisioned alternatives. At its worst, such compelled involvements breed resentment and violence.

The great *spiritual* value of a just and open society is the fallout of maximum opportunities for its people to follow ministries for which they truly are meant. However, part of justice is willingness to take out the garbage when it's your turn. True discernment thus involves not "private" decision toward exclusive pleasure or meaningful work at the expense of others, but a "public" decision that helps our gifts and situation build complementarity in sharing the burdens and privileges of community well-being. Such a basis respects a sense of participation in the Body of the cosmic Christ, rather than of isolated individualism.

In going through a discernment process with the person you may suspect that there are distorted perceptions of self and situation, perhaps ones that overrate or undervalue what is there, or express compulsive, guilty ministry, or focus on being cared for more than overflowing in care.

If there seems no openness to insight, but rather compulsion, paralysis, panicked anxiety, or other forms of blockage to true discernment, it may indicate that the person needs to be referred for special counseling before they can be free for real discernment. If this is the situation, it normally will be best to encourage the person not to make any unnecessary major changes in ministerial direction until such times as more free attunement to reality is possible.

If they do enter counseling with someone else, it certainly does not preclude their continuing relationship with you. You can be an important supportive presence and continuing bridge for attention to grace in their lives during this time.

Immediate Callings. You see someone injured lying on the street. Someone calls and asks if he or she can stay with you awhile, because there was a fire at home. Someone is out of a job and asks for help in finding another one. A single-parent neighbor suddenly dies without nearby family, leaving two small children to make provisions for. A friend is in trouble and needs to talk with you. A lonely relative's birthday is tomorrow and there is no one else to celebrate with them. It is a magnificent day that calls you to drop what you're doing to appreciate its giftedness. An old friend drops by for companionship.

On and on we could go with such immediate, unexpected callings, where we find ourselves the "right" person to respond.

Such callings normally don't lead away from our other levels of vocation. Rather, they supplement them with a general human calling to respond to an immediate human situation.

They are signs of the open-endedness, the surprising quality of life's daily passing. If we see them simply as disruptions of our controlled plans and settled vocations, we are likely to approach them with resentment and undue reluctance.

It will be different if we see them rather as part of our complementarity in life, i.e., our availability for another when he or she is down, trust that others are available for us when we are down, or our availability for complementing a beautiful day or a friend with our responsiveness. Then perhaps we can respond a little more easily, aware that such times do not necessarily deflect from but are part of our vocation.

Of course, there are times when someone else is available whose response at the moment is more appropriate than ours. We are not called to bear more than we can, and if we are overloaded, or sense a different priority, then we should not feel the load or appreciation compulsively need be ours. However, if this is so, we at least need to do what we can to help assure that someone *is* available: to meet an authentic need or to appreciate a gifted moment (if you can't enjoy the day at the moment, then encourage someone else to!).

In spiritual direction, you can help a person pay attention to the ways such immediate callings are perceived as graced, neutral, or cursed moments. For compulsive, over-burdened, guilty responders, you might help them sense a little more room for freedom and letting others respond in-stead sometimes. For those who tend to ignore response or resent such "disruptions," you might help them allow the freedom to include these events in their sense of graced voca-tion.

Indeed, they can be unexpected events that carry grace not only for another but for ourselves as well. At the very least they teach us that the Spirit always will try to find a way to unbalance our stagnating grasp for an overcontrolled, predetermined daily "plan."[36]

III. Rest

You have given room for cleansing and alignment in the person's life. He or she soon will leave you, perhaps not see-ing you again for some weeks. What can the person do to protect the healing process underway between visits?

This brings us to the protective "bandages" of spiritual disciplines.

Disciplines are very delicate affairs, because they so easi-ly become confused with trying to "make something hap-pen." The danger of turning disciplines into means of salvation has led Christian leaders at times to throw out most of them completely, recommending instead only confidence in salvation as already achieved in Christ, and life as thank-ful, free response.

The difficulty with this ideal is that there are so many subtle inner and cultural ways that our woundedness finds to evade full realization of life as a gifted, responsible, dy-namic "whole." Spiritual disciplines *rightly understood* can help with this realization. Right understanding needs to be closely wed with any particular discipline.[37] Let's look brief-ly at some examples.

Journal-Keeping.[38] This was mentioned earlier in relation to reflection on the spiritual journey and vocation. Such re-flection can give us a sense of grace operating in our lives in ways that not only help us understand its patterns, but help us relax our grasping. If grace is there, our job is to be attentive, to be cooperative. There is transcendent caring happening. We do not have to attempt creation of a protective island and stoke up aggressive powers to *force* this caring, or defend ourselves against a sense of an ultimately hostile or neutral world. There are *relatively* hostile forces that require vigilance and strength. However, Christian experience points to trusting not primarily in our own isolated prowess, or in the *ultimacy* of these blind or hostile forces, but in a collaborative flow of the "Powers of Light" in and around us.

Journal-keeping, in helping us be in touch with this flow, can include any form of writing: poetry, prose, dialogue, picture. These can be spontaneous or focused on some particular situation or theme. They can deal with thoughts, feelings, intuitions, and dreams, the past, present, and future.

The more casual our writing, the better. If it is too "heavy," too full of expected "good" insight, ego easily becomes attached. No longer is something flowing freely through us, but we are "trying" to do something, trying to make something happen. There is an extreme form of avoiding this tendency in a Zen Buddhist writing practice, where no pronoun is allowed to be used (e.g., "hand moves across page," not "*my* hand writes in *my* journal").

Frequency of entry in a journal is a very individual matter. As a rule of thumb, if the person is just beginning, then a more disciplined practice of daily entry of the first few weeks or months might be called for, as a way of letting the "habit" set in. Later, it can be more sporadic, as it seems helpful.

The *amount* of time taken also is a very individual matter. It may be for a minute, it may be for an hour.

Since we need to be free to write openly, we may have written what is not meant for public knowledge. To help insure privacy, we can invent certain key code words that disguise what we are saying to all but ourselves. Another possibility is periodically burning the journal, which may have the additional value of helping us let go an overbearing past.

Sometimes it might be helpful to read over the patterns in the journal over a period of weeks or months. You may sense your addictions that need healing and the grace that is healing—and calling. Suggesting that this be done before coming to a direction session with you can provide an incentive. However, another approach is to suggest making entries simply as a way of letting things go, with no intention of returning to read them.

Too much time and attention to journal-keeping can tempt to overfascination and overconcern with ourselves. For some people, it is a practice that, once tried, just does not show itself to be needed.

There may be particularly important periods when much writing time is called for. However, if it takes up too many hours, I think journal-keeping can lose the general "lightness" that needs to be present in all spiritual disciplines, lest we subtly find ourselves turning them into ends in themselves that try to force grace.

It is crucial in this and every discipline to realize that you cannot make happen or understood what you are not ready for or called to. Every discipline is a form of "attentive patience," a way of allowing what is needed to happen, a way of reinforcing trust in a promised, incipient, and dynamic wholeness that unfolds as it unfolds. Every discipline then potentially frees us to be a little more attentive to the loving, painful truth given in our lives, and less obedient to fantasies we in our wounded nature would substitute.

Prayer. Under "cleansing" I spoke of "bodily confession" and prayer related to the direction session itself. These also can be taken into a daily discipline.

As with journal-keeping, if a person never has had a daily prayer discipline, you might suggest they undertake a consistent pattern in the early months. This discipline normally is more important than journal-keeping and should be encouraged on a permanent basis.

Paradoxically, I believe a personal prayer discipline is as or more important for clergy and many people in formal religious communities than for lay people, even though they more likely will be involved in many formal and informal times of prayer with others during the week. These public times of prayer tend to be done "in role," however: the clergy or religious community person is leading liturgical prayer and prayer with the sick, school classes, etc.

A separate personal time for prayer each day is "naked soul" prayer, where the person's intimacy and openness can be cultivated as an end in itself rather than only in connection with an expected leadership role. Such separate time can save the person from slipping into the subtle temptation to hide that basic naked soul from God in the shielded, distanced security of a public position. Succumbing to such temptation can ossify the living, uncontrived, mysterious, intimate character of our participation in the Holy.

For anyone, the discipline of a separate time can be a "mini-Sabbath," an opportunity to simply "be," "listen," and appreciate the giftedness of life happening in and around us. It is a different quality of time where we allow our striving egos to relax, to deroutinize their crowded demands and feelings. It is a time that feeds the freshness and openness of the whole day.

Such time also can allow other people and situations to surface in our minds for prayer. There need be no words; it may be simply picturing or sensing these people in a very open way, holding them up for the Lord's caring power.

If you suggest such a possibility to your directee, it may be valuable to help the person explore his or her understanding of intercessory prayer. Whether the person sees it as directly effective at one end of the continuum, or as symbolic and self-motivational at the other, valuing intercession in some way expresses the communal and complementary nature of all life in Christian understanding.

The particular appropriate form for prayer will vary with the personality of the person. If you ask the person how he or she naturally seems to find God and prayer, this can give you some clues about what forms to support. Though such psychological typing as that of Carl Jung has the inevitable limitations of any categorizing instrument, nonetheless such typing at least points to the differences inherent among people, with consequences for prayer forms. C. R.

Bryant helpfully points out some of the implications. Here is
a brief schematization:[39]

Primary Ways of Dealing with the World	Introvert	Extrovert
Sensation	Imaginative activity in prayer, with external aids as with extrovert.	Corporate worship and support of community; books and material aids.
Intuition	Mystical union with God.	Cooperation with God in service of mankind.
Thinking	Theological reflection as prelude to prayer.	Theological reflection with others.
Feeling	Affective prayer.	Corporate affective prayer.

The *length* of time for these "special times" can range
from five minutes to an hour or more, once or twice daily.[40]
They will be longer if the person includes "bodily confession" first: some way of relaxing and energizing attentiveness so that he or she can be present more fully.

The ideal *place* is one that is quiet, familiar, simple, and
ideally furnished only with what will aid prayer and meditation: a light-colored candle, ikon, rug, cross, flowers, bowl of
water, or whatever seems right for the person. This could be
in the corner of a room or in an entire room set aside for the
purpose.

The *content* can range from various forms of active and
quiet prayer, chanting, bodily confession, and examination
of conscience (or consciousness)[41] to the reading of scripture
or other spiritual reading,[42] to journal-keeping or some artistic medium. If the person has an hour or more, particular
kinds of music might help openness to deeper dimensions of
awareness that can bring insight, new openness, and healing.[43]

If the person is not familiar with *habitual* prayer, you
may want to introduce some form or forms, as an aid to
bridging "Sabbath" and "ministry" times. This may involve

slowly repeating the Jesus Prayer, Centering Prayer,[44] or some word or phrase of scripture for a few minutes during special prayer time, and then letting it "surface" in the spaces and beneath the "stuff" of the day. It can be a steadying reminder and opening of the person's deepest identity and purpose, saving from the dominance of petty ego graspings and fears of the day.

With such a discipline of personal prayer, a person is likely to participate in corporate worship more deeply and easily. Liturgy grounds personal prayer in the community and tradition of faith, a necessary and mutually enriching complement for personal prayer.

Other Disciplines. You may refer back to Chapter Four and review the forms of guidance mentioned for stimulus as to other ascetical disciplines that might be helpful for the person, including moral disciplines of attentiveness, stewardship, and action related to particular human needs and community.

Moreover, since selection of disciplines is so wedded to our personality, experience, and intent, it is very important to deal with them in relation to each individual's unique point of unfolding.

If a person has a very oppressive and legalistic sense of discipline, then it might be appropriate to suggest lightening what they are doing to something as simple and spontaneous as possible.

If, at the other end, he or she is hungry for some ways of being attentive and has little experience, then the situation may call for limited experimentation with different possibilities.

In our cafeteria culture especially, there is the danger of running across the surface through many disciplines without giving any an opportunity really to assist "attentive patience." Over a century ago F. W. Faber warned of this:

> Don't [over] stimulate to new directions [with the directee], taking up devotions and throwing them down again,

N B

like a child restless amid his toys, heaping practice on
practice, and getting the fruit out of none of them. . . .
Don't apply remedies, and then apply others before the
first have had time to take effect. This is driving God.[45]

This warning must be balanced with a person's need for
a certain amount of exposure to the possibilities for disciplines as a way of discovering which ones are right to "stick"
with. Each of us in some sense is an "experiment in continuity," a mystery of unfolding that we grope on the surface to
understand and allow.

We cannot force this unfolding, but we can let go im-
pediments as these are ready to drop away. Spiritual disciplines can help us attend to this always evolving process.

Other Dimensions of the Relationship. In the last chapter I
detailed other dimensions of the relationship that are important. These include factors that affect the relationship: age,
sex, experience, personality, spiritual path, faith tradition,
situation, and opportunity. They also included the value of a
"covenant" agreement concerning the purpose, structure,
and content of meetings, and the helpfulness of periodical
evaluation together of the relationship.

Finally, and perhaps most importantly, I mentioned the
value of the director's ongoing prayer for the person. This is
crucial, not only for its intrinsic value, but also as a constant
reminder that you are attending to a process of unfolding in
the person's life that is *not* in your hands. Intercessory prayer can be a constant reminder of your humble place in this
process. Then perhaps you will be less tempted either to try
and "make things happen" or to feel guilty if nothing seems
to be moving.[46]

Spiritual unfolding is a slow, long-term process. Loving
patience and trust in the hidden ways of grace are crucial
qualities in the director. You cannot rush the incubation periods between stages.

I have avoided speaking of specific *stages*, since the unfolding process is so unique and nuanced in each person.
Christian tradition does have a long history of seeing devel-

opment in terms of rough stages, however (as I mentioned in Chapter Two). We should have some awareness of these, along with remembering that you cannot apply them to any one without taking into account the unique ways that person's qualities, freedom, and grace mesh and develop.

The classic stages and the "clinical" comments of great Christian masters about each are described perhaps best in Part Two of Evelyn Underhill's great classic, *Mysticism.*[47] She moves through the complex stages of awakening (conversion), purgation (self-knowledge), illumination, surrender (the Dark Night), and the unitive life, with special sections on particular interior experiences along the way.[48]

Combining Underhill with A. Poulain's classic *The Graces of Interior Prayer*[49] (which includes specific suggestions for the director) can give you a little more sense of confidence in knowing the range of possibilities that might occur in a relationship and how others have understood and dealt with these.

Most people we encounter are not likely to be far enough along for much of the material presented in these books. However, it is just the person going through some of the more unusual experiences who most needs a director, one who will have some sense of possible authenticity in what is happening, beyond merely pathological possibilities. Two books that can help you understand some of the psychological dynamics at certain stages are William James's *Varieties of Religious Experience* and Roberto Assagioli's *Psychosynthesis.*[50]

One more recent work on stages is a very interesting empirical attempt by James Fowler to determine the ways people perceive and value basic reality, an underlying orientation to life that precedes any particular faith symbols used. He tries to do for faith development what Jean Piaget has done for cognitive, Erik Erikson for psycho-social, and Lawrence Kohlberg for moral development.[51]

Though the empirical data is limited, the categorization of six stages inevitably arbitrary for such subtle data as faith development, and the descriptions abstract, I have found his work sensitizing me to the different ways people subconsciously approach themselves, each other, God, and the Church at various points in their development. I would recommend it, as with the other works, with the caution that its main value is its suggestiveness for our sensitivity rather than any definitive statement that would lead us unjustifiably to "pigeonhole" our directees.

Such readings will suggest many signs of progress for you to note along the way in a long-term relationship. Sandra Schneiders speaks of the "surest" manifestations of growth as:

1. An increasingly unfearful, loving, and maturely obedient attitude toward God, and

2. An increasingly unselfish, compassionate, and responsible commitment to other persons—toward "perfect friendship," a capacity to lay down your life for the other.[52]

The signs of growth and connectedness with the Spirit of Truth can be subtle and deceptive. William Connolly exemplifies this in terms of Paul's list of the fruits of the Spirit:

> Witless enthusiasm can look like joy, torpor like patience, relief at decision like peace, suppression of anger like patience.

Connolly goes on to say that when these gifts appear *together*, their origin *is* the Spirit. "Though growth may be unequal, never are they *conflicting* elements. If they conflict, then suspect illusion."[53]

Relevant Learnings From Asian Practice. Before leaving this chapter on the ways of being a spiritual friend, I think it is important to call attention to the potential contributions of selected Asian religious guidance practices for Christian spiritual direction.

Perhaps the greatest overall contribution is their living reminder of neglected Christian apophatic tradition, of which I have spoken at length in Chapter One and elsewhere.

Thomas Merton in many ways helped pave the way for recent serious Christian investigation of these potential Eastern contributions. This affirmation of his in the final speech before his death on Asian soil is an example:

> By openness to Buddhism, to Hinduism, and to these great Asian traditions, we stand a wonderful chance of learning more about the potentiality of our own traditions, because they have gone, from the natural point of view, so much deeper into this than we have. The combination of the natural techniques and the graces and the other things that have been manifested in Asia and the Christian liberty of the gospel should bring us all at last to that full and transcendent liberty which is beyond mere cultural difference and mere externals—and more this or that.[54]

The subject of relationship between these Eastern and Western religious traditions is very complex and the subject of much ongoing research and experiment. In these few pages I simply want to outline three selected practical contributions to Christian guidance as I and others I know have experienced these, related to *bodily energy, intuitive awareness,* and *flexibility.*

Bodily Energy. Though the incarnate quality of Christian tradition sporadically has required seriousness about the positive place of the body in spiritual development, the strong influence of Platonic thought and other factors have led to much less directly aware concern about this dimension than we see in much of Asia.[55]

We are only beginning to take seriously a very old and long-tested series of assumptions and practices related to a proposed subtle spiritual energy in and around us that, when blocked in our bodies, leads to illness, and when allowed to flow evenly, leads toward healing and an open mind. I think such a holistic view of spiritual psychosomatic dimensions lends itself to a Christian interpretation of life with greater ease than our currently dominant allopathic medical view that tends to deal with the body primarily in material and mechanistic terms.

My experience with various Yogic practices of breath-

ing and bodily postures, and its confirmation with others, is
behind my earlier suggestions for attentiveness to "ener-
gized relaxation" in spiritual direction. This does not mean
that any particular Yogic practices are necessary, but that
some form of positive attentiveness to the body is very helpful (through sports, walking, or whatever).

A tense and tired body can have its way of impeding our
attentiveness to grace. For me, particular physical practices
have been very helpful in freeing my mind for prayer and
compassion. The value of certain Yogic practices is their capacity to open us gently to more subtle layers of our consciousness, as well as opening and balancing our bodies'
renewing energies.

Taken up in the context of Christian faith, and with
clarity that they are simple means of opening but in no way
insure anything of spiritual sight, they can be helpful ways of
preparing the ground in us not to miss or reject the "still
small voice" when it comes.[56]

Intuitive Awareness. Christian practice in recent decades
has conditioned the director to come to a relationship armed
with all kinds of analytical knowledge about the faith and
spiritual and human development. Such analytical knowledge can be invaluable for our understanding, perspectives,
and communication of what is going on. However, unless
such analysis is balanced by at least a rudimentary intuitive
awareness, we will miss our great potential of knowing intuitively what is happening with the person.

Cultivation of this awareness is basic in the preparation
of a spiritual director, a guru, in many Eastern traditions. It
is in fact still the ideal in Eastern Orthodox Christian practice, insofar as they have maintained continuity with the Desert Abbas.

Kallistos Ware, a Greek Orthodox monk-scholar, reflects this when he describes an ideal quality of the spiritual
father (or mother) as:

> Insight and discernment: the ability to perceive intuitive-
> ly the secrets of another's heart, to understand the hid-
> den depths of which the other is unaware. . . . To know

immediately and specifically what it is the individual needs to hear.[57]

Such a director comes to a relationship primarily *dis-armed*. He or she has a quality of "innocent presence" wherein so little mediating ego exists that the director can be capable of direct contact, direct coinherence with, the direc-tee's mind. In such moments, words come through the direc-tor that are not predetermined. They just come spontaneous-ly, guided subconsciously by the basic motive of desiring the transcendent loving Presence to flow through the other, in the way it is needed.

This is different from *impulsive* speaking, which comes from the director's particular ego fears or desires rather than from what is "called out" through naked contact with the mind of the other. Maintaining a trace of analytical aware-ness can help maintain discernment between the two.

How can you be helped to develop such intuitive pres-ence? Each of us has a different degree of natural intuitive giftedness, but I believe most of us are capable of nourishing this gift at least to the point of glimpsing more surely what it is, and the different quality of appreciation it can bring to a relationship. Here are several possible aids:

1. *Meditation:* Practice thirty to sixty minutes a day let-ting your mind be "cleansed" in some such way as I suggest-ed earlier under "cleansing." Lightly noticing thoughts and images and letting them go by without "identifying" with them can free you for a more open quality of awareness. You can begin noticing the space between your thoughts as very free, alive, and in touch with reality more directly than the words and images that come to describe it.

You may begin to discern the difference between the "closed," "interpreted" qualities of mind events, and the open or driven energy from which they come. You may be-gin to distinguish between the particular *contents* of the mind, and the open *structure* that allows them; between your "little" self possessively identified with the contents, and your "big" self, more attuned to the image of God.

This image I believe is unpossessively aware, openly

present and knowing at all times, even though often hidden by the efforts of "little" self.

You may begin to sense the dynamic, unified gestalt of awareness, and no longer "divide off" unique presentations in this field as though they *ultimately* were isolated categories, *fully* separate realities. You may begin to sense the coinherence, the substantive unity, of words and silence, content and structure, foreground and background, you and other, God and creation. Such realization brings incredible intimacy with all that is. Neither uniqueness nor unity is destroyed; both are inextricably present together.

Such subtle awareness is graced intuitive awareness, one that Christians might identify as a shadow of the Kingdom.

If a flash of this subtle awareness emerges for you in meditation, you may find that it corroborates what you already vaguely know from your own experience elsewhere. If it is true awareness, it reveals a quality of mind already belonging to us all, when we have eyes and grace to see.

How such awareness is *interpreted* moves us into the symbols of different religions, cultures, and personalities. At that point we have moved beyond the "pure awareness" to its translation in ways we and others around us might understand. For our purposes here, though, what is important is the practice of such preinterpreted "direct seeing," and discerning the different yet connected interpretations of this seeing. In a direction relationship, it is this "preinterpreted" presence that allows intuitive awareness.

Except for very holy and/or gifted people, any such awareness is likely to be very brief. It is lost the moment we "look" at it to see what is happening. It is never uncovered while we are "self" conscious and driven by contrived ego schemes. Its price is living a moment *without* knowing, "*unknowing*" the normally (abnormally?) complex, dividing, grasping way to which we are accustomed.

The more your presence is innocent, unpretentious, uncalculating, simple, undivided, yet open, the more your intuitive awareness will see what is needed to be seen. There is a certain grace, a certain giftedness, a total intimacy about such moments. They cannot be forced. They require us to be, as Jesus recommended, "like a child," with that mind that "sees" with wide eyes for a minute, before self-consciousness and manipulation set in.

It is such an innocent, intuitively discerning mind that helps make the Eastern guru and the Desert Abba "master." It is such a mind that he or she seeks to cultivate in the disciple. There may be great compatibility here with the intimate mind Jesus sought in his disciples, and Paul described as being *"in* the mind of Christ."

Where personal compassion and a sense of compassionate, intimate Source radiate among non-Christians, then surely we must be dealing with the "other sheep" (Mt. 10:16) manifesting the cosmic Christ.[58]

2. *Watching:* Another way of cultivating intuitive awareness for spiritual direction involves watching another person. One way this can be done is at a distance, without another person's knowledge. Just watch someone (known or unknown to you) from where you cannot be noticed, for as long as an hour. Let your mind be open, just as in meditation, yet very "aware" of the whole being of the person. Watch your mind judge, label, interpret, feel all kinds of things toward the person. Watch your sense of "self" consciousness. Each time you notice such a mind event happening, gently let it go. Sometimes this can be helped by asking yourself "who" is judging, labeling, etc., a way of freeing your sense of identity from these "hooks."

Let your mind be more and more simply present, with less and less "between" you and the other person. Notice the intimacy, the close proximity to "direct seeing" that emerges the longer you are uninterpretively, openly "with" the person.

Perhaps you will sense that you have come to "know" that person a little in an inexpressible way. At least you will have had practice noticing how much your active mind "does" something to the relationship that reflects your own projections and interpretations, rather than "innocent knowing."

The more that "knowing" emerges (as there is less and less "between" you to *prevent* that direct knowing), the more you will be able to sense that the images and words coming to your mind simply describe the way the person is, less "polluted" by your own distant analytical guessing. However, even in this instance, once you have *interpreted* the images and words that come, you have been removed from these direct mediational vehicles into your own world of more subjective understanding. Such understanding still is connected to the more "direct seeing," but you need to be aware of its polluting effect.

If you do this within a deeply appropriated faith framework that sees Holy Love naturally connecting you, I think that this faith can help draw out those perceptions that would be most needed by the person, were you in a direction relationship. Such faith can dampen the temptation of ego to select perceptions that fit its own fears and desires, rather than the other person's real situation.

You also can do such "innocent faithful watching" briefly from time to time within a direction relationship. If you have been practicing watching another for a longer time, that can feed the quality of these short moments.

One other way to practice this intuitive attentiveness is to sit face to face with someone in silence for up to forty minutes at a time (with another spiritual director, for example). Look at the bridge of the person's nose, or *through* the pupil of one eye, as a way of letting your eyes remain still and your mind unselfconscious.

Let yourself be just as confidently, unexpectantly, openly, energetically present as possible. Proceed as described in looking at the person from a distance. Afterward, rest a few minutes, lying down with your eyes closed, still maintaining the same quality of mind, if possible. Then you can repeat the process once more.

The second time, you may want to let yourself subtly be "exchanged" with the other person, allowing yourself to "become" the other, and the other to become you. This need involve no internal "interpretation"—just an innocent "allowing" of the exchange to happen.[59]

Flexibility. Such intuitive awareness within a relationship seems to enhance the great flexibility of response seen in some Eastern masters (again paralleling the Desert Fathers and Mothers). What that awareness reveals to be needed by the person can range very broadly: kind or angry words, a (harmless) physical blow, a question, ignoring the person, suggesting they do some act of labor or charity, humor, crying, a discussion, silence, a massage, a riddle, a seemingly irrelevant comment.

If your job as director includes providing an environment for the person to allow the Spirit of Truth to rise up through the thinning walls of the mind, your hopefully graced perception of the readiness or nonreadiness for "new birth" of sight or action will determine what kind of a response is needed. If the time seems very close for such birth, then perhaps some gently "shocking" kind of response is called for. If it seems far away, then more supportive and patient response may be called for. The appropriate kind of response will vary, of course, in relation to the unique qualities of the person and of the direction relationship.

In my group work with the Tibetan Lama Tarthang Tulku, I was impressed with his capacity usually to be with a person as he was needed. This did not normally involve pleasing the ego of the person (a sometimes mutual complicity that can stymie a direction relationship) except when he felt that was all the person could bear.

Unless a person was at a very weak point and could only receive sustaining response, he seemed to respond in a way that kept people slightly off balance, just enough to keep them open, attentive, and not complacent. He was particularly adept at becoming humorously playful with persons whose plodding, heavy, grasping egos were in the way of the "light clarity" of their souls.

I have noticed this "off-balancing" tendency also with both a Japanese and a Korean Zen Master with whom I have worked briefly. Such an approach has a way of "cutting through" dullness and habit, freeing a person sometimes to let the "real truth," a sharp awareness, come through the mirage of surface barriers.[60]

Very few of us have had the intensive conditioning for intuitive awareness of such gurus to allow us their "free audacity," and I would recommend caution in any such responses unless they seem just simply to "come through" you with spontaneous confidence.[61] We perhaps have not known such a free, flexible, carefully cultivated tradition of direction in Christian history except through the Desert Abbas and their relatively few successors.

One of the ironies of our time is the way grace seems to be working to help Christians rediscover and enrich some of their own lost depth of intuitive guidance through the gifts of seemingly very distant traditions.

We cannot reclaim this subtle dimension of direction overnight. I believe it will take at least another generation of careful attention before this apophatic dimension can flower again in the West.

The process already is underway, especially within some Christian contemplative communities, which provide long-term setting and motivation for apophatic depth. The new ecumenism involved here is not between Christian and Christian, but between Christians and the grace of other intuitively deep religious traditions.

As a spiritual director, you might begin with a few of the little practices suggested here (and in the readings referred to). Adding intuitive depth to our analytical sophistication can be a rich and mutually correcting marriage, whose fruit will be more flexible and penetrating spiritual friendship.

Conclusion

I have presented you with a wide range of content for the spiritual direction relationship. This range, kept loosely in the back of your mind, may provide a certain "check list" of areas and approaches that will help insure that nothing major is ignored by oversight in an extended relationship.

However, with any given person who comes to you, you may be called upon to focus more narrowly. Early on you need to sense what the priorities are with the person. Is he or she coming with a vocational decision? Particular temptations? Questions about prayer and discipline? Questions of faith? Special problems? Or readiness to grow in the spiritual life as a whole?

If this last question really is central and your relationship is compatible, then you are likely to have a sustained relationship, perhaps over years. If the focus is more narrow, the relationship may be shorter and more sporadic.

Though our ideal may be long-term relationship with a broad focus on the ways of grace in our lives, in actuality many people seem not ready and willing for such a sustained focus. Some may already have had this in their lives and currently sense no need for it. In any case, these and others may want to be with you for a brief time, with specific questions, and that is enough for now.

Where these questions overlap into psychological problem-solving, you will need to discern how much their primary concern is for the grace running through "problems," or how much it is on psychological analysis and resolution of them, calling for a therapist.

If they clearly come with both concerns, then perhaps they need to see you and a therapist, each with a different "focal setting" on the same reality.

How do you provide *support and perspective for yourself* in looking at such questions and at your whole approach to spiritual friendship? This is an important question to which I will turn in the last chapter. A "colleague group" and/or special educational program can be invaluable for your direction ministry.

There are infinitely varied situations and possible approaches in being a spiritual friend; this book can open up only certain barest foundations for you. It is in ongoing exposure and dialogue with other spiritual directors that you can be helped to see more clearly what you need to see for your evolving ministry.

7. Group Direction

Group spiritual guidance is the *standard* form of guidance in Christian tradition. In Chapter Four I mentioned some of its current forms. These include sacramental guidance for groups gathered for Eucharist, rite of reconciliation, and healing; also, guidance manifest through preaching, teaching, writing, and leading groups for faith sharing, scriptural reflection, singing, and prayer.[1]

One other important form of group guidance comes closest to the intents of one-to-one direction as I have described it. This is the small group focused on the spiritual appreciation (Sabbath) and vocation (ministry) of its members, with the clear leadership of a particular "group director." This form of group direction will be the focus of this chapter.

Such a group has great potential value in our time. It can be a short-term group, as in a retreat, or a long-term one, meeting regularly over a period of months. It is capable of combining all other forms of group guidance mentioned above as these might become appropriate, together with a limited amount of one-to-one direction.

It fills a gaping hole today between minimally guided "sharing" groups, and the nondialogical guidance of "general" direction (preaching, teaching, writing, etc.). It also can help fill the gap left by the shortage of visible, experienced, qualified one-to-one spiritual directors.

For some people, such groups might actually be *more* helpful than one-to-one direction.[2] The richness of insight available in a group can outstrip what is available in a one-to-

174

one situation, even though there is less opportunity for direct personal focus. Also, the corporate nature and energy of a group can be mutually supportive and stimulating.

It can be a small community reflecting the larger corporate nature of life and the Church, drawing a person into a larger sense of identity. In a culture so focused on the individual, this corporate quality can be particularly valuable.

Indirectly such a group can be an incubation ground for more in-touch, existential, responsible participation in the larger communities of church, family, work, and society. It can be a corporate Sabbath time that provides authentic sanctuary which feeds real ministry.

More specifically, what are the merits and demerits of such a group in relation to one-to-one direction?

Shaun McCarty has put together such an excellent comparative list that I would like to quote him at length.[3] He writes:

> Some of the *benefits* of *individual* spiritual direction are:
> 1. A greater ease in communicating more deeply with a director.
> 2. Less chance of evasion.
> 3. A more rapid getting to where the directee "is" in prayer and in their relationship.
> 4. A greater freedom and ability to talk when the right moment arrives.
>
> Some of the *disadvantages* of *one-to-one* direction are:
> 1. The danger of dependency.
> 2. Undue influences by one person on another.
> 3. Diminishing returns, perhaps, from one person.
>
> Some of the *benefits* of *group* direction are:
> 1. A greater richness through diversity and the possibility of being affected by other people's prayer.
> 2. Easier communication for some who have difficulty in relating one-to-one.
> 3. The benefits of communal experience.
> 4. Less danger of dependency developing.
> 5. The impetus of group accountability.
>
> Some of the *disadvantages* of *group* direction are:
> 1. A possible lessening of individual accountability through hiding within the group.

2. A greater threat to confidentiality.
3. The difficulty of self-disclosure in a group for some.
4. The practical difficulty of finding a time when all can
   get together regularly.

We need not choose between group and individual direction. One can be an excellent complement for the other. At a given point in a person's life one may be more valuable than the other.

For example, a *group* probably will be best for a person in need of general exposure to a range of interior spiritual disciplines, together with some reflection on their relationship to his or her unique spiritual journey, or for a person who simply needs focused, attentive "sanctuary" time.

One-to-one direction is most crucial for a person in the midst of some hard vocational discernment, or for a person going through unusual or confusing interior experiences. In general, such personal direction is best for anyone who has any kind of immediate, up-front issues that need much ongoing dialogue.

Groups can be structured in ways that include some time for focus on individual issues, but such time will be limited compared to a one-to-one session, and persons in great need of much dialogue likely will be frustrated in a group, and the group frustrated by them.

If such persons want the benefits of a group, then for their own sake and for the group's, they also should be in one-to-one direction (or therapy, if their issues so warrant). The delicacy of group life is such that just one person consistently demanding attention can be disruptive of the group's intent.

Selection

Screening by the leader of potential group members can be very helpful in preventing such situations. Sometimes such screening can be done adequately in writing. A description of the group can make its intent and process very clear, distinguishing it from the problem-solving or other interactional focus of therapy, encounter or discussion groups. Written applications from potential participants can include questions like:

"What are you looking for in this group?"

"What are you *not* looking for?"

"What in your basic spiritual experience has led you to feel the need for such a group at this point in your life?"

If a group is being gathered within a *parish* such screening is more difficult, since many congregations have tacit norms that every activity ought to be available to any member. The fear of exclusivism and elitism can lead potential leaders to resist any screening. Also, a sense that the Holy Spirit calls whom He wills, beyond our limited knowledge of who is "right" for a group, adds more pressure to keep it open.

In such situations we can assess a continuum of possibilities for group selection with these high points:

Leaders can risk exclusivism and choose people by invitation only, based on their knowledge of people in the community.

Moving toward the middle of the continuum, leaders can issue an open invitation, but include the requirement of a personal interview to aid mutual discernment of the appropriateness of a group for a particular person. An alternative can be a written statement by a potential member, as previously suggested, with interviews only with persons about whom the leaders have questions.

At the other end of the continuum, anyone who wants is allowed to join the group, but with clarity as to commitment in time and standards for group life. If certain persons prove destructively disruptive, *then* the leader can take them aside and gently guide them toward alternative behavior in the group, or failing this, toward alternative sources of help.

My experience with such groups within parishes leads me to sense that more experimentation is needed with options less loose than this last one. My sense of the tacit norms in most parishes is that Sunday worship is the one thing that everyone is accountable for. The second most important thing is accountability when called upon to help in some crisis. The third is assistance with institutional maintenance. Accountability for one's ongoing spiritual development is very low on the list of important things.

The fallout of this low priority is the looseness with which a series of group sessions on spiritual development can be approached. Some are late for sessions. Others leave early. Others attend sporadically or drop out completely after one or two times. Reflection within sessions can be diverted by defensive or irrelevant comments. Then more serious people may drop away, feeling frustrated about the group's refusal to center down.

As I have tried to make clear earlier, facing in to one's "deepest self" in God is both threatening and alluring at the same time. Surface ego will struggle to stay in charge in some way, struggle to "keep things the same." The power and value of a group is its capacity to help us pay more attention to the lure than to the threat. Providing and enforcing clear guidelines for serious participation can help a group provide such an inviting environment.

My sense is that at any one time there is a small group of people ready for such a serious group in any religious community (and in the larger community, as well). Such people are at a particular point of openness and vulnerability in relation to their deeper self in God. They are, so to speak, "pregnant" with the Spirit. Such a group can provide a midwifing environment for these people, and an opportunity to nourish and support whatever new life is born (or perhaps already was born before the group).

It is at this point of identifying and aiding people's readiness for more serious spiritual development that parishes often fail. My hunch is that many spiritual births are stillborn or deformed because they are inadequately attended. Perhaps the complex tasks of parishes mean that they have built-in limitations in this area, and it is other centers of Church life that need to be most accountable here (monasteries, retreat centers, and institutes such as Shalem).

Historically the parish always has been but *one* center of the Church's life, and it is not fair to expect it to be a sufficient structure for all dimensions of people's spiritual lives.

However, I do sense that more assistance is possible here, if there can be agreement in a parish about its importance. A serious agreement would insure that gifted leaders are released from other duties for such work, or that other leadership is cultivated or brought in. Such an agreement also would support group membership that *stresses* serious readiness and accountability.

Over a generation in the life of a parish, perhaps most people would have been involved in such a group, as they were ready, once or many times.[4] Others may have found equivalent or more appropriate assistance elsewhere. These people, and others on a "plateau" in their spiritual life, will be content to let the parish be a stabilizing center of sacraments, community, and service.

Such groups would be consonant with Bruce Reed's view of the "extra-dependency management" function of the Church. They certainly are in keeping with the Church's historic pastoral function, focused in this instance on that pastoral dimension that the Church is most uniquely qualified and commissioned to attend. spiritual nurture.

Direction groups also can be valuable in *theological school* communities. These can be "attentive sanctuary" and spiritual discipline learning times for students. Such times can help fill the gap between highly evaluative and function oriented supervised ministry, class, and advisory session times on the one hand, and corporate worship and personal prayer times on the other.

A direction group can help provide a perspective, personal integration, and support that complements other dimensions of seminary formation. Such groups, as well as one-to-one direction, can help protect that "naked soul" time that keeps us aware of our larger and more spacious self in the image of God, a nonstrictly functional, open, loved sense of self that is crucial for a spiritual leader.

Primary Functions

The primary functions of direction groups essentially are or can be the same as those of one-to-one direction. These

I consider the most important functions of such groups, combining both apophatic and kataphatic dimensions:

1. *Sanctuary.* Protecting, securing, enabling a quiet, open environment in which persons can relax their normal driving, coping, doing behavior, and become free simply to be attentively present.

This I believe is a pervasive function that guides all the others. Many people have told me that this sense of sanctuary is the greatest value of the group in their busy lives, regardless of the particular *content* this sanctuary is given in any particular session.

2. *Teaching.* Introducing particular spiritual disciplines, especially ones that allow for more attentive presence and open compassion.

These disciplines can include (among others) "bodily confession" discussed in the last chapter; active and quiet forms of prayer in words, chant, visual symbol, and imageless presence; journal-keeping; forms of attentiveness to the subtler controlling emotions and self-images that impede our naked presence; meditation on scripture and other spiritual reading; and fasting.[5]

These disciplines in my experience are best taught in a roughly progressive order, from the more relaxing and simple to the more subtle and demanding.

The assumption that needs to be made clear in the beginning is that not *all* disciplines are appropriate to a given person at a given time. Rather, the teachings provide an exposure to a range of possibilities, among which perhaps two or three might be appropriate for some to maintain in their lives.

Such an explicit assumption helps relieve people of guilt and perhaps anger at not being able to respond well to a particular discipline. It also helps people to avoid the temptation of skimming the surface and not going down deeply through any one discipline.

The number of disciplines introduced should be limited to what can be absorbed by the group. In a long-term group, I think at least two sessions (along with between-sessions practice) need to be spent on any one before introducing another.

In groups composed of people who already have been experientially introduced to a number of disciplines, a steady rhythm of much attentive presence and some reflection, using a few agreed upon methods, normally becomes central. This at least has been the experience of Shalem groups over the past seven years.

3. *Reflection.* Providing opportunity for describing and interpreting experiences in prayer and other disciplines, and periodically for reflection on one's spiritual journey and personal sense of vocation at the different levels described in the last chapter.

This function can be met through plenary, subgroup, and one-to-one frameworks. Plenary sessions are least valuable where there is need for everyone to share. These larger sessions can be used more for questions and probing stimulated by subgroup or one-to-one sharing.

4. *Accountability.* Offering people a "checkpoint" in their lives where, as in one-to-one direction, they know someone cares about their spiritual journey and whether and how it is being attended.

The director can offer specific suggestions for "homework" between sessions, especially ones focused on the forms of discipline being introduced. Accountability for a daily personal discipline is much more likely when we know others are involved also, and that you may be reflecting on your practice in the next group session.

Such "in-between" session attentiveness helps to integrate the group's learnings and insights into daily life, and in turn helps to integrate the nitty-gritty of daily life into sessions.

The focus, though, is not "problem-solving" of daily ego-management problems. Rather it is the grace and "background" open attentiveness present through such problems. Problems can indeed be lightened in this way, since such practice prevents us from overidentifying with particular "foreground" ego desires and fears. But this is a by-product of the focus on the transcending yet incarnate larger Self in God's image.

Conditions[6]

Attention to the various conditions of group life is a central task of the group director. Here are some dimensions that I have found important.

Environment. If the group is to have sanctuary time, it is ideal (just as in one-to-one direction) if the physical situation can reflect an inviting sanctuary.

The ingredients of such an ideal setting would include a quiet, rugged room with low lights. The "open" space of a minimally furnished room where people can sit on cushions in a circle on the floor if they wish has a way of inviting a grounded, open mind. (If people do sit on the floor, introduction to positions that aid long-term stillness is helpful.)

A candle lit in the middle of the room can provide attention for wandering minds, and also be a symbol of the Spirit's presence.

Size. The best size I and others have found for a long-term group ranges between eight and twenty people. The larger number can be accommodated if it is broken into subgroups for part of each session.

Groups of fewer than eight people can lose the richness of diverse insight, especially when sickness and emergencies are likely to make actual attendance even less.

More than twenty can make plenary sessions unwieldy, with less opportunity for dialogue and sometimes more difficulty in being able to hear each other.

Time. Sessions in a long-term group can last from a bare minimum of one and a half up to three hours. Shorter periods allow inadequate time for depth. Longer periods are more than most people can absorb or need.

Ideally groups would meet weekly, for a committed minimum of six weeks and a maximum of ten months. An opportunity for recommitment, without pressure, can be offered at such evaluation points. Some people are ready to be on their own, with a different group, or in one-to-one friendship after such a period of time. Just as in one-to-one direction, no one should be pressured toward long-term dependency.

It *may* also be right for a particular person to remain with a group. This needs to be discerned carefully. If a group stops for a period of time after its commitment, it can be a good test of whether or not it needs to reconvene.

Standards. I have found it helpful in the seven years I have led such groups to agree together on a set of standards that will give them some common guidelines for being a specifically focused "temporary community."

These have included such standards as the following.

Within the group:

1. Giving priority to group sessions.
2. Beginning and ending on time.
3. Silence in room (except during group reflection and after sessions).
4. No smoking, drinking, eating in room (you can do these outside).
5. Attentive patience: with doubts, frustrations, boredom, judgments, restlessness, elation. Neither repression nor necessary expression. Letting come, letting go.

Outside the Group:

1. Daily discipline of open attentiveness: in solitude and in daily activity, using methods introduced in the group where appropriate, including journal-keeping, and specified scriptural verses.
2. Reading is secondary to firsthand experience, but taking on at least one relevant book during the group's life might aid your motivation, confirmation, and clarity.
3. Discrimination in sharing of your personal experience with others outside the group. Sometimes you need to let your experience develop quietly, without discussion. Also, others will not necessarily be able to make sense out of what you're talking about.
4. Remembering that it is the fruits of the Spirit, trusting mind, and open heart that are important, and not experiential "highs" and "lows."
5. Teach others what you learn only when and if you

feel confident about it in your own experience. With this qualification, we encourage your sharing where others have need and openness.

6. Prayer for those in the group, especially for those in your subgroup; in-person meetings with one or more of them by mutual agreement and need for additional support, encouragement, clarification, gentle challenge, and sharing of experience related to spiritual awareness.

Rhythm. As in one-to-one direction, beginning with "body confession" helps clear the body of accumulated tensions and dullness. You can move from this to some "way in" to attentive presence, using scripture, prayer, or another discipline, which flows in to a period of corporate silent meditation.

This can be followed by a few minutes of silent journal-keeping or rest time. Then there can be a period for subgroup[7] and plenary reflection, describing and interpreting personal experience in the silence and during the week. "Homework" may be given in plenary session.

Ending with open intercessory prayer can help bridge the group into daily life and concerns beyond themselves, actualizing and symbolizing a sense of development and solidarity within the larger Church and societal body, rather than as isolated individuals.

This reflects the basic rhythm I have "settled into" over a period of years, based on my own and group members' evaluations, and the work of other group leaders.

This normal session rhythm fits within the larger rhythm of the group's whole life together. I have found that beginning and ending with a full day provides opportunity for establishing a relaxed community at the beginning, and a relaxed and adequate closure and evaluation at the end. Sometimes a full day in the middle of a lengthy group also is helpful. An extended retreat together, for example, over a weekend, also might be considered.

Many specific suggestions for ways of beginning with a group are available in *Pilgrimage Home.*[8] One suggestion not included there that I have found of special value in the past two years is short personal interviews with each person in a separate room, while the group is involved in some long written biographical or evaluative assignment on the first and last days.

In these five- to ten-minute periods with each person, it is amazing how much can be exchanged. It can be a way of putting both director and participant in more clear touch with some of the "nitty-gritty" sense of basic personal and spiritual relationships and reality as these are being experienced by the person.

At the beginning of a group this can help sensitize the director to what may be going on with the person during the ensuing weeks, along with information gleaned from other written and oral material given in group sessions.

Sometimes individuals during these times bring up important feelings or issues that they do not want to bring up in the group itself. It may be enough to hear and briefly question or comment on them. They may indicate need for more individual time, with the director if he or she has it, or by referral to someone else, depending on the nature of the issue. Having seen the director privately may stimulate and ease the way for seeing someone else more extensively, if this is needed.

I usually include personal prayer with and for the person at the end of these brief sessions. In group contexts, such individual prayer and questions can help reinforce a sense of unique, cared for, responsible spiritual journey, a journey that the director cares about in God's name with the person.

This personal uniqueness sometimes is drowned out in the corporate rhythm of the group's life and focus. One result of this "drowning" I have found in the past is that some people just drift away without telling anyone. Sometimes this means that the group just is not right for them. In other cases, however, I sense they just have not had adequate opportunity to connect and communicate their own situation adequately with the group director, or sometimes with group members.

The private session at the beginning not only helps to incorporate the uniqueness of the person into the group spiritual journey, but also helps to bond the relation between director and individual.[9] This bonding can help the person to feel a little more at ease in letting himself be present in group sessions without personally distancing, controlling, or slipping-away behavior.

The value of being able to trust the leader is precisely the resulting freedom to allow oneself that extradependent mode of consciousness about which I spoke at length in Chapter Three.

A good director, of course, will always be concerned about more fully intradependent behavior in daily life. The process of extradependent "Sabbath rest" in the group has a spontaneous capacity to serve that inner coping strength afterward without the director "trying to make it happen," apart from providing a good environment and rhythm for it. Toward the end of a group's life, though, it can be helpful to spend more and more time reflecting on specific individual senses of *callings* to intradependence (vocation), and on people's daily *rhythm* of extra and intradependence, Sabbath and ministry. Such reflection can help wean people from the group without leaving its values behind.

If the director understands the need of people in the group for such extradependence, he or she will avoid relinquishing leadership to the group.[10] The oscillation theory described by Bruce Reed and reflected in the historic Judaeo-Christian rhythm of Sabbath and ministry time has been amply verified in groups I and others have led.

Very active, independent people who come to groups in my experience consistently seek a different mode of participation in reality during sessions. They do not want to have their egos in the driver's seat trying to achieve something, compete, assert, defend, etc. They are searching for a quality of "being" time marked especially by a simple openness.

It is the director's job to sacrifice much of his or her *own* "being" time for the sake of the group, so he or she can be trusted enough to be "in charge" for them; then they are free just to be openly present.

If that "in chargeness" truly is trustworthy, the director simply will be providing an environment and rhythm for the larger Holy Presence to be "in charge" in place of our intradependently grasping and coping egos. The more the director is in touch with where people are, and with what they can bear and need in the content of the group's rhythm that will serve Sabbath time and bridge back to ministry time, the more he or she can be worthy of trust.

This "in touchness" can be fed by the initial interviews, by reading over initial written material on their spiritual journeys, and by listening to them share in subgroups.

I also have found it helpful to include a *written evaluation* midterm that focuses on: 1) where individuals are now in their own clarity and confusion about their journeys, 2) how valuable they are finding different dimensions of the group's life and leadership, and 3) anything different they would like to see in the group's life and leadership.[11]

Directed Retreats

All that has been said about the long-term group essentially applies to directing a retreat. The main difference is the shortness and intensity of time.

Retreats of several days or longer have the advantage of a long block of time, allowing participants greater opportunity to relax the "driver's-seat" ego and become more and more simply and appreciatively present.

They have the disadvantage of normally lacking "follow through." Much that might have opened up during the retreat is in danger of being stillborn, because there often is no way, support, or accountability to keep going after a person has been "dropped" at the end of a retreat. This makes it particularly important to pay attention at the end of a retreat to helping people who seem to need it to determine what their next step needs to be and who will support them in this.

The intensity of group retreats can be particularly exhausting for the leader, especially if it is a "strange" group to him or her and to each other. A clearly structured rhythm of liturgical offices, much silence, free time, and guided group meditation and subgroup sharing sessions can provide a securing and facilitating framework for everyone.

It is important to provide opportunity at particular

points in the retreat for one-to-one counsel. Much of importance can emerge for people on retreat that sometimes needs
reflection with another. A very wide range of issues can be
brought up during these short sessions, some needing much
more time than is available. When this occurs, it is important
to suggest resources for the person to go further.[12]

Qualities of a Good Group Director

The kind of group I have described involves a paradoxical attitude of leadership. On the one hand, there is need for
awareness that the director cannot make anything spiritually
important happen. He or she is providing a structure, an environment, a rhythm through which what is important
(whatever this may be for a given individual) *can* perhaps
more easily happen. He or she is providing a setting for attentiveness to the Deep Spirit of our lives, who alone is director. The human director at best is a transparency for this
Spirit in the way he or she structures and responds to people.

On the other hand, as I have described the group, the
leader is clearly other than a facilitator of a participatory democracy, where everyone's views regularly are weighed, decisions negotiated, and leadership shared. The *group* cannot
make anything spiritually important happen either.

I have found the greatest hostility in attempting that
kind of facilitation in my early days of group leadership,
stemming I believe from my lack of appreciation of the
unique quality of presence needed by people in such a "Sabbath" group.

Though the director is just another brother or sister in
face of the shared Spirit for whom all await, he or she is in
some sense a father or mother in protecting and encouraging
that "waiting."

Such a director ideally will incorporate those same qualities mentioned for the one-to-one director, plus special capa-
cities for appropriately structuring and attending to groups
of diverse people.

The particular qualities I would hold up as most important for you, if you are considering or testing such leadership, are these:

1. *Attentiveness to your own journey.* A deep desire for communion with God and all that is real. Firsthand experience with a range of spiritual disciplines, enough for you to understand some of their possibilities, limitations, and temptations. Continuing involvement with a spiritual friend and/or group for yourself, where you are *not* in charge. Awareness and acceptance of your own gifts and limitations.

2. *Trust in the Spirit's guidance.* Clarity that you cannot manipulate the spiritual growth of anyone; you can only provide a climate for attentiveness. Trust that beneath the barriers in everyone the Spirit is there, and in its own time and way, related to the person's readiness, it will open the person, obviously or obscurely.

Trust in that Spirit within yourself, yet not naively or egotistically identifying it with whatever you do as leader. Still, you need to be able to maintain deep, calm confidence in yourself as servant-leader, beneath whatever tentativeness you may feel on the surface. The group needs to sense such confidence in you, so that its members can feel free to relax their own intradependent controls.

3. *Caring for the group.* Even though you are aware that progress does not depend on you, nonetheless you are aware that it might be impeded by you. Therefore you need to pay attention to providing an environment that constantly invites attentive presence, you pray for the members, and you meet with them one-to-one in spiritual crisis situations to the extent your time allows, and to the extent that you are the appropriate person with whom to meet.

4. *Respect for the uniqueness and shared journey of each member.* Awareness that each person is at a unique point in his or her journey, with unique gifts, limitations, ways to the truth, vocation, and mystery.

At the same time, awareness that each person is an interdependent part of a dynamic *corporate* (and even cosmic) spiritual journey wherein there is much overlap, common pattern, and gifted complementarity.

Given this situation, you need to pay attention to what

is appropriate in response to a given person at a given time, always attempting to evoke the truth that is in them, not merely imposing your own way. You need to be able not to push a person beyond what he or she can bear, yet press toward all he or she is ready for, doing this in the way you probe, question, and support the person.

Given the group setting, you need to be able to give *brief* questions and comments, holding back the temptation to fill the spaces with your words all the time. Spacious silence is a powerful teacher, much more so than most of our chattery words.

5. *Flexibility.* You need some understanding and feel for designing a group's rhythm and content. You need to be willing to plan sessions ahead of time. But you also need to be free to throw out what you plan, if the Spirit surprises you and catches up the group in a way you did not predict.

Your own leadership style ideally should be capable of a large spectrum of possibilities, from strong and bold expression to quiet, patient listening, from support to gentle challenge, depending on what is called for in the moment.

6. *Awareness of basic group dynamics.* You need to be aware and capable of responding to certain "constants" of small group life and leadership.

Who is silent out of lack of confidence, yet seems to need to speak (and thus needs drawing out by you), and who is silent because they are content to let what is happening within develop without interfering comment (and thus needs being left alone)?

Who is too talky, dominating the time, needing gentle halting (and perhaps a separate word outside the group)?

The leader also needs to be able, where helpful, to relate what one person says to another person's comments, to summarize, integrate, and help clarify what has been said, to hear and test suggestions, and deflect unwarranted encounters and discussions that sidetrack the group.

As much as possible you need to protect "space" for the group to "be," avoiding temptations to become a problem-solving or personality-dissecting therapy group.

The leader also needs to be able to sense the mood of the whole or parts of the group and to respond appropriately: to such things as tiredness, restlessness, lostness, and the sudden "kairos" of deeply silent in-touchness.

7. *Basic knowledge of Christian ascetical tradition and human development.* You need to have enough working knowledge of scripture and ascetical tradition that you are able to "tie in" people to their heritage, as appropriate, freeing them for deeper identity with it.

Such connectedness can help persons enlarge their own sense of valid belonging within a deep religious lineage, offsetting the a-historical, overly individualized sense of life with which many people in American culture come. This awareness in the long run can provide a new sense of freedom for larger participation in and accountability for the spread of the richness of Christian tradition and its corporate caring for authentic life in the society.

At the same time, you need to be able to criticize and not merely propagandize the tradition. If the group picks up from you merely whitewashed, all-knowing answers and rightness in the tradition, members will be tempted either to alienation or to fundamentalist oversecurity and imperialism.

If you are free to recognize human pollution, narrowness, irony, and injustice in the tradition along with the true glory, then you will be helping people to join an always reforming, purging, evermore universal and less narrowly sectarian yet still integral, spiritual lineage.

Some awareness of the basic dynamics of psychological-social human development and its barriers also is valuable knowledge. You do not have to be a psychologist, but you do need a basic sensitivity to the way human fears, yearnings, and experiences condition, if not determine, the way people respond in the group. For some people, such sensitivity is intuitive out of their general life experience, rather than something they need to learn.

This sensitivity can add both to your patience and insight, though such groups are not the place for direct psychological analysis. Your attentiveness is to the way grace may be operating or impeded through whatever development process members have undergone.

Your trust is that the disciplines of the group may help to lighten and loosen the "dark" side of that development and foster the light side, though certain people may need special therapeutic help to assist this process.

Conclusion

If you feel a certain lack of confidence after reading this ideal list of qualifications, then welcome to the human family! Our first response rightly is one of humility before our own inevitable limitations.

On the other hand, since your *primary* work as director is simply providing a sensitive structure for people, you need not let your sense of inadequacy in particular areas stop you from being such a leader, if you sense a particular calling and basic gift for it.

If you never said *anything* in the group beyond giving structured instructions and presiding over its basic rhythm, it is likely the group would be very valuable for its members.

If people are ready, then the environment you provide can be enough. Their attentiveness to the rising Spirit of loving truth will carry the group. The leader's role ultimately is a very humble midwife position in this mysterious process.

If you have not led such a group, the best preparation is first to have been a member of one. The next best preparation is to work as an apprentice leader with someone else whose experience you trust. A third and complementary preparation is through some such program as I describe in the next chapter.

Coleadership of groups has proved valuable in Shalem's experience, especially where personalities are complementary. Male-female teams have been particularly helpful.[13]

The potential value of and need for such groups, as I

earlier affirmed, is very great. Leadership of such groups is a particular form of spiritual direction that deserves much more widespread encouragement and careful preparation today. It is a position to which clergy, religious, and lay people may equally be called.

8. Bringing It All Together:
A Program for
Spiritual Directors

Is there need for a special program better to prepare spiritual directors as I have described them? If so, what kind of program is needed? What kinds of people should be in it?

Such questions have been on my mind for a number of years now. This chapter will share some of my own and others' answers, and their elaboration in a particular experimental program now underway.

Need

Perhaps the first need is for us to remember the many forms in which spiritual guidance is already being offered (cf. Chapter Four). One-to-one and group spiritual direction as I have described them supplement these other forms.

They are most valuable when practiced *along with* some of these other reinforcing ways. They are not meant to be sufficient means of guidance in themselves. They do not take place in a vacuum, but in the context of a whole way of life and range of practices that mediate the loving truth of God in our lives, as this is understood within the experience of Christian tradition.

Within this larger context, however, the dimension of spiritual direction is much more potentially valuable both to Church and society than is apparent by the scant disciplined attention given it by the institutional Church.

194

We can see an increasing realization of this neglect today in seminaries and churches across the American continent. Now that direction has been purged of its pre-Vatican II Roman Catholic authoritarian connotations, many Protestants are included in this fresh interest.

This interest has been reinforced by the current "religious awakening" and by our cultural dis-ease, both of which contribute to increasing requests by people for assistance with personal spiritual guidance at all levels of the Church's life and ministerial training.

One way of answering this need is to say that it will be met informally by other Christians in the Body who are at hand. Given the priesthood of all believers, every Christian has the right and responsibility to be a spiritual friend for someone in need.

There is a certain truth to this response. Every serious Christian in fact probably does provide valuable spiritual friendship for others occasionally. On the other hand, St. Paul makes it clear that there are different gifts of the Spirit that complement each other. Everyone may be called to be a friend at times, but a few seem to have a special gift for giving more extensive and conscious time to this calling.

If it is a special gift, then what need is there for a developmental program? Few great spiritual directors have been through any special preparation for this ministry (apart from their general spiritual formation and probable experience with a director for themselves). It was a gift that developed through experience and grace.

The same could be said, though, about most of the other special ministries of the Church historically. Preaching and various forms of pastoral care also are gifts that develop with experience. Yet they normally have been seen as gifts that can be given perspective and depth by special assistance in seminaries or elsewhere.

The same is true with spiritual direction. It is not a technical skill that can be developed in one-to-one correlation to a given training program. But it is a gift, an art, like any gift and art, that can be given perspective, depth, and support in a special program.

A major problem today, however, is that there has been no well-established, broad-based "school" of spiritual direction to offer such assistance. With the centuries-old split between rational and experimental knowledge in the life of the Church described in Chapter One, the bridging discipline of spiritual theology, of which spiritual direction is a practical expression, has been neglected to the point of oblivion in many seminaries and other educational centers of the Church.

As with any other dimension of the Church's life, there is need for a specialized teaching discipline in this area, if it is to be insured depth of historical and current perspective and approach. An ongoing "lineage" of mutually illuminating experience and cumulative, tested knowledge is needed.

On the other hand, there is something peculiarly "non-institutionalizable" about authentic spiritual direction. Since it is focused centrally on the "naked soul" of a person, rather than on a particular function or role, it does not necessarily *directly* serve visible institutional Church or societal operations. What emerges from truly open spiritual direction may in fact lead to resistance to smoothly but falsely functioning roles in institutional life.

Spiritual direction indeed is a paradox in the Church's life. Though it often has taken place as a charism on the fringe of the institution's formal life, and cannot be depended upon to be a smoothly meshing gear in the institutional box, at the same time it stands at the very heart of the institution's purpose: nourishing people's disciplined appreciation and discernment of the Spirit's life in their midst.

Indirectly it can serve profoundly the long-term renewal and maturity of the Church and the society it serves. If it is authentically established as part of the infrastructure of the Church's life, much fruit can be expected.

Thus we see the need for spiritual direction on several levels:

1. The need to bring this resource more broadly and carefully to the attention of people.

2. The need for more and better prepared spiritual directors who have a special gift for spiritual friendship, and a

calling to give more time to it than the average Christian in casual encounter.

3. The need for a more established discipline of spiritual theology and guidance that can provide teachers who will be especially helpful in the preparation of spiritual directors.

Response

Across the continent there is increasing activity afoot for meeting these needs. Literature slowly is becoming more available and widespread, helping to bring attention to the field (though much more is needed, especially among Protestants). Spiritual directors increasingly are finding ways of meeting with one another for mutual help and support, and are encouraging others to consider their calling in this area.[1]

A number of long-term programs have sprung up in recent years to prepare directors and, hopefully, some teachers.

All but three of these programs to my knowledge are Roman Catholic in staff and primary constituency, reflecting the greater formal place spiritual direction has had in that tradition, especially within religious communities. Most of these are staffed primarily by Jesuits, indicating the dominant place Ignatian spirituality and direction has held in the Roman Catholic community. One that is not Jesuit-run is especially designed for charismatic Christians at the Benedictine Community in Pecos, New Mexico.

The two most intensive Roman Catholic programs to my knowledge are the master's degree programs in spiritual direction run by the Jesuits of Weston, Massachusetts (now adding a doctor of ministry degree), and by the Duquesne Institute of Formative Spirituality in Pittsburgh (founded by Adrian van Kaam). This latter program—the oldest in the country—is just adding a doctoral degree as well, which should aid in supplying teachers of spiritual theology and guidance.

Both these full-time programs basically combine a number of academic courses together with supervisory practicums related to work with others in direction.

This is true also of the one non-Roman Catholic master's program in spiritual direction I know of, offered by the Center for Christian Spirituality at the General Theological Seminary (Episcopal) in New York (which may also be offering a doctor of ministry or doctor of theology degree in the future).

The other long-term, nonexclusively Roman Catholic sponsored programs besides this one to my knowledge are Shalem's in Washington, D.C., begun in the fall of 1978, and another begun the same time at Wainwright House in Rye, New York, under the Guild for Spiritual Direction.[2] This latter program is two academic years in length, given in twenty-four hour residential periods once a week in the first year, and for seven weekends in the second year. It gives special emphasis to Jungian psychology and Judaeo-Christian spiritual heritage. It can be related to a degree program through the New York Theological Seminary.

Now we will turn to Shalem's experience.

Shalem Programs

Background. The Shalem Institute for Spiritual Formation's first experiment with long-term group spiritual direction began in the fall of 1973. The eventual desire of many participants in that first ecumenical, clergy and lay group led to experiments in pairing group members into spiritual friends. These pairs met with each other for twenty to thirty minutes during part of many weekly group sessions, and some pairs met outside the group on a regular basis for longer periods.[3]

Over the years since then, more groups were formed, with leaders besides myself. It became apparent that we needed time to share with each other how we were leading groups, and to grapple together with various questions arising about their nature and purpose.

About the same time as Shalem group leaders began helping and checking each other more regularly, a movement arose for providing assistance for one-to-one spiritual directors. Father Shaun McCarty, S.T., called an informal meeting of people he had heard about who offer such direction in the Washington area in the spring of 1975. Over 100 people responded (most of them Roman Catholics), far more than expected.

That meeting made it clear that most directors did not talk with anyone about their direction work, and most had little specific preparation for such ministry.

The outcome was the establishment, under Shalem's administration, of a number of spiritual director colleague groups focused upon informal mutual supervision and support.

Colleague Groups. These groups have continued to meet, with varying membership, ever since. Over the years they have evolved a pattern that would be fairly easy to duplicate elsewhere. Because of this potential transferability to the reader's situation, I will describe the basic learnings of these groups in some detail.

Membership. The groups normally have included a mixture of members of religious communities (both men and women) and lay people (mostly women). Sometimes parish pastors have been involved as well.

Those from religious communities have steadily predominated. These people consistently have found it important for lay people and parish pastors to be present to help broaden their perspective.

The optimum size for these groups has been found to be between eight and ten.

At the beginning of each academic year a general organizational meeting has been held for those who wish to continue for another year, and for potential new members.

Membership standards have been based on: 1) a person's existing work with others, formally or informally, focused on dimensions of prayer and vocational discernment; 2) willingness to give priority to group meetings, and occasionally to present a direction situation to the group.

The more secure group members become with one another, the easier it has been to absorb new members later in the year. In early years membership was closed after the first meeting or two. The steady core of directors continuing each year, though, has shifted this norm to allow new members at any time (with the permission of the group).

Time. Groups from the beginning have met once every two weeks, from October through April. Members for the most part lead very active lives, and this frequency has proved most realistic and helpful.

Specific times are agreed upon at the initial joint organizational meeting. Usually there is one day-group that meets for an hour and a half, and one night-group meeting for two hours.

Structure. Initially we attempted to use a tightly structured case-study model.[4] However, groups tended toward a looser model. The basic pattern of a normal session has gone something like this:

A convenor (elected for the year) starts and/or ends the meeting with prayer and/or scripture.

One person previously has volunteered to present a situation at this meeting. The presentation takes about twenty to thirty minutes. It is presented in such a way as to guard the confidentiality of the person. The background of the person and his or her situation are sketched, along with a history of the direction relationship. The focus then may be upon a particular incident or on the ongoing situation. The presenter summarizes his or her concerns, often in the form of a few questions to the group.

The group then responds as members are moved, often beginning with questions of clarification. The focus then as much as possible is on the director: his or her perceptions about the relationship and situation, and the assumptions of faith and direction underlying these. However, despite this norm, there is a tendency to slip into advice-giving focused on the directee. Also, despite the norm of focus on spiritual dimensions, psychological diagnosis and prescription, or broader issues of pastoral care, sometimes come to the fore both in presentations and discussion.

Hilary Hayden, O.S.B., has described the process as one requiring a high degree of mutual trust:

> The director must be able to express the intimate details of his/her actions and reactions with confidence. A like confidence is required of the colleagues, if they are to make the observations and ask the questions that can lead to fresh insight without wounding.[5]

A great deal of learning takes place in the groups for the colleagues as well as for the presenter. Everyone seems to be able to read into most presentations enough to cull many insights for himself. Also, accountability and stimulus for attentive direction seem generally enhanced.

Over the years, groups also have joined together occasionally for workshops on special subjects, such as "group spiritual direction," and "beginning a direction relationship."

Evaluation. Groups normally spend part of their last session in April evaluating their process and life as a group, and determining issues for discussion at a joint evaluation session in May.

This joint meeting provides some cross-fertilization of learnings, relationships, and resources. Planning for the next fall is begun, based on the stimulus and evaluation of this session.

One of the side-benefits of the groups is the way they have informally established a loose network of persons concerned with spiritual direction as a resource for Church and society.

Members refer potential directees to one another, call upon each other for teaching assistance in different Church situations, exchange much information about what is going on in spiritual-direction programs, and stimulate one another to further think through the meaning, place, and form of spiritual direction in today's world.

In effect, members have been building a loose "lineage" of spiritual-direction understanding, mutual challenge, and support. The insights of laity and Protestants often have been a new factor for many of the Roman Catholic members of religious communities. The often long, disciplined experience of these community members has been equally stimulating for the others.

This rich mix of people—ecumenical, clergy-religious-lay, male-female, and at times interracial, I believe is helping in its own way to prepare the ground for the more collegial ministry of the Church. This is particularly heartening to see evolving in an area so close to the formative heart of different traditions and orders of the Church: personal spiritual nurture.

Long-Term Development Program

By 1977 another organic step seemed called for. Shalem group leaders' meetings and the colleague groups did not provide the kind of long-term, more intensive development program for spiritual directors that a number of people were beginning to ask for. Something with more systematic, sustained, theoretical and practical focus was needed—a full-fledged, long-term program, building on our evolving experience, for those wanting to give a larger amount of time to development as spiritual companions.

This "next step" was given impetus by a special grant from the Rockefeller Brothers Fund for Shalem to plan and mount an experimental program in spiritual direction, under the auspices of the Association of Theological Schools in the United States and Canada, and in cooperation with the Washington Theological Union,[6] with myself as director.

Goals. The *primary* goals for the program have been twofold:

1. To help *increase the number* of better prepared and tested spiritual directors available for theological schools, churches, chaplaincies, retreat centers, and related bases in Church and society.

2. To pilot a *new structure* for such preparation, which would aid in developing the theoretical and practical knowl-

edge needed for the development of similar structures elsewhere.

A number of important *subsidiary* goals also have been significant in the program's development:

1. Development of a *collegial arena* wherein clergy, religious, and lay people, men and women, could teach and learn together as peers in this ministry. The aim here is twofold: a) the practical purposes of enriching one another's understanding from such breadths of background; b) the symbolic purpose of expressing both the just collegial nature of the Church's people and the history of spiritual direction itself, wherein it has been a democratically distributed gift of God to people regardless of their status in the Church.

2. Provision of an *ecumenical arena* for mutual learning and sharing, again both for its practical value of mutual learning and for its symbolic value of holding up the ultimate vision of a united Church. Such an aim also would express the historical reality that Christians (and in fact those of other deep religious traditions) usually have been much closer to one another in their spiritualities than in their polities and doctrinal emphases.

3. Provision of an opportunity for critically *exploring authentic possible spiritualities* for our time, taking into consideration both historical knowledge and current learning and need.

4. To hold up for attention neglected *apophatic dimensions* of spiritual development along with complementary kataphatic approaches.

Staff. Who is needed to staff such a program? And who is available? Given the unprecedented nature of its collective goals, no staff is "ready made" for it. The need was for people with a certain pioneering spirit, who are able to work well collegially, who have a depth of experience in spiritual direction, and who share a broadly consonant sense of intent and process in Christian spirituality.

Given the collegial and ecumenical nature of the program, the staff also ideally should reflect these dimensions. Given the intertwining nature of psychological and spiritual development, the staff additionally should include someone with this specialty.

Finding such a right combination of people, and ones with the time to give to a fairly demanding part-time program, was my first major task. I decided that several layers of resource people were called for.

Associate Staff. Three people were chosen as collegial associates with me to assist with the overall detailed planning and ongoing execution and evaluation of the program:

The Rev. Shaun McCarty, S.T., a Roman Catholic priest, member of the faculty of the Washington Theological Union with a specialty in spiritual theology, a highly experienced spiritual director and retreat leader, and a consultant on spiritual renewal both nationally and internationally.

Dolores Leckey, D.H.L., a Roman Catholic layperson, director of the Secretariat to the Laity for the National Catholic Conference of Bishops, member (on leave) of the faculty at De Sales Hall School of Theology in the area of Christian education and spirituality, and an experienced spiritual director.

Gerald May, M.D., a psychiatrist, Protestant, director of Shalem's two year research study on spiritual development that resulted in *Pilgrimage Home,* author of several other related books, and a person whose private practice and leadership of groups frequently has focused on the relation of psychological and spiritual development.

Special Resource Persons. A number of persons who supplement the core staff's experience have been asked to lead particular seminars during the first year of the program.

In addition, a small pool of highly regarded spiritual directors were asked to be available for program participants who were in need of a director.

Finally, a curriculum advisory committee was formed (and later a national advisory committee).[7]

Curriculum Advisory Committee. This committee was formed to provide outside consultant perspective on the program's development.

Its make-up purposely was broad: Catholic and Protestant, lay, religious, and clergy, black and white, male and female. We also selected people who were graduates of both the Weston and Duquesne direction programs mentioned earlier, as well as the director of the program at the General Theological Seminary.

It has met twice in its first year, and individuals have responded to mailed materials and personal questions. The committee has provided broad support and helpful perspective for different dimensions of the program.

Areas for Consideration

In the staff's long process of thinking through how to put together the program, we were determined to examine as many of our assumptions about spirituality and spiritual direction as possible. The more we did so, the more apparent it became that mounting such a program inevitably involves an enormous range of considerations: theological, moral, educational, and psychological.

Some of these will be exposed as I lay out the three key areas of consideration in which any such attempted program must struggle: participants, structure and content, and evaluation.

Participants

Who is appropriate for such a program? After much reflection ahead of time and with the experience of the first year of the program now completed, a number of criteria for selection have been established.

Underlying these is a sense that there is a need to raise up a new level of spiritual companion today who falls between two historic models: the graced master and the gifted but unpolished friend.

Graced masters I think are given, they cannot be developed. Gifted friends, too, basically are given, but sometimes their helpfulness is unnecessarily limited by lack of perspective and support. They can end up providing others with an environment for first aid, when in fact they could be providing a fuller, deeper, more flexible long-term environment.

It is the cultivation of these already-gifted friends who are the focus of the program. As with artists of any kind, the gift is there or it is not. It cannot be made. But the gift can be nurtured.

Clergy, seminary faculty, religious educators, and religious community members usually are legitimized by their positions to offer such assistance. Some of these do not have a motivated gift as spiritual friends. Those who do often have little preparation for applying it, and few or no places to turn for help in its development. This situation is exacerbated by the increasing demand for such help in many of their religious structures.

It has become increasingly clear to many such persons that neither psychological pastoral counseling nor theological knowledge hits the nail on the head as adequate preparation for helping someone in depth with his or her prayer life, charity, and discernment. The "on-target" need is for spiritual direction/friendship.

Nonprofessionally church-related lay people usually are not positioned to offer assistance except in a very informal way. One result has been the neglect of a great potential resource pool.

In my experience with Shalem groups, I have been very impressed with the number of mature lay people, especially women, who demonstrate special gifts of spiritual sight and friendship. These people often are sought out by others in their neighborhoods, families, parishes, and jobs for informal counsel that includes the spiritual dimension of life. However, I find that the gifts of such people are not recognized by the Church as a whole, and that they often lack confidence and perspective in what they do as spiritual friends.[8]

As a result of this experience, I have been particularly concerned that these people, as well as more professionally positioned ones, be legitimized and prepared as a resource for Church and community. There never will be enough professional Church people for such direction work, especially with all the other complex tasks in which these clergy, educators, etc., usually are involved. And in any case, many of the best potential directors, as well as those often with more time for it, are among the broad spectrum of laity.[9]

The *chief* criterion in our selection of participants has been to see whether others spontaneously seek out the person for spiritual counsel. This criterion can be met equally by laity, religious, and clergy.

Since historically this has been an unpaid service (at least financially), we have assumed that most spiritual directors will experience this ministry on a part-time basis. It is an area largely of "volunteer" ministry, though it is more directly related to some people's "jobs" than others.

With the great need for qualified spiritual directors today, perhaps more religious institutions need to consider providing a full or part-time salaried position for such persons. This would allow highly gifted people to be able to afford using their gifts more broadly, yet without having to "charge" persons a fee. Such "fee professionalization" I think would have a more negative than positive outcome for this ministry.

There is, of course, the old tradition of someone making a voluntary contribution for the work of the director to his or her organizational base. Some approach to continuing this tradition could be another way of dealing with the realities of financial need.

In selecting participants we therefore have looked for persons who are positioned to be able to offer direction without needing it as a basis of financial support, except as it may be part of the work of a salaried position, or otherwise non-fee supported.

Since we are approaching direction largely as a part-time vocation, it seemed important to offer a program that also would require only part of a participant's time.

This was reinforced by our criterion that points to the best directors being more mature people in the second half of life (cf. Chapter Five). Such persons normally are in established family, community, and work situations that would make it extremely difficult for them to drop everything for a full-time program. Also, we assumed that many ongoing experiences in people's normal lives are valuable ones that inform spiritual direction; with the program as an ongoing backdrop, their whole lives can be seen as data for reflection and insight.

It became clear in the applications for the initial program that many could not have participated if we had required full-time direct participation, as opposed, in effect, to full-time attentiveness to spiritual awareness through whatever work and life experiences were there in their lives.

Here now is a summary of the nine criteria used for selection, each of which has demonstrated its value in the first year and is being used as a basis for selection of future groups. The first year's experience clearly has demonstrated the priority of the first two and the enhanced importance of the last.

Criteria for Selection

Individuals who:

1. Sense a call to spiritual companionship for others, i.e., attention to a person's growth and sharing in the ego-transcending and transforming life of God.

2. Have had this call tested by others coming to them for assistance with this area of their lives, who can vouch for his or her potential helping gifts.

3. Desire an experientially and academically exploratory two-year program with an ecumenical mix of peers.

4. Have a B.A. degree or equivalent.[10]

5. Express commitment to Truth through a particular major religious tradition and at the same time are open to learning from other traditions.[11]

6. Have sufficient life experience.[12]

7. Ideally, are affirmed or sponsored for the program by a jurisdiction, religious community, seminary, local church counseling center, or other settings that will help legitimize and encourage their work.[13]

8. Ideally, have some background in one-to-one and group counseling theory and skill development.[14]

9. Ideally, are (or have been) in spiritual direction/ friendship with someone else over a period of time.[15]

In the future, we also will plan more focused supplementary work than we had in the first year for those with little background in the study of scripture, theology, and the history of Christian spirituality.

First Program Participants. Roughly fifty people applied for the first program scheduled to begin in September, 1978, from a broad variety of backgrounds.[16]

Our main disappointment was in having no black applicants in a metropolitan area with a 25 percent black population, though interest in the program had been expressed by the Dean of the Howard University School of Religion, which is predominantly black.[17]

Apart from this gap, the range and quality of applicants was great enough to allow us to choose a group of almost equal numbers of men and women and of Roman Catholics and Protestants, and a good mix of parish clergy, religious community members, chaplains, seminary faculty, advanced students, formation directors, and laity working in various church and community situations.

Twenty-five persons were accepted, despite our announced limit of twenty. This was done partly because of the high quality of the applicants, and partly because we expected that for various reasons there would be attrition. In fact, by the beginning of the second semester the group leveled off at twenty-one members.

The rich mix of participant backgrounds again and again has proven one of the most important bases of learning in the estimation of many participants.

Structure and Content

What do people really need to help them be better directors? Apprenticeship to a master? In a relatively "masterless" time, this is not likely to happen. But they do need to be with someone who is their director, who can help them attend to the Master of Loving Truth within.

Technical skills? Yes. Yet direction is an art, and such skills at best can only draw out the gift that is there.

Academic knowledge? Yes. But such knowledge is an arrow of comprehension that can go just so far in a ministry that essentially involves apprehension.

Personal spiritual disciplines? Yes. But these *guarantee* nothing.

Indeed, there is *nothing* a program can do to *make* a better spiritual director. Just as in direction itself, a program can provide an *environment* that invites one to see what one needs to see and hear. If a person is *ready* to see and hear more deeply, even a relatively "bad" program might be helpful. If a person is not, the best structured program in the world can do little.

This reality means a certain humility is called for on the part of the staff. We cannot engineer one-to-one correlations between program and product. We are dealing with the subtlest, most integrative dimension of a person's life in spiritual direction, and this always remains to a large extent an area of mystery and awe.

To attempt its reduction to some clinical technical model would be to defy the very heart of spiritual direction awareness. That awareness points to the necessity of patient waiting for healing sight. It means willingness to sit beside a person with words and methods and support, yet clearly aware that you wait outside his or her chamber of awareness for the Spirit to open heart and mind.

It is this depth of mystery that resists programmed "problem-solving" and "skill development." There is that dimension of charisma involved that can only be attended as an unfolding process. A program can provide launching, sensitizing, and securing platforms, but oh, how puny these look beside the Spirit's movement in a person when the time has come.

A program at its best stands as midwife, attending the birth of deeper spiritual sight through cleansing, aligning, resting. This faithfully appropriated integrative sight is what "makes" a good spiritual director. It is not the accumulation of knowledge. It is the nakedness of sight. Woe to the program that would bank on the pretense of that accumulation for qualification, rather than upon the stripping of whatever may come between the nakedness of the person, the director, and God.

Such nakedness is too much for any of us all the time. We will cover ourselves with many things that secure our identities and analytical knowledge. These coverings, like bandages on our wounds, are valuable, as long as we know that they are bandages and not the healing, knowing power in themselves.

A directors' program, too, must recognize our human need for coverings. At the same time, of all programs I can think of, it must remain the most iconoclastic, the most suspicious of anything that would manipulate the mystery, and most attentive to the unpredictable nuances through which a person actually hears an integrating word.

It is because of this unpredictable process of development that we agreed not to move the program toward a degree offering or toward a qualifying certificate. We felt there was no way we could guarantee a more qualified director at the end of the program. We wanted to maintain a sense of the centrality of the historic charismatic dimension of direction, rather than a focus on academic achievement.

At the same time, we did recognize the realities of human need for an objective document enough to agree that we would give a certificate of completion to those who satisfactorily finish the program, which simply will describe the disciplines undergone.

The program also can be taken for graduate academic credit where this is needed by students, though we try to arrange this on a pass/fail rather than grade basis to offset the temptation toward an attitude focused on expedient work for extrinsic reward rather than on the intrinsic attentive unfolding so valuable in such a program.

Several students are taking it as part of academic doctoral programs in Christian Spirituality at Catholic University. Some others are taking it as part of master of divinity programs.

It is with these important cautions that I now turn to the specific dimensions of the program we have put together. All the dimensions "surround" the growth process of participants with invitations to see and hear. We may plant the seed, but the Spirit gives any growth of significance that may occur.

Individual participants come with need for different emphases. Just as in group direction, there is no way to provide a perfect one-to-one match for just exactly what every individual is ready for. Given the mystery of the growth process involved, I don't think there is a way for individuals themselves to know exactly what is right for them, even if we could tailor-make a program exactly to their stated specifications.

Given the range of needs and mystery involved, our approach has been to provide a range of different "environments," which we hope are mutually connecting and reinforcing. Particular ones are likely to prove especially right for particular participants. Following are the different dimensions we have required, with some of our learnings related to them in the first year of trial.

Spiritual Director. Each participant must meet at least once a month with a spiritual director of his or her own choosing.

Most participants entering the program already were in direction with someone. Others knew whom they wanted. The few who needed help were given the names of several directors in the program "pool" earlier mentioned, after discussing with them the kind of person who might be best.

For those with no or little direction experience, it seems best to encourage them to see a director more than once a month if possible, at least for the first two months. For those with a great deal of experience, it might be best to be looser about this requirement if they are at a point in their lives where less frequent meetings seem best.

For most participants, though, this direct participation

in the "oral tradition" of direction is crucial. It symbolizes our assumption (a classic one in spiritual direction) that the best preparation of a director is constant attentiveness to his or her own spiritual journey rather than to any external skill development, and the value of a spiritual friend in this attentiveness.

Personal Discipline. Participants are expected to have their own discipline of *prayer and attentiveness,* with accountability to God through their directors.

In addition, each person is expected to keep an inclusive *journal.* It should include: reading and seminar notes; a log of personal prayer/meditation practice and reflection; notes from sessions with director, directees and staff; log of relevant personal daily experience (including dreams); and any integrative reflections on these dimensions.

This journal is considered the "primary text" for the program. It is treated as a process workbook, the main thread of reflective coherence through the many facets of the program. No one is asked to share it, except as someone might want to. It is a private document, so that it can be written as freely as possible.

Early in the program we give instructions about different ways such a journal can be kept, and ask for the shared experience of participants.

Some people have a great deal of past experience with journal-keeping of one form or another. They may be at a point in their lives where it is natural for such written reflective work to be more sporadic. For others who are just beginning, such journal-keeping can be an important and needed daily or frequent discipline. In hindsight, it would have been valuable to reflect on journal-keeping methods and issues periodically through the year, rather than just at the beginning. Some participants seemed to become bogged down in their writing and needed the stimulus of others' experience.

Directees. Participants must work with at least two individuals, meeting with each at least once a month on a long-term basis. Some people work in group direction as well, but two individuals a month still must be seen by them.

Working with directees is the ongoing reality testing ground for whatever one may learn elsewhere.

The majority of participants either already were working with two directees, or were positioned in such a way that those wanting to be directees came to them after knowing their eligibility.

However, a number of participants, especially the Protestants[18] and students, needed help in finding directees.

This sometimes proved a delicate matter. It is not good for a potential directee to have a staff member (or anyone else) refer him or her to a participant for direction just because that person "needs" someone. Attention to the right "match" is important. Also, if for some reason a participant really seems confused about the nature of direction, perhaps confusing it with pastoral counseling, or seems ill-prepared to be a director at the moment because of pressing personal issues, then referring potential directees becomes all the more problematic.

The reality of dealing with the spiritual lives of real people takes it out of the realm of guinea-pig experimentation. This is no game. Referring directees is a serious business for which the "referer" is accountable.

This reality makes it particularly important that participants are selected who really can be trusted to understand enough about spiritual direction, and have enough personal maturity, that worry about whether or not potential directees appropriately can be referred to them is mitigated. If a person despite screening turns out to be in the program without these qualifications, then they may need to leave, or their work with directees may need to be delayed for some months.

Peer Groups. Each person is preassigned to a subgroup of four people for the year, using heterogeneity and complementarity as the primary criteria.

Each peer group meets monthly for two hours, by mutual arrangement. The time is strictly structured around two participant presentations, focused on a particular directee relationship.

Staff normally do not attend these. This is due both to

the limitations of staff time, and to our learnings in colleague groups from some people who have been through heavily supervised direction programs. Their comments centered around the relief of being able to "travel together" as peers, more focused on letting the directee "work it out with the Lord" rather than on the director's "performance"—"doing it right."

We also trusted that the group would be made up of unusually mature and experienced people who could be trusted to have sufficient insight among themselves.

The experience of the first year was mixed. Some peer groups proved very compatible, reliable, and highly appreciative of the process. Others foundered on the basis of 1) differing expectations of the degree of self-revelation desired; 2) differing views of spiritual direction (some interpreting it more broadly than others to include dimensions of pastoral counseling); 3) personality differences; and 4) differing degrees of accountability in attendance.

In the second year for this group we will experiment with: 1) staff attendance at these sessions to see what difference it makes (a request of many participants); 2) new mixes of people; and 3) gathering all groups together at the same time and place, with some opportunity for plenary reflection.

In hindsight, if it could be arranged practically, I think it would be valuable to have these peer groups meet twice rather than once a month, and to include a staff member more often, especially at the beginning.

Retreats. Four full days of retreat together were required for the first year.

These group days were divided into two residential retreats at a country retreat house, one at the start and one at the finish of the year.

The *opening orientation retreat* began at 9:30 A.M. on a Friday and ended at 9:00 P.M. on Saturday. Four goals were set for it:

1. To provide a significant block of time together that can build the foundation for a two-year temporary community marked by a spirit of shared prayer, awareness of one

another's backgrounds, and a quality of mutual ease that can aid the flow of communication and learning.

2. To provide an overview of different dimensions and selected issues of spiritual guidance.

3. To form peer groups.

4. To have the first private staff-participant advisory sessions, with particular focus on the participant's proposed area of specialization.

As it turned out, the retreat was an excellent way of beginning for most participants. Some would have liked more opportunity for silence and formal retreat than we allowed. A few wished it had been less exhaustingly "packed" with presentations and work. Most of Saturday afternoon was a free and silent period, except for a half-hour interview, but the rest of the time was very full.

In the future I think we will relax the schedule a bit and give more time for absorption of what is presented and for evoking insights from participants (this latter need being an important learning from the seminars, as we shall see).

The *final group retreat* was held at the end of the first year over the same days and time. Its goals included these:

1. To provide opportunities for program and self-evaluation.

2. Review of proposed structure for the second-year program, and joint planning of content.

3. One-to-one participant interviews with staff members for review of program participation and relevant personal needs.

4. Meditation and prayer, alone and together.

5. Informal fellowship and learning with each other.

This retreat proved an invaluable opportunity for integration. A part-time, nonresidential program particularly needs such sustained periods of time together.

A minimum of *two silent retreat days* (alone or with others) also are required in the first year. These days have the symbolic purpose of holding up the importance of the spiritual journey as a unique, pioneering endeavor for everyone, a journey on which one's naked faith and trust is foundational beyond the security of any particular roles, institutions, or other support systems. These days are meant to provide a minimal link with such a spirit of the Desert Mothers and Fathers, and a counter to any overdomestication, securing, and institutionalization of the spiritual life.

Such an attitude I believe is crucial to maintain on the part of a "soul friend," one which counters the temptation to succumb to a womby, comfortable, sectarian view that presumes overfamiliar, oversecure knowledge of the Spirit of Truth's awesome, mysterious ways among us.

Practically, these days invite participants to take a little serious "Sabbath time" during the year. Perhaps "commanding" such appreciation and unambiguous listening time might help put predictably overproduction conscious American participants a little more easily in touch with the fourth "commandment": Sabbath rest. Again, for a good soul friend, experience and awareness of this dimension of life is crucial.

We asked participants to plan for these days in consultation with their spiritual directors and with a staff person. We also asked that they selectively share journal reflections on the retreat, if they liked, with the staff members with whom they were scheduled to meet the month following the retreat.

When these days were taken was up to them. We suggested the possibility of taking them during Advent and/or Lent, to tie them into a collective Church preparatory season.

In fact, these retreat days only sporadically were discussed by participants with staff, given the crush of other requirements and possible subjects for discussion in the generally very busy lives of participants. However, the harried quality of participants' lives just reinforces the importance of insisting that these days be taken.

Seminars. Every Tuesday night the group met from 7:15 to 9:30, with myself always, and the fluctuating presence of other staff and resource persons, depending on the subject.

Goals for the seminar were these:

1. To provide a broad historical and contemporary theoretical background in the development, forms, and values of

spiritual direction/friendship, together with assumptions concerning the nature of God, person, and world, through lectures, discussion, and readings.

2. To provide an exposure to selected spiritual disciplines, especially methods of prayer and discernment, together with reflection on their appropriateness in different situations.

3. To provide opportunity both for the deeper personal integration and understanding of these areas in participants' own lives, as well as a better sense of their application in working with others (conjointly with other activities of the program).

As we thought through what seems important for a spiritual director to know and face, the breadth of subjects became larger and larger. If we were to deal with all of the assumptions and potentially useful knowledge involved in approaching spiritual direction, we would in effect have to construct an entire theological education.

This awareness reinforced the reality of spiritual direction for us as an integrating discipline. Everything in life is relevant to it. And yet it is how "everything" subtly falls together into single-sightedness and single-heartedness that is involved in spiritual direction. It is easy to miss this underlying subtle simplicity amidst the complex fragments of different subjects and dimensions of living.

As it turned out, we were too ambitious in the weekly objectives. Though everything we did was relevant, we forgot the reality of how much a person can present or absorb. Each seminar subject was worthy of a course in itself. We found ourselves opening (or reopening for many) vast fields of knowledge, without time to integrate insights before we were into yet more subjects.

We had assumed a certain background knowledge in many of the subjects on the part of most participants. We had hoped we could narrow the focus to specific dimensions directly related to direction. However, we easily became bogged down in the complex and varying assumptions of particular subjects without adequate time to integrate them well with spiritual direction, much less with the particular issues of participants.

We in effect set out to "cover" everything possibly related to spiritual direction, with lectures trying to squeeze the essence out of vast quantities of material in a very short time. By the time a lecturer reached a point of wrapping up this essence, seminar time virtually was gone and many participants were left with many loose ends.

Over time, with the assistance of assigned readings, we hoped everything eventually would fall in place. Instead, many participants found themselves more and more confused, fragmented, and frustrated. There was no way everything could fall in place if we continually added new material and gave little time in the class for personal integration.

At the end of the first three months I tested this growing sense of mine with participants, and found that for almost everyone I was right. One participant put it very well when she said, "We should use the same central methodology in the seminar that we use in direction itself: *evoking* the truth from participants rather than trying to *tell* it in lectures.

We shifted the methodology thereafter to approach subjects differently. We gave up the desperate attempt to cover all the content we felt important. Instead, we shifted toward weighting the readings more for this end[19] and saving the seminar time for short lectures (twenty to thirty minutes) leading to individual, small group, and plenary reflection on particular questions that could help integrate the subject, spiritual direction, and the existential experience of each participant.

We also began giving more time for corporate prayer forms and related experiences, which also had been neglected in the press to cover everything didactically.

On the whole, participants breathed a sigh of relief. I began to sense that we finally were on target with an inductive method that better fits an arena of apprehension. What is most important is that participants be able to "catch" certain key insights in their own living/directing situations. There is no way that anyone can "catch" everything available to be caught. But they can catch what they are able and need to catch at a given time.

This approach reflects more consonance with our sense of the required journal, i.e., that knowledge is a permanent process of unfolding, not a product to be covered in a stated period of time. We can expose people to a full array of subjects, but what each needs to and can effectively learn will relate to where they are personally and what grace of insight they need for themselves and their work.

The best value of having begun the seminars on the more conservative academic model of long lectures is our firsthand negative learning about the inappropriateness, or at least inadequacy, of this model for the subtle, integrative, existential arena of spiritual direction.

Some teachers, of course, are excellent lecturers and just don't have either the training or gift for more inductively experiential teaching. But persons capable of this second mode of learning I believe are the most valuable ones to raise up for the future development of spiritual theology and direction.

The basic seminar pattern into which we finally settled included a brief lecturette related to the subject, followed by individual and small group work related to particular integrative questions. This was followed by up to half an hour for some led prayer/meditation/reflection discipline, and a short break. The seminar then ended with opportunities for plenary questions and comments related to the subject, and some ways of tying it in with the previous and following week's seminar themes.

Another frustration of the seminars was the shortness of time. The initial retreat had begun relationships and informal learning among participants that were impeded in the seminar by the great amount of work we needed to do together.

Since we are dealing with an area of apprehension, the opportunity to "turn over" subjects in various ways both formally and informally over a period of time is important. Appropriating linear information about a subject is not enough. A more personally insightful appropriation, integrated with other knowledge, is needed.

Our proposed way of aiding more "mulling and turning over" time for the future is to have fewer seminars for longer periods (six hours) on a theme, including a meal together where more informal learning and relationships can be enhanced.

One final frustration of the seminars was the lack of time for integrating assigned readings. Next year, with a longer block of seminar time, and with more weight on the readings for systematic coverage of content, we plan to integrate them into each session through particular relevant questions.

Though we did include special weight on understandings and practices in apophatic tradition, we did not provide a systematic, consistent focus here. To have done so would have provided a more clear and less potentially confusing focus. However, it also would have denied access to and integration with the broad, dominant kataphatic approaches that are primary for many participants, as well as with many of their directees.

Our main motive in giving the apophatic as much attention as we did was because of its serious neglect in recent Christian practice, as I have pointed out earlier in this study. We rightly assumed that most participants would have had far less exposure to apophatic than to kataphatic approaches.

In the future, these two approaches perhaps will need more conscious dialogue and integration than was apparent in the first year. My sense, though, is that such correlation is a subtle, organic process in people's lives that cannot be forced, and that should not lead to overcategorization of two valid and interrelated modes of participation in the same reality.

It should be mentioned here that some persons have the time and need to include more learning than that provided by the seminars. We encourage these people to enroll in other courses along with ours, particularly those focused on spirituality, prayer, discernment, direction, and related subjects offered through the Washington Theological Union and other area schools.

Reading. A large bibliography on spirituality and spiritual direction[20] was put together, with inputs from the staff and from bibliographies of other programs and courses that I had been collecting for several years.

Included was a list of current periodicals that regularly include relevant articles.[21] Much of the material directly related to spiritual direction is found in periodicals rather than books. Most of these are Roman Catholic in editorship, though a number include articles of non-Roman authors.

The split between theological and devotional life has tended to be sharper in most Protestant traditions.[22] This factor, together with normally greater Protestant weight on justification by faith alone, on moral rather than ascetical development and, in liberal Protestant traditions, upon psychological models of growth, has managed to reduce emphasis on or even leave a place for the bridging disciplines of spiritual theology and spiritual friendship.

As I earlier pointed out, there is growing interest in these areas today among Protestants, but not enough to be reflected, to my knowledge, in any special periodical.

Perhaps the more free ecumenical climate of our time will mean in the future simply more denominationally varied authorship of articles in the already established Catholic periodicals, together with occasional articles in more general Protestant journals, rather than the foundation of any specialized Protestant periodicals. Protestants in any case do not have the special impetus and resources of the Roman religious communities, who frequently are the sponsors of such periodicals. The "nonexceptions" to this are the periodicals of Anglican religious communities, which publish relevant articles from time to time.

Post-Vatican II Roman Catholic thinking and practice have veered so much closer to many Protestant traditions, and vice versa (at least in attitude, if not always practice), as I earlier have discussed, that literature across these lines is increasingly "absorbable." The main difficulty for Protestants in reading Roman material has been getting used to a certain terminology that often is new to them.[23]

Protestant participants on the whole have shown less confidence in their grasp of spiritual direction, given its more veiled presence in their traditions. Some of the basic readings as a result I think have been particularly important for them.

On the other hand, though Roman Catholics are more familiar with a skeletal vocabulary for spiritual direction, the meaning of some of these terms has undergone such dramatic change since Vatican II that their sense of "newness" to the subject often doesn't seem much different than the Protestants'.

Together I think both the Catholics and Protestants vaguely have sensed that we share a time of groping together toward an emerging, reconstellated understanding of direction in which none of us is yet thoroughly confident. Thus, in regard to readings, as in all other dimensions of the program, there is a common sense of humble searching and equality.

Five levels of reading are involved in the first-year program.

First is a general text that we suggest everyone buy: *Soul Friend, A Study of Spirituality,* by Kenneth Leech. Leech is an Anglican whose book I believe is the most succinct, balanced, and lucid work yet available on spiritual direction. Indeed, it may be the *only* comprehensive, ecumenical book on the subject ever written (which is one impetus for the writing of this book). It includes sections on history, the present climate, prayer, and the relation of spiritual direction to therapy, social justice, and the rite of reconciliation, as well as a selective bibliography.

Leech shows sensitivity and information about selected Protestant as well as Roman Catholic and Anglican traditions. He also is sensitive to apophatic as well as kataphatic approaches.

The *second* level of reading involves a small sampling of *required* basic readings related to spirituality and spiritual direction to be read at leisure during the first year (cf. *Appendix* for these and other readings).

The *third* level involves a selection of *recommended* readings.

The *fourth* level involves reading assignments and recommendations for particular seminars, normally given out a week or two beforehand.

The *fifth* level involves extra reading from the bibliography[24] (or elsewhere) that fills in some of the particular major gaps in the knowledge of the participant. We particularly recommend attention here to the reading of writers who demonstrate an experiential and not just academic knowledge of God.

The historical series of Louis Bouyer is recommended as the most comprehensive available compendium of Christian spirituality (though new books are needed badly on scriptural and Protestant spirituality—nothing currently available is adequate). Part Two of Evelyn Underhill's *Mysticism,* together with Bouyer, are recommended as primary resources for gaining an overview of particular Christians with demonstrated, experimental spiritual knowledge.

I have already mentioned that our too-infrequent references to readings during packed seminar times have encouraged some participants to be spotty in this area. In the future, as I have suggested, we will pay more attention to this. Discussion of readings also might aid participants in sorting out any confusion these works may engender relative to kataphatic and apophatic emphases.

Research. The requirement of a research paper has three primary purposes behind it:

1. An opportunity to plow into some particular area of interest which will give the participant a sense of more in-depth knowledge at a particular point.

2. In the process of researching a particular area, an opportunity to find how various dimensions of spirituality and personal experience connect with it, serving to aid a more integrated understanding.

3. An opportunity to add to the printed body of knowledge related to spiritual direction, which is so thin at this point compared to other subjects.[25]

We wanted participants to choose a subject area as soon as possible, so that they could use it as a focus for their ongoing experience and reading during the year. During the summer before the program began I drew up a list of specialization areas that seemed to me to be in need of further research today. With some modification by the staff, this list was circulated to participants. They were not restricted to working in one of these areas, but we hoped the list might stimulate their thinking and direction.

Oral presentations of basic research insights were made to the whole group in the spring term. These on the whole proved very stimulating. They presented the best opportunity of the year for sharing the mutual resources of participants. I suggested that these be treated as opportunities for testing certain insights or questions with the others.

I also suggested that participants listen to the presentations with one ear listening for relevance to their own research area. My assumption here is that all knowledge is interrelated, and integral thinking in an integrating discipline such as spiritual direction is particularly important.

Advisory Meetings. The plan for the first year was to have each participant meet with each of the four staff persons twice during the year. This would give staff an opportunity to develop a more firsthand knowledge of each person's situation, and give each participant an opportunity to utilize the different resources of each staff member.

These meetings average out one meeting a month for each person. Each was scheduled for up to one and a half hours, except the first and last meetings, which were restricted to half an hour during the opening and closing retreats.

Guidelines given to participants for these meetings included the following:

Meetings can include a brief review of the learner's work in these areas:

1. Work with directees: any general or specific problems or important learnings.

2. Personal discipline: journal-keeping, reading, relation to spiritual director, etc.

The bulk of time can be given to a specific topic/question/problem which is to have been selected ahead of time by the learner. This can include issues raised by his or her practical work with others, conceptual issues, etc., ideally with special reference to the particular experience and resources of the staff person with whom he or she is to meet.

It is important that the learner review his or her work ahead of time with regard to the above and come to the meeting with an agenda. The journal can be used to work with this preliminary sifting. He or she is encouraged to bring the journal to the meeting for possible reference.

The staff had hoped these meetings could be used by learners to help them integrate confused or fragmented dimensions of the program in their experience, as well as to give opportunity for in-depth reflection in a particular area.

The staff also saw it as an opportunity to check on how learners were progressing in selecting and moving into a special research area, and how they were sensing the value of particular dimensions of the program, especially the peer groups, which staff do not normally attend.

As it turned out in the first year's experience, many participants had difficulty with the "open agenda" dimension of the meetings. Perhaps because most of them lived such busy lives, the opportunity to reflect carefully ahead of time on some issue worth discussing seemed rare. With all the other dimensions of the program, this one seemed a little more of a luxury, an optional "extra," than we had anticipated in many cases, relative to the travel and meeting time involved.

Nonetheless, learners ranked these meetings unusually high in evaluations. These ratings may have been skewed by an unwillingness to look as if they did not appreciate the staff time. I think more basically, though, that the meetings did have a way of supporting and attending to the individual situations of participants that was an important "personalizing" dimension of the program for them despite the sometimes vagueness of agenda. They fulfilled on a larger scale some of the functions of the private interviews mentioned in the last chapter on group direction.

Learners were not allowed to utilize staff as spiritual directors. "Outsiders" were required in order to assure a "cleaner," more open relationship unpolluted by evaluative dimensions. Nonetheless, these advisory sessions often did include spiritual dimensions of learners' lives. This "corroborative" opportunity for counsel seemed an important resource for many.

Probably the most consistent subject of conversation was the research area. Some learners had particular difficulty "settling in" to an area. Some changed their area in midstream. Opportunities to encourage clarification, confirmation, and resources for this research seemed important for many.

Our proposed revision in this area for the future is to reduce the number of required meetings to four, one with each staff member, spread through the year. The staff also will be available at other times for special assistance, on a needs basis.

Second Year Program

The second year is designed to be a "lighter" one, with fewer meetings and less general time involvement. It is meant to be a transition between an intensive initial year, and the years after the program when participants will maintain contact only through ongoing colleague groups. All the dimensions of the first year will be maintained, with these differences:

Seminars will be held once a month rather than once a week, with a focus on particular issues and readings related to spiritual direction, chosen in relation to a consensus of learner needs.

Peer groups will meet once a month together, with rotating staff participation in each, and opportunity for some plenary sharing. Groups will be reconstituted to provide broader experience with others in the program.

Retreats will be reduced to one day at the beginning and end. The initial retreat day will overlap with the new first-year group's initial retreat, as a way of giving the new group some opportunity for exchange and learning with the second-year group.

Advisory sessions will be reduced to one required meeting each semester, with other meetings as needed.

Readings will be focused more on individual needs.

The paper will be focused more personally: on the learner's understanding of spirituality and spiritual direction, and its valid ways of being utilized in his or her own particular ministerial context.

If a person has time and interest in pursuing a particular area of research, this also can be an additional focus of the paper.

We plan strongly to encourage learners to form or join a colleague group after they have finished the program, and commit themselves to this or some other form of mutual supervision and support for as long as they practice spiritual direction.

Evaluation

We have developed both formal and informal means of evaluating the learners and the program itself.

Learner Evaluation. Informally, staff attend to learner participation at retreats, seminars, and in advisory sessions. These sessions also include a special opportunity to check on accountability in different dimensions of the program.

Formally, the research paper provides a major opportunity for staff to sense how much reading and integration have been going on. In future years, we may need to provide a further check on reading, perhaps through reports of books read as well as relevant questions in seminars. One possibility we are considering for the second-year group is asking participants to select a few especially important sentences or paragraphs from their special readings, which we will collate and distribute to everyone for mutual edification.

Since we are dealing with a basically mature and intrinsically motivated group in such a program, we have not wanted to be overly restrictive watchdogs who do not respect participant motivation to do what is important for them.[26] This is counterbalanced in our experience of the first year by the great busyness of most participants, so that they perhaps need a little extra sense of external accountability to lead them to give the program's work sufficient priority.

Learners are given an opportunity for self-evaluation relative to the different dimensions of the program in a midterm and final written evaluation.

They also are given this opportunity in relation to their work as a spiritual director in the peer groups, together with feedback from other members of that group. To mark the importance of this particular dimension, a careful written and oral evaluation procedure has been put together for attention before, during, and after the final peer-group meeting, including a summary report for the staff. This procedure includes evaluation of a list of important qualities in the spiritual director's attitudes and behavior.

Program Evaluation. Informal ongoing evaluation happened through occasional questions asked the group in seminars and staff advisory meetings.

The staff met monthly together to assess the functioning of different dimensions of the program and to plan for any changes in course. They also provided some basic information for one another about the progress of the learners with whom each had been meeting in advisory sessions, as a way of sensitizing the staff member who would be seeing them next. This was important, for example, in providing information on where a learner was in his or her research area, so that he or she did not have to start from scratch each time the learner shifted to meeting with a different staff member.

Formally, two detailed written evaluations are built into the program, one in late December, and one during the final retreat (conjointly with written self-evaluations).

On the final evaluation the overall average rating of the twelve different dimensions of the program was 5.4, on a scale from (7) (highest value to participant) to (1) (lowest val-

ue). The ratings were closely clustered. The highest dimension (6.1) was "Relating to the variety of participants."
Closest to this one was the "Research paper" (6.0) and
"Times with your directees" (5.9). The lowest rating was for
the "Seminar" (4.5), closely followed by the "Readings" (4.6)
and "Journal-Keeping" (4.6). Every dimension of the program demonstrated sufficient value both to staff and participants to warrant retaining them all in the future, with
modifications that I have indicated.

Conclusion

On balance, the first year's experience points to a viable
and valuable program that fills a gap in available educational
offerings.
    Its distinctiveness relative to other programs includes
the particular and broad mix of staff and participants; the
balancing of apophatic and kataphatic approaches; the primary qualification for participation: someone whose sense of
calling is verified by the spontaneous coming of others to
them for help; and the particular constellation of dimensions
offered.
    Its greatest overlap with other programs includes its
concern for historical, theological, and psychological dimensions of understanding, and concern for supervision of participant direction work with others.
    In the future I think there will be great value in the pe-
riodic meeting together of those responsible for such programs, so that our emerging learnings can be exchanged, and
we can be mutually correcting and enriching.
    Though such programs can draw some people on a na-
tional and full-time basis, if they are to attract persons who
are settled into jobs and families where it is not feasible to
leave the area or take on anything full time, there will need
to be more "regional," part-time programs available. Our experience I think shows that the intent and quality of such a
program can be maintained without its having to be full
time. This is especially true if it is stretched over several
years, and if participants are encouraged to maintain a sense

of the ongoing process of their learning and unfolding so that they continue in colleague groups on a long-term basis.

Such regional centers would also have the advantage of being able to stimulate local concern for identifying, cultivating, and utilizing direction gifts in church settings. They also would allow participants to continue direction work with those already seeing them, rather than having to find new people with whom to work in a new setting, from whom they would be cut off at the end of the program.

The difficulty, of course, is to find adequate staff and re sources to establish such centers. As more persons become prepared and experienced through existing programs (or through other relevant experience), and as more people become aware of the long-term value to Church and society that spiritual direction can provide, I think such difficulties can be overcome.

It is a time of experimentation and reawakening in the classic art and ministry of spiritual direction. My hope is that the Shalem program, and the other materials in this book, will serve in some small way to provide a sense of the promise and possibilities of this ministry. There is much more to be said about it historically, theoretically, and practically than I have offered here. I look forward to an evolving and deepening dialogue and literature in the years ahead.

As I have reiterated again and again, spiritual direction or any other discipline cannot guarantee spiritual sight However, I believe it can provide an important environment for slowly letting the scales fall from our eyes, to the extent grace is given. As this happens, we hopefully will be less prone to miss, distort or be so frightened by the wondrous ways of the Holy One in our midst.

And Yeats's ever-lurking apocalyptic monster will shrink, God willing, a little further from our shores.

Notes

Introduction

1. Though increasingly many therapists have moved to its fringes, as in existential and transpersonal psychologies.

2. Cf. Gerald May, *Pilgrimage Home* (New York: Paulist Press, 1979), which summarizes Shalem's work and learnings thus far.

3. Under the auspices of the Association of Theological Schools in the U.S. and Canada, based at the Washington Theological Union, with the assistance of a grant from the Rockefeller Brothers Fund (cf. Chapter Eight).

4. "Ego" has many different uses in philosophy, psychology, psychoanalysis, and colloquially. My use of it in this book has this connotation:

Ego is a self-construct that provides functional secondary control of the mind. It is an extra layer of willfulness, centered on a constructed self-image that seeks to protect a particular sense of territory, by manipulating whatever is not included in this self-image territory.

In authentic contemplation, this constructed self-image territory dissolves, allowing a more spontaneous, natural will to live. Theologically, one might say that when this will is at its height, then it is God discerning and willing through us.

Such ego comes between us and our firsthand awareness in God. At the same time, such ego informs us of God and of our existence, but only through a process, a sense, of separation from them. Thus such ego is valuable, but only of relative value to firsthand awareness. When such ego is too heavy, too reified, then it is mistaken for that awareness and for our very existence, and we fear its suspension.

I am indebted to Dr. Gerald May, a psychiatrist and Shalem colleague, for this understanding.

5. "*Knowledge* (apprehension, experience) is wider and deeper than *science* (comprehension, reflection). We get to know realities in proportion as we become *worthy* to know them, i.e., less self-centered." This insight of the great nineteenth-twentieth century lay Roman Catholic spiritual di-

233

rector, Friedrich Von Hügel, is complemented by his wide definition of spirituality: "The deepest experience of the deepest fact." There are non-spiritual facts and experiences, too, he says, which are necessary to our health, balance, and religion (physical, sexual, artistic, social, etc.), yet spirituality concerns them all—in a *total* person's stance before, and as partner of, the *total* real, finite and infinite, secular and sacred, historical and eternal. The spiritual life is a dynamic process, full of dualisms (not dichotomies) in arduous process of resolution.

Several other definitions of spirituality: "The process of becoming a human being in the fullest sense" (John Macquarrie, *Paths in Spirituality* (New York: Harper and Row, 1972); "The lived unity of human existence in faith" (Thomas H. Gannon and George W. Traub, *The Desert and the City* (New York: Macmillan, 1969).

More comprehensively, we can distinguish "spirituality" and "Christian spirituality" as follows:

Spirituality refers to our probing and responses to that basic mysterious human yearning for the infinite. It is that underlying dimension of consciousness that openly waits and searches for a transcendent fulfillment of our human nature.

Christian spirituality involves such probing and response in the context of historical and contemporary Christian experience, faith, and community. It can take many forms, but it always takes seriously an intrinsic love of God for Creation (especially humans), and a wounded yet partially free human nature that is called and empowered toward conversion, i.e., toward ever deeper sight and life in the image of God. This ongoing conversion involves such fruits as compassion, humility, healing, spontaneous creativity, just reconciliation, peace, and joy.

6. Sometimes "*k*ataphatic" is transliterated as *c*ataphatic from the Greek.

7. Cited in Thomas O'Meara, "Meister Eckhart's Destiny," *Spirituality Today*, Vol. 30, No. 4 (December 1978).

8. A good argument for their complementarity in more formally philosophical terms is found in John D. Jones's "The Character of the Negative Theology for Pseudo-Dionysius Areopagite," *Proceedings of the American Catholic Philosophical Association*, Vol. 51 (Washington, D.C.: Catholic University of America, 1977).

9. I know there are particular exceptions to this, and that most theologians are very sincere, faithful people struggling in the still anti-intellectual climate of our culture. Their work is important. I just want to point out the loss of an *integrally* cultivated intuitive, affective, analytical consciousness in their normal preparation.

10. From her spiritual autobiography, *Waiting for God* (New York: Harper and Row, 1973).

11. Quoted by Richard Drummond in "Experience of God Outside Judaeo-Christian Context," *Spirituality Today*, Vol. 30, No. 2.

12. The historian Guntram Bischoff provides a helpfully succinct statement of how broad the end of this "becoming" has been seen:

Man is in process of becoming. The only thing certain is that man at present is not what he ought to be, could be, and, one hopes will be. This is a religious statement, a "mythical" sentence (i.e., symbolic representation of the sacred, the really Real). True man is identical with the "sacred." The goal is union, assimilation to and identification with God, apotheosis. Man may be truly and fully man only in the One (Plotinus), in Christ (Paul), in the darkness of Light (Eckhart), in the coincidence of opposites (Nicholas of Cusa), in the absolute spirit (Hegel), in his archetypal self (Jung), in the identity of his true humanity (Marx), in the depth of his species-consciousness (Feuerbach), in the vision of "the new man" (Castro), or in the *raptus* of La Verna. All of these have differences in symbols, but not in structure of the Myth.

"Dionysius the Pseudo-Areopagite: The Gnostic Myth," *The Spirituality of Western Christendom* (Kalamazoo Mich.: Cistercian Publications, 1976).

13. In pre-Communist Tibetan culture it was customary to ask a visitor not *where* he was from, but from what "deep tradition" he came. The profound assumption behind this is that a tested lineage of experience and interpretation concerning our purpose and liberating way through life is what shapes our inmost being and offering to others. Though we live in an experiential time of transitional and "broken open" inheritance, the value of mutating a particular tradition into the future, enriched and chastened by other deep traditions, current knowledge, and historical situation, is greater than abandoning all traditions and attempting to build from scratch on a *tabula rasa*, or drawing from all traditions as an outsider, without depth in any.

Perhaps most of us inevitably are a little more "outsiders" to any exclusive tradition today, given our vastly greater awareness of other possibilities than were known in the past, and the individualism of our time. Yet, however tenuous our ground, we can stand but one place at a time. That is only human. Moving from particular depth to mature universality seems the human way. Trying to shortcut this by starting out everywhere is likely to lead to shallow watering holes that dry up, never going deep enough in sweat and commitment to find the deep ground whose hidden depths nourish all.

1. *The Spiritual Sea in Which We Swim Today*

1. From "The Second Coming," *The Collected Poems of W. B. Yeats* (New York: Macmillan, 1974), p. 184.

2. Other religious bases than Judaeo-Christian, of course, are increasingly visible and actively available to Western people today: Moslem, Buddhist, Hindu, shamanistic, and various syncretistic groups. In Chapter Six I will refer to the value of incorporating certain disciplines developed in some of these traditions for spiritual guidance in Christian settings.

3. E. Rozanne Elder puts this more inclusively: "After the 12th century, there was a break in the integrity of man's response to God, becoming affect *vs.* rationality, love *vs.* reason, action *vs.* thought, being *vs.* do-

ing." "William of St. Thierry: Rational and Affective Spirituality," *The Spirituality of Western Christendom.*

Dom François Vandenbrouke speaks of the chasm opening at the beginning of the fourteenth century: "The *theologian* became a specialist in an autonomous field of knowledge, which he could enter by use of a technique independent of the witness of his own life—of its personal holiness or sinfulness. The *spiritual* man, on the other hand, became a "dévot" who cared nothing for theology, whose experience became an end in itself, without reference to any dogmatic content to be sought in it." "Laity and Clergy in the Thirteenth Century," in Louis Bouyer, ed., *A History of Christian Spirituality* (New York: Desclee, 1970), Vol. II, Pt. 2.

4. Cf. *Ibid.*

5. Cf. Introduction where these two ways are first explained.

6. Cf. Chapter Six for a few particular uses. Examples of adaptation can be seen through such books as Herbert Slade, *Exploration into Contemplative Prayer* (New York: Paulist Press, 1975), and Enomiya Lasalle, *Zen Meditation for Christians* (Lasalle, Ill.: Open Court, 1974).

7. Cf. Paul Tillich's *Systematic Theology* (Chicago: University of Chicago Press, 1951), Vol. I, pp. 97f., for a helpful elaboration of ecstatic knowledge beyond (but including) reason, and controlling technical reason.

8. The older these groupings, the more likely the brittle edges will soften and lead to greater inclusiveness. No group can be completely static (for long) without great coercion to enforce its position.

9. The theologian Urban Holmes speaks of current religious polarization and reconciliation in different language, but which I believe moves in the same direction. He speaks of the contemporary mind tending to be either rational and cynical, or irrational and sentimental, each usually being a reaction to the other. His solution lies in what he calls the "sensible" mind (borrowing from T. S. Eliot), i.e., the ability to be deeply aware; to devour the whole experience, with all its contradictions, and to make a new whole meaning without leaving anything out, without sentimentalizing chaos or maintaining control through cynicism. Eliot laments the "disassociation from sensibility" in Western, particularly English, literature since the seventeenth-century metaphysical poets. Cf. *The Priest in Community* (New York: Seabury Press, 1978), pp. 70ff.

10. Many persons belong to or overlap with this school in the past and present who never have heard of the word "apophatic." The boundary between apophatic and kataphatic approaches is fluid, as I have tried to make clear. Nonetheless, I think the term "apophatic" does provide a helpful umbrella for covering certain neglected emphases in Christian spirituality.

It should be noted here that a primarily kataphatic way also is capable of encompassing intellect, affect, intuition, and volition. But I think it often is more difficult to do so on that path, since the more formless intuitive "ground" more easily is missed, leaving the other dimensions more readily overcategorized, isolated, and reified, subtly losing their intimate connectedness and relativity to the Mystery.

11. "Tradition" increasingly touches more than Christian experience for many contemporary people in predominantly apophatic tradition. The

special place in that tradition of preconceptual intuition frees it to relate sympathetically to the preconceptual awareness found in other traditions of human experience with the Holy.

12. The great seventeenth-century French spiritual director Francis de Sales puts this imaginatively when he says, "Many people would keep the pleasure of loving rather than love, if they could; the honey without the bread." *The Love of God* (Westminster, Md.: Newman, 1962), p. 382.

13. The early Church Father, Diadochus of Photiké, optimistically pointed out the grace inherent in the relation and difference of theologian and contemplative.

> . . . the theologian tastes something of the experience of the contemplative, provided he is humble; and the contemplative will little by little know something of the power of speculation, if he keeps the discerning part of his soul free from error. But the two gifts are rarely found to the same degree in the same person, so that each may wonder at the other's abundance, and thus humility may increase in each.

Quoted by Alan Jones, citing Andrew Louth, *Theology and Spirituality* (Fairacres, 1978), p. 14.

14. This approach I believe reinforces a philosophical-theological position of symbolic realism: religion symbolizes unities in which we participate beyond both the "subjective" and "objective," which we know, as Michael Polanyi puts it, "not by observing but by dwelling in them." Polanyi points out that we have forgotten that such "implicit" knowing is fundamental, since all "explicit" knowledge depends on its unconscious assumptions (cf. *Personal Knowledge* (New York: Harper and Row, 1965).

Robert Bellah believes that if the theologian comes to his subject with the assumptions of symbolic reason, as many seem to be doing,

> Then we are in a situation where for the first time in centuries theologian and secular intellectual can speak the same language. Their tasks are different but their conceptual framework is shared. What this can mean for the reintegration of our fragmented culture is almost beyond calculation.

Beyond Belief (New York: Harper and Row, 1970).

15. Cf., for example, Evelyn Underhill's classic work on *Mysticism*, where, despite its brilliant coverage of this neglected third way, there is virtually no mention of the value of historical process, and an implicit related acceptance of Platonic categories.

16. Margaret Furse has written a very helpful article showing the possible reconciliation between such Neo-Orthodox theologians and classic and contemporary apophatic mystics: "Mysticism: Classic Modern Interpreters and Their Premise of Continuity," *Anglican Theological Review* (April 1978).

17. Hegel and his various successors, including Karl Marx, elaborated this as a dialectical process, ideational, historical, or otherwise. The apophatic tradition would give weight to an intuited always-present dynamic unity of Source for both ends, even as they unfold on the surface in different configurations.

18. This is the central insight of the great fifteenth-century German Cardinal, Nicholas of Cusa, an heir to the Rhineland mystics, and an irenic island in a sea of philosophers/theologians of his time still leaning on Aristotelian denial of such coincidence. His thought has fresh relevance for our day.

19. The sociologist Robert Bellah insightfully remarks on the American Founding Fathers' view that the Republic could not endure without such a transcendent bond. He elaborates the importance of biblical covenant in American history, and its importance in more open form today as an antidote for the growing destructive edges of atomistic individualism. Cf. "The Normative Framework for Pluralism in America," *Soundings*, Vol. 61, No. 3 (Fall 1978).

20. This tendency in part is related to the very individualism just discussed: a reaction to its potential societal chaos by coercive social ordering. Cf. *ibid.*

21. "Spirituality for Protestants," *Christian Century* (Aug. 2, 1978).

22. *Ibid.*

23. In Chapter Three I will imply another social value of the apophatic way: its assistance with a rhythm of contemplation and action.

24. Harvey Egan, S.J., provides an illuminating comparison of the *Cloud of Unknowing* and Ignatius's *Spiritual Exercises* in terms of their mutual affirmation of both apophatic and kataphatic paths. The kataphatic is the necessary door to the apophatic in the *Cloud;* also, the contemplative is meant to become an "icon of Love," a kataphatic moment. For Ignatius, the kataphatic also is meant to lead to the apophatic, though without an explicit call to "forgetting" and "unknowing."

Egan also helpfully spells out the potential aberrations of both paths. He sees both, at their best, as authentic ways in the mystical journey, chosen on the basis of temperament, situations, and calling. "Christian Apophatic and Kataphatic Mysticisms," *Theological Studies* (Fall 1978), pp. 399ff.

25. Perhaps the height of sustained, subtle dealing with such interior development over time is found in the works of John of the Cross and Teresa of Avila. Part II of Evelyn Underhill's *Mysticism* provides a synopsis of the way great Western mystics approached this development, categorized by the classical stages of awakening, purgation, illumination, and union. A. Poulain's *The Graces of Interior Prayer* (1910) is another and more practical attempt to bring to bear the developmental experience of great Christian mystics for our use, though his overconfident, overcategorized, and premodern psychological language is somewhat out of place today.

26. St. Joseph's Abbey, Spencer, Massachusetts.

27. "Wholesomeness: Approaches to Diagnostic Assessment," in Tarthang Tulku, ed., *Reflections of Mind* (Emeryville, Calif.: Dharma, 1975).

28. An unpublished comment of Dr. Terrence Tice, University of Michigan.

29. Unfortunately, many such holistic psychologists, while yearning for this religio-communal wholeness, still find themselves operationally individualistic. They seem unable to be part of a "whole" committed communal way of life, and are unable to model or offer those who come to them for help such a whole way. Many factors enter into this difficulty, ranging from the individualistic conditioning focus of psychology itself and of our culture, to the perceived inadequacy or demandingness of the religio-communal ways that present themselves.

30. Not only a greener pasture geographically somewhere else, but also in time. There is a widespread search for and indiscriminate romanticism about the archaic and esoteric today, beneath which I believe is a subconscious searching for the intuitive human discoveries of history that are sensed to be suppressed in the analytically dominant West of recent centuries, with which many identify the Western Church as well. I'm thinking of such subjects as astrology, alchemy, esoteric religious strands of practice, and psychic phenomena.

31. Perhaps this is one basis for Don Browning's comment that "specialized pastoral counseling and psychotherapy in the U.S., in spite of honest efforts to the contrary, is gradually losing contact with the moral and spiritual context of the larger church." Quoted in Kenneth Leech's *Soul Friend* (London: Sheldon, 1977), p. 101. Elsewhere Browning remarks on another contributing factor: the wedding of Neo-Reformation theology and clinical pastoral education, whereby *religious* methods are given negative connotations, yet *CPE* methods are given *positive* ones, as ways of serving a realization of grace, forgiveness, acceptance, liberating justification, maturity. "Method in Religious Living and Clinical Education," *Journal of Pastoral Care*, Vol. 29 (1975).

32. Don Browning, *ibid.*, notes that for the last forty years theologians have wrongly assumed people would know what to do once grace and forgiveness are experienced. They have neglected method to protect the sovereignty and initiative of God.

33. *Ascetical*, from the Greek *askein*, referring to learning a skill (especially athletics) by exercise, was picked up by the early Church to refer to what humans can do in their search and preparation for realizing the holy, with particular foundation in the writings of St. Paul (I Cor. 9:24–27, Phil. 3:13–14, II Tim. 4:7, Acts 24:16, also cf. Mt. 5:45, 6:33, Mk. 8:34). Von Hügel describes asceticism as "the energetic, largely indirect attack on whatever prevents our encounter with the real from occurring, in its full drama of otherness, interiority, actuality, and promise." Joseph P. Whelan, *The Spirituality of Friedrich Von Hügel* (New York: Newman, 1971), p. 209.

Mystical most simply refers to an awareness/experience of unity or communion with the Holy, and its fruits of deeper wisdom and compassion. Cf., for example, Joseph de Guibert, *The Theology of the Spiritual Life* (New York: Sheed and Ward, 1953), pp. 5ff., for elaboration. For different uses of "mystical" by the early Church Fathers, cf. Louis Bouyer, ed., *History of Christian Spirituality* (New York: Desclee, 1960), Vol. I, p. 405.

34. Unless one turns to Eastern religious models.

35. Cf. William A. Clebsch and Charles R. Jaekle, *Pastoral Care in Historical Perspective* (New York: Aronson, 1964), pp. 68ff.

2. *Living Waters of the Past*

1. G. K. Chesterton, quoted by Gervais Dumeige in "History of Spirituality—A Key to Self-Understanding," *Chicago Studies*, Vol. 15, No. 1.

2. See Chapter Nine of Gerald May's *Pilgrimage Home* for a summary of these interviews.

3. Cf. John T. McNeill's *A History of the Cure of Souls* (New York: Harper and Row, 1951) for elaboration of Jewish, Greek, and Christian approaches. The later guidance given by Wisdom literature (Proverbs, Job, Ecclesiastes, etc.), focused on reverent attitudes and moral habits, should be mentioned here separately, since it does not necessarily draw back to Torah, but is a parallel stream of wisdom drawn from a large Near Eastern pool. Cf., for example, Ecclesiasticus 6:5–17 on friendship, which includes this gem: "Let your acquaintances be many, but your advisers one in a thousand."

4. Browning critiques contemporary therapeutic settings and Protestantism for losing or undervaluing this insight into a basic human/societal need. Mental health, he believes, depends on having resources and methods for making value decisions. Without these, there is value confusion, emotional conflict, and general dis-ease. *Op. cit.*

5. See Thomas Luckman's *The Invisible Religion* (New York: Macmillan, 1967), for a sociologist's view of the isolated individual as the central reality of all Western institutions today, our de facto religion of self.

6. See Louis Bouyer, *The Spirituality of the New Testament and the Fathers* (New York: Desclee, 1960), Vol. I, p. 31.

7. Varieties of story-telling are frequent modes of spiritual guidance in all deep religious traditions. Jewish and Sufi traditions are particularly rich in this medium.

8. For a helpful elucidation of Jesus's practice and teaching about prayer, cf. Joachim Jeremias, *The Prayers of Jesus* (Naperville, Ill.: Alec Allenson, 1967).

9. It is interesting to note how frequently such a preparation alone in the wilderness is found with great religious figures the world over.

10. The importance of the First Epistle of John related to *discernment* in spiritual guidance also should be mentioned here. I will return to this subject shortly.

11. I will speak to the implications of this male/female complementarity for choosing a spiritual friend in Chapter Five.

12. I am indebted to Dr. McNeill for many of his insights concerning Greek contributions. See *op. cit.*

13. See "Sin and Guilt in Classical Greek and Hellenism," in Gerhard Kittel, ed., *Bible Key Words* (New York: Harper, 1951).

14. According to McNeill (*op. cit.*, p. 35), the twelfth-century Sufi master Al-Ghazzali anticipated later Puritan practice by keeping a daily *journal* of achievements and defects to test personal progress in holiness. Mental examen was recommended in the early Church by such saints as Antony, Chrysostom, Basil, and John Climacus.

15. Aelred of Rievaulx, *On Spiritual Friendship* (Washington, D.C.: Consortium Press, 1974).

16. "Aelred in the Tradition of Monastic Friendship," *ibid.*, pp. 36ff.

17. "Marriage and the Contemplative Life, *Spiritual Life*, Vol. 24, No. 1 (Spring 1978).

18. *Ibid.*, p. 56.

19. *Ibid.*, pp. 78–79.

20. Cf. Chapter Five for criteria in looking for such an outside spiritual friend.

21. "Sex as a Sacrament East and West." (Unpublished paper.)

22. This is an oral tradition of higher practice that is not meant to be learned from books, or outside the context of a deeply committed spiritual path. Cf. John Blofield's *The Tantric Mysticism of Tibet* (New York: Dutton, 1970), pp. 226ff.

23. Cf. Thomas Merton, "Notes on Spiritual Direction," *Sponsa Regis*, Vol. 31.

24. Thanks to Athanasius's *The Life of St. Antony*, Ancient Christian Writers Series (Westminster, Md.: Newman, 1950).

25. *Ibid.*, pp. 25f.

26. Their practices probably are the closest parallel existing in Christian tradition to certain Buddhist and Hindu ascetical traditions, though the abbas were strongly centered in content on Christ and scripture.

27. Athanasius, *op. cit.*, pp. 50ff.

28. Cf. *The Praktikos* and *Chapters on Prayer* (Spencer, Mass.: Cistercian Publications, 1970).

29. Cf. Athanasius, *op. cit.*, pp. 37–68. How much Athanasius's own ideas may be interpolated here no one knows; but the thoughts are in keeping with other sayings of the abbas. For a well-selected compendium, cf. Thomas Merton's *Wisdom of the Desert* (New York: New Directions, 1960). For a more scholarly treatment, see Helen Waddell's *The Desert Fathers* (Ann Arbor, Mich.: University of Michigan Press, 1972). For the *Conferences* of John Cassian, see *The Nicene and Ante-Nicene Fathers*, second series (New York: Christian Literature Company, 1894), Vol. 11. For *The Sayings of the Fathers* cf. Budge's *The Paradise of the Fathers*, or Benedicta Ward's *Sayings . . .* (Oxford: Mowbrays, 1975).

William Walsh makes interesting parallels between the procedures of the Desert Fathers and those of reality therapy, both being focused on intense personal commitment, rejection of irresponsible (immoral) behavior, and learning responsible behavior. "Reality Therapy and Spiritual Direction," *Review for Religious*, Vol. 35 (1976), pp. 372–385.

30. Merton, *op. cit.*, pp. 281, 286.

31. Merton, "The Spiritual Father in the Desert Tradition," *Contemplation in a World of Action* (New York: Doubleday, 1965), pp. 281f. The great contemporary Eastern Orthodox Archbishop Anthony Bloom,

standing as he does in the whole Eastern Church's sustained closeness to desert tradition, powerfully expresses the importance of obedience for spiritual maturity:

> Obedience begins the moment you accept what is beyond your understanding, beyond what your will is capable of accepting freely. If you *do* understand, then it is not obedience, but a way of doing your own will at the moment when it coincides with the will of another. This is not learning to be detached and listen to the will of another. If you can't obey in little things, it is impossible to obey a Gospel that is contrary to all common sense and logic. God's ways are above ours. Whatever he asks is always absurd by the standards of human wisdom.

"My Monastic Life," *Cistercian Studies*, Vol. VIII, No. 3 (1973–1974).

32. Cited by Kallistos Ware from the *Apophthegmata Patrum*, alphabetical collection, in *Cross Currents*, Vol. 24, Nos. 2–3 (Summer-Fall 1974), p. 306.

33. Merton, *Contemplation in a World of Action*, p. 286.

34. This attempted blending of roles always has had its difficulties, and in more recent times they often have been separated into different people. Perhaps one learning from this historical tension is the value of maintaining spiritual directors in fringe, horizontal positions with those they see lest, as in our discussion of marriage earlier, the complexity of relationship (especially if it involves legal power) eclipses the simple presence to one another crucial for spiritual friendship.

This was part of the value of the thirteenth-century mendicant orders, the Franciscans and Dominicans, both of whose members (especially the latter) functioned frequently as spiritual directors of others from their "outside" positions.

35. See Catherine de Hueck Doherty, *Poustinia* (Notre Dame, Ind.: Ave Maria Press, 1975). The community she has founded, centered at Madonna House in Canada, blends Orthodox and Roman Catholic traditions of spiritual community, including the *poustinia*, with special power.

36. Cf. *Discernment of Spirits*, trans. by Innocentia Richards from the *Dictionnaire de Spiritualité: Ascetique et Mystique*, Vol. III (Collegeville, Minn.: Liturgical Press, 1970).

37. Cf. *Ibid.*, pp. 42ff., for a helpful interpretation of such scriptural bases.

38. Louis Puhl, *The Spiritual Exercises of Ignatius Loyola* (Chicago: Loyola University Press, 1951), pp. 175–187. Also cf. *Discernment of Spirits*, pp. 84ff.

39. For example virtually every issue of the monthly *Review for Religious* for many years has contained an article on some aspect of spiritual direction, usually by an Ignatian-influenced writer. A major "modern" application and extension of the method is found in John English's *Choosing Life* (New York: Paulist Press, 1978). Also cf. the St. Louis periodical, *Studies in the Spirituality of the Jesuits*.

40. Compare, for example, Ignatius or any of his interpreters with any article by Anthony Bloom (one reference has already been cited) or by

Kallistos Ware (e.g., "The Spiritual Father in Orthodox Christianity," in *Cross Currents,* Vol. 24, Nos. 2–3 (Summer-Fall 1974).

41. Cf., for example, the journals and writings of George Fox, John Woolman, Rufus Jones, and Douglas Steere.

42. Cf. Bouyer, *The Spirituality of the New Testament and the Fathers* (New York: Desclee, 1960), pp. 307f.

43. Cf. *ibid.,* for a description of some of the formative community Rules, especially those of Basil and Benedict. Volumes II and III describe later developments.

44. In an exchange of Thomas Merton with the Dalai Lama shortly before his death, Merton was interested in the Dalai Lama's questions concerning the progress of monks after vows. In effect, he seemed to be asking, do you Western monks just vow to "hang around" or to attain progress? See Merton's *Asian Journal* (New York: New Directions, 1973), p. 124.

45. Merton comments that the Marxist goal of "From each according to his capacity, to each according to his needs," is in fact a definition of monastic community and, he believes, the only place in which it can be realized (*Asian Journal,* p. 334).

46. Something of this regularized intent also is found in the early left wing of the Reformation and in the eighteenth-century Methodist small-group meetings for mutual edification and correction (and their various Protestant successors). Ways of approaching a *group* context for direction will be taken up in Chapter Seven.

47. In Chapter Seven I will elaborate more fully the differences between therapy and spiritual direction.

48. Quoted by P. A. Sorokin in *The Ways and the Power of Love* (Boston: Beacon Press, 1954) in the chapter "Monastic Psychoanalysis, Counseling, and Therapy."

49. Descriptions of great masters' experience and advice in these stages is lucidly compiled by Evelyn Underhill in Part II of her *Mysticism.* Also cf. Kenneth Leech, *Soul Friend,* pp. 157f. One value of these views of progress today lies in their aid to people's resistance to becoming unduly enamored with or depressed by particular interior experiences along the way, such as voices, visions, and dry periods. Another value is their positive help to people in understanding what is happening to them, and how to respond.

However, these stages develop and spiral uniquely in each person, and the intuition and experience of the guide is primary. This raises up the importance of a careful oral tradition, which we largely have lost, and need again to try and establish. The program described in Chapter Eight is a very humble beginning, along with other beginnings underway today.

50. Merton says in this regard that, "The director, if not essential for the spiritual life, is considered in practice to have had a decisive part to play in the lives of saints and mystics, with a few notable exceptions. [Great directors] have clearly exercised a providential function in the lives not only of individuals but also of religious congregations and of certain social milieux, indeed of the Church itself." *Contemplation in a World of Action,* p. 269.

51. John's "Ladder of Paradise" is regarded by the sociologist P. A. Sorokin as being "at least as effective and scientific as any therapeutic and educational system of our times." Sorokin develops a careful case for the enduring value of monastic practices in "The Monastic System of Techniques" and "Monastic Psychoanalysis, Counseling, and Therapy," excerpted by Abbey Press (1973) from his *The Ways and Power of Love*.

52. Reference to the particular contributions and writings of these spiritual guides can be found in Bouyer. The title "spiritual director" does not seem to have been employed until the sixteenth century.

3. The Eternal Rhythm

1. *Shabbos* is Yiddish, *shabbat* is Hebrew for the English transliteration Sabbath.

2. Both of these rabbis are university teachers and not responsible for synagogues, thus their absence from leadership in synagogue services that evening.

3. Cf. Amos 8:4–6; Hosea 2:4; Isa. 1:13, 56:2–8, 58:13f.; Jer. 17: 21–27; Ezek. 20:12–20. For further commentary and references, cf. "Sabbath" in Alan Richardson, ed., *A Theological Word Book of the Bible* (New York: Macmillan, 1959).

4. Cf. Ex. 16:22–30, 31:13–17, 35:3; Lev. 23:2f.; Num. 28:9f.

5. Cf. Mk. 1:21, 29; 2:23; 3:6; Mt. 12:11; Lk. 14:5, 13:10–16; Jn. 5:1–18; 9:10–16; and Col. 2:16 (where Paul infers a Sabbath freedom similar to that of Jesus for Christians). Cf. also Richardson, *ibid.*, for further commentary.

6. Cf. Acts 20:7. Also cf. "Sabbath," in F. L. Cross, ed., *Oxford Dictionary of the Christian Church* (London: Oxford, 1958).

7. Cf. "Sabbatarianism," *ibid.* In seventeenth-century Scotland, even books and music not strictly religious were disallowed.

8. *Turning East: The Promise and Peril of the New Orientalism.* (New York: Simon and Schuster, 1977), Ch. 5.

9. *The Sabbath: Its Meaning for Modern Man* (New York: Noonday Press, 1951).

10. *Ibid.*, p. 13.

11. *Ibid.*, p. 10.

12. *Ibid.*, pp. 14, 32, 73.

13. *Ibid.*

14. *Ibid.*

15. *Ibid.*, p. 27.

16. *Ibid.*, p. 59.

17. *Ibid.*, pp. 87, 91.

18. *Ibid.*, p. 89.

19. Cf. Victor Turner, *The Ritual Process* (Chicago: Aldine, 1969), pp. 129f.

20. An interesting and desperate historical Christian use of the quality of Sabbath time is seen in the Middle Ages when, during times of constant warfare, bishops sought to install periods of "The Peace of God," especially during liturgical high seasons such as Lent, when no fighting could take place.

21. An Institute of applied organizational research and consultation, working with many kinds of organizations including churches.

22. Reed recently authored a book summarizing his thesis and experience: *The Dynamics of Religion* (London: Darton, Longman and Todd, 1978). A less developed but shorter work is his "The Task of the Church and the Role of its Members" (June 1975), available from the Alban Institute, Mount St. Alban, Washington, D.C., 20016.

23. *Ibid.*, p. 22.

24. *Ibid.*, p. 15.

25. Reed quotes a number of recent psychotherapists' positive senses of regression, including Winnicott, Kris, Hartmann, Bion, Balient, and Kahn (cf. *ibid.*, pp. 22, 36).

26. *Ibid.*, p. 23.

27. *Ibid.*, p. 52.

28. *Ibid.*, pp. 54–57.

29. *Ibid.*, pp. 74–100. Also cf. Henry Selvey, "The Spiritual Experience: Speculations On Its Nature and Dynamics," *Journal of Pastoral Care*, Vol. 31–2 (1977), for further insights into the regressive process. In terms of worship, Paul Philibert gives other insights related to ways of understanding and helping to cultivate a more "bicameral" (intuitive and unpredictable as well as rational) mind in worship. "The Mental Ecology of Worship and Spirituality," *Spirituality Today*, Vol. 30, No. 4 (Dec. 1978).

30. *Ibid.*, p. 148.

31. *Ibid.*, pp. 149, 182–183.

32. *Ibid.*, p. 215.

33. In fact, Reed believes that with its limited energies, the Church needs to concentrate on its primary task stated earlier as its real, unique service to the society, and not dissipate its energies trying to do everything. "In the world of politics and economic life the Church is smalltime and amateur; but in leading worship and coping with the crisis transitions in life the Churches possess the highest level of competence and skill. It is by their serving society in that capacity that the nation and its citizens will derive the greatest benefit." *Ibid.*

He warns that if the Church is shunted into a siding, no other religious movement is likely to prevail in Western society to provide a coherent pattern of symbols by which societal values and culture can be shaped for the benefit of the whole. Without this, "Our national life will degenerate into a cacophony of hymns and devotions to many deities while cults and mystery religions flourish in glades, caves, and sitting rooms" (*Ibid.*, p. 220). This warning is akin to Robert Bellah's previously cited view of the importance of a shared covenanted biblical transcendence for the society's health.

34. Cf. *ibid.*, Chapters Five and Six. He compares the Christian Paschal Mystery to the authentic oscillation process: dying is regression to extradependence, or death *to* the world. Resurrection is transformation to intradependence, life *in* the world (p. 132).

35. Turner draws on his experience with the Ndembu tribe of Northwest Zambia, as well as anthropological theory, being especially inspired by Arnold van Gennep. His basic relevant text is *The Ritual Process*. He applies these views further in a two-part article published in *Worship* maga-

zine (Vol. 46, Nos. 8 and 9), entitled, "Passages, Margins, and Poverty: Religious Symbols of Communitas."

36. Cf. Turner, *The Ritual Process*, pp. 94, 127, 128, 132, 185.

37. *Ibid.*, pp. 111, 127, 176.

38. Turner, "Passages, Margins, and Poverty," *loc. cit.*, p. 492.

39. Cf. the sociologist Richard Stivers's penetrating analysis of this current pathology in revolt against technological culture. "A Festival of Sex, Violence, and Drugs: The Sacred and the Profane in our World," *Katallagete* (Winter 1979).

40. Turner, *The Ritual Process*, pp. 129, 139.

41. *Ibid.*, p. 139.

42. "Passages, Margins, and Poverty," *loc. cit.*, p. 492. It should be noted that the historical experience of the Church, just as of political societies, is full of conflict over the relation of communitas and structure. The many divisions of the Church reflect this. It is also apparent in the historical controversies over the relative values and relation of contemplation and action, the apophatic and kataphatic ways, and the eternal and historical. These tensions are a basic theme of Gannon and Traub's *The Desert and the City* (London: Macmillan, 1969).

43. *The Ritual Process*, p. 177.

44. An outstanding additional support would be the German philosopher Josef Pieper's great essay, *Leisure, the Basis of Culture*, (New York: Pantheon, 1964), where he describes the rhythm of leisure, epitomized in "divine worship" and the seventh day, with the rest of human life.

Another important source of support is Robert Bellah. He contrasts interior and exterior life, regression in worship and normal defensive ego functioning, and describes the integrating functions of "other-worldly" religious symbols. His view of their social importance is seen in such statements as these (taken from *Beyond Belief*):

"The price of neglect of the interior life (implicit knowledge) . . . is the reification of the superficial, an entrapment in the world of existing objects and structures" (p. 253). "Worship involves a partial regression from normal defensive ego functioning so that there is a greater openness to both inner and outer reality" (p. 211).

He quotes the Protestant theologian Herbert Richardson sympathetically: "Transhistorical symbolism always retains the "vagueness" and conceptual openness that prevent man from expecting any absolute fulfillment in time. Only transcendent religious symbolism can undergird an infinite development of society at a controlled pace. Only "other-worldly religious symbolism can preserve the system from falling into an intra-historical stasis." *Toward an American Theology* (New York: Harper and Row, 1967).

Bellah believes these religious symbols are relational, overcoming the dichotomies of ordinary conceptualization (e.g., objective and subjective, cosmological and psychological) and bringing together the coherence of the whole of experience (*op. cit.*, p. 202). This speaks, I believe, to the importance of maintaining religious symbolic language in spiritual guidance, and not substituting psychological or political language as though such substitution could be made without net loss.

Mircea Eliade provides still further support. Cf. *Sacred and the Profane*

(New York: Harper and Row, 1961). Also cf. Gabriel Marcel's *Being and Having* (Westminster: Dacre Press, 1949).

45. With some people "up-front" problems may be so dominating that they must deal with them directly for awhile before they are able to move on into more extradependent spiritual guidance.

46. *Op. cit.*, p. 183.

47. Where there is openness, time, and skill, certain arts also can be utilized in a session to encourage positive childlikeness: e.g., focus on an ikon or other painting, and listening to music. I will return to this subject in Chapter Six.

48. Reed has a strong sense of this different quality of task and relationship from that of therapist in what he calls a "pastoral" relationship. Cf. *op. cit.*, pp. 182–183.

49. Cited (without source, but probably from *Conjectures of a Guilty Bystander*) by John Crocker in "Switching Mentalities: From Campus to Parish," *Fellowship* (Jan.–Feb. 1979).

50. Quoted in a lecture by the Rev. George Maloney at St. Anselm's Abbey, Winter 1979, Washington, D.C.

Much later, in the fourteenth century, John Ruysbroeck poignantly describes this nature and rhythm of reality: "God is absolute repose and fecundity reconciled.... The Spirit of God breathes us out that we may love, and do good works; and draws us into Himself, that we may rest in fruition, and this is Eternal Life.... Action and fruition never hinder, but strengthen one another.... They are the double wings ... that take us Home." From *Gradibus Amoris*, quoted in Evelyn Underhill, *Mysticism*, pp. 434–437.

4. *The Many Colored Coat of Spiritual Guidance*

1. For a very lucid, succinct, and irenic description of historic Protestant and Roman Catholic approaches to spiritual guidance up to the Second Vatican Council, cf. "Common Frontiers in Catholic and Non-Catholic Spirituality," *Worship* by Douglas Steere (Dec. 1965).

2. Cf. Galatians 5:22–23: "The fruit of the Spirit is love, joy, peace, patience, kindness, goodness, trustfulness, gentleness, self-control."

3. For a helpful discussion of the rite of reconciliation today in relation to spiritual direction, cf. the Appendix on this subject in Kenneth Leech, *op. cit.*, pp. 194–225. The history of this rite as spiritual guidance is a basic theme of John T. McNeill's *History of the Cure of Souls*.

4. For a helpful guide to spiritual reading, cf. Susan Muto, *A Practical Guide to Spiritual Reading* (Denville, N.J.: Dimension Books, 1976).

5. William Connolly sees the *similarities* of direction and counseling as their use of the same initial questions, and their looking to gradual change in attitudes, eschewing authority, striving for free decisions, and mutual trust. The *differences* he sees as the experience of contemplation in direction, and a focus on receptivity and response to the Lord of Reality, vs. the focus on insight, healing, and new directions in counseling. "Contemporary Spiritual Direction," *Studies in the Spirituality of Jesuits*, Vol. 8,

No. 3 (June 1975). Personally, these seem to me to merge potentially at the point where there is listening to one's "deepest" self.

Gerald May, the psychiatrist member of the Shalem staff, has been evolving a sense of the integration of counseling and spiritual direction at the point of simple openness together before the Mystery, allowing direction *and* therapy to "happen" through humble attentiveness, rather than through trying to *make* something happen. Cf. his *Simply Sane* and *Open Way* (both Paulist Press). He does, however, see operational differences between them, as I will describe in Chapter Six.

6. *Pastoral Care in Historical Perspective*, p. 66. This situation is fed by Protestant weight on individual responsibility and the sole mediation of Christ, reinforced with Evangelicals by focus on redemption (initial conversion) to the neglect of "stages of further yielding and communion." (Cf. Steere, *op. cit.*)

5. Seeking a Spiritual Friend

1. Perhaps such an attitude is responsible in part for the fundamentalist reaction, wherein people swing vehemently the other way and cannot seem to *stop* talking about their relation to God. It is as though a long pent-up dam had burst, and they need a very long time before getting their fill of "pouring forth."

2. Bernard of Clairvaux bluntly responds to such questioning with this: "He who sets himself up as his own teacher becomes the pupil of a fool." Quoted by Joseph de Guibert, *The Theology of the Spiritual Life*, p. 155.

John of the Ladder asked, "Is it possible to think a man leads a Divine Life, in accordance with the Will of God, if he lives without a guide, pandering to himself and obeying his own will?" Quoted by Merton in "The Spiritual Father in the Desert Tradition," p. 287.

3. The Jesuits Hugh Kay and James Walsh speak of the importance of this readiness in a bit extreme but helpfully provocative terms. They describe the goal of direction as the "total transformation of human into divine will—a death to self. If you are not ready for this, then you are deceiving yourself. If you think you need spiritual direction, you really are looking for a partner in crime.... When you find yourself face to face with your own impenitence and stay with it, when your desire to be pursued by the Lord is genuine, when you feel the need for prayer so much that it becomes an ache, then what you need is spiritual direction." "A Plea for Direction." *The Way*, Vol. 2, No. 3 (July 1962).

Another Jesuit, William Connolly, puts readiness more gently: Direction is for "the adventurous sensing their journey with the Lord attracting them." He adds that your prayer, spiritual restlessness, etc., need to be approached "not as substitutes for life, but as dimensions of a fuller life." "Contemporary Spiritual Direction: Scope and Principles," *Studies in the Spirituality of Jesuits*, Vol. 7, No. 3 (June 1975).

F. W. Faber in the last century said that "You are called to choose a director whenever a real attraction to a devout life becomes manifest, i.e., more than transient caprice of fervor." *Growth in Holiness* (Baltimore: Murphy, 1855 original).

Thomas Merton speaks of finding someone who can help us accept what we already know: "Kindly support and wise advice of one we trust often enables us to *accept* more perfectly what we already know and see in an obscure way." "Spiritual Direction," *Sponsa Regis,* Vol. 30 (1958–59).

4. Cf. first footnote, Chapter Eight.

5. Cf. *Modern Man in Search of a Soul* (New York: Harcourt, Brace, 1933), p. 229.

6. Rita Anne Houlihan, a Cenacle Sister with much experience in direction, believes that *younger* people especially should not choose a peer, but someone older. "Discernment and Spiritual Direction" (publisher unknown).

7. An unpublished paper by Dr. Dolores Leckey, a Shalem Associate Staff person, was one result of this concern: "Growing in the Spirit: Notes on Spiritual Direction and Sexuality."

8. The most famous of these would include Teresa of Avila and John of the Cross, Francis de Sales and Jane Frances de Chantal, Vincent de Paul and Louise de Marillac, Francis of Assisi and Clare, Catherine of Siena and Raymond of Capua, and Catherine of Genoa and Don Marabotto. Cf. Paul M. Conner, O.P., *Celibate Love* (Huntington, Ind.: Our Sunday Visitor Press, 1979).

9. Leckey, *op. cit.*

10. I am aware that these qualities do not necessarily have anything to do with *physical* maleness and femaleness. It seems clear today that many of these characteristics are culturally conditioned. Jung himself borrowed masculine-feminine stereotypes from the culture in a time before such conditioning was culturally conscious.

11. Complementarity may also be present in the different experiences each may bring to prayer, and perhaps even different ways each experiences the Holy. Such differences may or may not be communicable and mutually enriching across sexual lines. (I am indebted to Dr. Francine Cardman of the Weston School of Theology for stimulating this insight.)

12. *C.G. Jung* (New York: Viking, 1973), cited by Leckey, *op. cit.*

13. For an elaboration of the value of these particular complementarities, cf. the commentary (based on Jungian opposites) in the *Myers-Briggs Type Indicator,* by Isabel Briggs Myers. Distributed by Consulting Psychologists Press, Inc., 577 College Avenue, Palo Alto, California 94306. The test included in this can give you a sense of your own personality type. It is not foolproof, but it does at least point to important differences among people, and the potential value of pairing with someone who can help elicit our "shadow" side.

14. Cf. *The Denial of Death* (New York: Free Press, Macmillan, 1973).

15. Michael Griffin comments that "In English-speaking countries clergy are enterprising and practical-minded; [they have] difficulty in offering spiritual direction, [since] so little seems to happen fast." "How to Profit from Spiritual Direction," *Spiritual Life,* Vol. 13 (1967).

16. *Method in Theology* (New York: Herder and Herder, 1972), pp. 115–119.

17. Speaking of such advanced directors, Teresa of Avila in the sixteenth century said, "Not one in one thousand is capable." A century later St. Francis de Sales said not one in ten thousand. Thus this is not a new problem. Quoted in Charles Hugo Doyle, *Guidance in Spiritual Direction* (Westminster, Md.: Newman, 1959).

18. Teresa of Avila says that "The Lord will give you a director if you are really humble, and *desire* to meet with the right person." Quoted in A. Poulain, *op. cit.*, p. 477.

19. Shaun McCarty has a helpful relevant section on "negotiating expectations" in his "On Entering Spiritual Direction," *Review for Religious*, Vol. 35, No. 6 (Nov. 1976). This is an excellent article for those considering spiritual direction: either as director or directee.

20. Thomas Merton adds depth to this clarification when he says, "The director has to know what we really want, for only then will he know what we really are." "Manifestation of Conscience and Spiritual Direction," *Sponsa Regis*, Vol. 30 (1959). Elsewhere Merton says, "The directee needs to bring the director into contact with our real self, as best we can, and not fear to let him see what is false in our false self. This implies a relaxed, humble attitude in which we *let go* of ourselves and renounce our unconscious efforts to maintain a façade." "Notes on Spiritual Direction," *ibid.*

21. The great Franciscan Bonaventure in the thirteenth century gave these rather austere marks of passing from a "spiritual" to a "carnal" relationship:
1. Long and useless conversations.
2. Mutual looks and mutual praise.
3. One excuses the faults of the other.
4. Exhibition of little jealousies.
5. The absence of one causes inquietude in the other.

Quoted in Pascal Parente, *Spiritual Direction*, (New York: St. Paul Publications, 1961), p. 50.

22. Catherine of Siena spoke of the director as "a visible guardian angel." Quoted in Parente, *ibid.*, p. 49.

23. As an example, Evelyn Underhill's great spiritual director, Friedrich von Hügel, helped her to the discipline of giving a day a week to work in a soup kitchen, apparently to balance her ethereal intellectual and prayer life.

24. Merton comments, "The life that is peaceful, almost commonplace in its simplicity, might perhaps be quite a different thing without these occasional friendly talks that bring tranquility and keep things going on their smooth course." *Ibid.*

6. Being A Spiritual Friend

1. I am indebted to Gerald May, a psychiatrist and colleague in Shalem's work, for this analogy in his *Simply Sane*. (New York: Paulist Press, 1977), p. 74.

2. Gerald May, *Pilgrimage Home* (New York: Paulist Press, 1979), p. 158.

3. *Ibid.*, pp. 158–159.

4. Quoted in Merton, "The Spiritual Father in the Desert Tradition," p. 286.

5. *Ibid.*, pp. 271, 286.

6. Cited in A. Saudreau, *The Degrees of the Spiritual Life* (London: Burns and Oates, 1926), Vol. II, p. 245.

7. Cited in A. Poulain, *op. cit.*, p. 477.

8. *Introduction to the Devout Life* (New York: Harper, 1950), p. 45.

9. Cited by Joseph de Guibert, *The Theology of the Spiritual Life*, pp. 100, 155.

10. "New Approaches and Needs for Spiritual Direction of Women in the Catholic Church," *Crux of Prayer* (Nov. 1977).

11. *Preparing for Spiritual Direction* (Chicago: Franciscan Herald Press, 1975), p. 98.

12. "Spiritual Direction: Training and Charism," *Sisters Today*, Vol. 48 (1976).

13. *The Dynamics of Spiritual Self-Direction* (Denville, N.J.: Dimension Books, 1976), pp. 304, 422. Van Kaam, who is both a psychologist and a priest, and founder of the oldest American center for the preparation of directors (at Duquesne), describes spiritual direction as "the discovery and unfolding of one's life direction in Christ as revealed by the Spirit," in distinction from psychological direction, which "fosters an awareness and development of ego management of one's life and helps identify its obstacles" (p. 367). As in all such distinctions, it is important, I think, not to so overcategorize as to obscure the fact that both deal with different overlays of *one* reality.

14. "Spiritual Direction," *loc. cit.*

15. Presented in the Howard Chandler Robbins Memorial lectures at Wesley Theological Seminary, Washington, D.C., March 22, 1979. The pastoral counseling definitions are influenced by William Clebsch and Charles Jaekle, *op. cit.*

16. Eugene Geromel mentions five helpful contributions (or reinforcements) of psychology to spiritual direction: a methodology that can bring what we do in focus; information on the working of a dynamic relationship; understanding of conscious and unconscious motivation; ways of monitoring our work; examination of what we do in the light of research. "Depth Psychotherapy and Spiritual Direction," *Review for Religious*, Vol. 36, No. 5 (Sept. 1977).

17. Human development in spiritual direction could be spoken of in many other images than healing. It could be portrayed as a process of inspiriting, empowering, unfolding, sanctifying, divinizing (a favorite of some early Eastern Church Fathers), enlightening, transforming, conversion, or full humanization. The analogy of physical healing, however, lends a particularly concrete and understandable structure to a description of the direction process. It also reminds us that direction reflects and participates in a larger universal process.

Finally, it is a frequent analogy to spiritual guidance in Church history. Cassian and Benedict of Nursia, e.g., focus on spiritual woundedness, and the necessity of going to your "physician," so he can expose the wound in order for it to be healed.

18. Thomas Aquinas, speaking for the incarnational theme of Christian experience, saw the body as a means of *all* the Spirit's actions. Cf. Aelred Squire, *Asking the Fathers* (New York: Morehouse-Barlow, 1973), p. 64.

19. Cf. Chapter One for a description of apophatic.

20. This Reality in Christian terms, of course, is symbolized as Triune God and Creation, which is described in an enormously rich variety of ways by those who claim its firsthand experimental knowledge, or who interpret this described awareness theologically. It is the same Reality beneath these always inadequate verbal descriptions (some of which are more adequate than others in the history of Christian doctrine).

21. This danger perhaps is greatest in those eclectic nonchurch related "spiritual" or "transpersonal" centers in the country that have no accountable connection with the moral traditions of the Church.

22. This tradition of moral-spiritual connectedness is reinforced in most non-Christian, deep religious traditions as well.

23. In the new Episcopal Book of Common Prayer, for example, there is a form of "Declaration of Forgiveness" that a lay person can use in place of Absolution (p. 452). One comprehensive book on concrete dimensions of confession is Bernard Haring, *Shalom: Peace* (New York: Farrar, Straus, and Giroux, 1967).

24. I am indebted to the Rev. George J. Rowe, S.M., for stimulating some of the basic questions in this section in lectures on "Theological Principles for Spiritual Direction" at the Washington Theological Union in spring, 1978, though most of the interpretations and elaborations are mine.

25. These examples are adaptations of some given by the Rev. Peter Damian Wilcox, O. Cap., in lectures on "The Theology of Spirituality" at the Washington Theological Union in the spring of 1978.

26. Cf. Ira Progoff, *At a Journal Workshop* (New York: Dialogue House, 1975).

27. Poulain says of such interior phenomena: "[They are] least suspicious if their end is solely the love of God and the saints; more suspicious if this end is instruction, even more so if they urge to action." He quotes John of the Cross: "No soul who does not deal with interior locutions as with an enemy can possibly escape delusions to a greater or lesser degree in many of them." Poulain recommends gently repelling them in the beginning. He does recognize their possible authenticity in origin (if not always in interpretation), citing Teresa of Avila's sense that the Lord became a "living book" by her visions. *Op. cit.*, pp. 312, 380.

28. Cf. "Voices and Visions" in Evelyn Underhill's *Mysticism* for a helpful description of great Christian masters' views of such phenomena. Also cf. A. Poulain, *op. cit.*, pp. 232ff., 380ff. on such phenomena, and pp. 7ff. on prayer. For a more positive view of the value of interior phenomena cf. the works of Morton Kelsey, e.g., *The Other Side of Silence* (New York: Paulist Press, 1976), and *Encounter with God* (Minneapolis: Bethany Fellowship, 1963). For a practical list of guidelines for interpreting possi-

ble "revelations," cf. J. S. Setzer, "When Can I Determine When It Is God Who Speaks to Me in My Inner Experience?" *Journal of Pastoral Counseling,* Vol. 12 (Fall-Winter 1977–1978), p. 42). You also might want to refer to Carl Jung's positive treatment of some religious experiences in his *Memories, Dreams, and Reflections* (New York: Vintage, 1965). For other experience, cf. William James, *Varieties of Religious Experience* (New York: Modern Library, 1936).

29. Excerpt from a lecture given at Union Seminary, Richmond, in July 1974.

30. This modern tendency, for example, I think is seen tacitly in Bruce Reed's assumptions about "intradependent" time, that normal work/coping time when we are living by our own wits, not by any special guidance, though "extradependent" (as in spiritual devotion) time can *inform* this work time (cf. Chapter Three).

31. Cf. the section on "Discernment of Spirits" in Chapter Two.

32. Cf. suggestions in the notes of that section in Chapter Two.

33. Kenneth Leech has an excellent little chapter on this subject, "Towards a Prophetic Understanding of Spiritual Direction," in *Soul Friend.* Attention to this dimension of covenant helps insure that spiritual direction will not tacitly focus on adjustment to the social order, but on the Reign of God in social structures, as well as in personal life.

34. Cf. John English, *op. cit.,* Chapter Two, for an elaborate procedure for such Ignatian-inspired reflection, including special suggestions for the way spiritual directors can aid a person in this process.

35. John of the Cross generalizes three qualities produced by the Spirit in any situation: tranquility, gentleness, and strength. Cited by Evelyn Underhill, *The Spiritual Life* (New York: Harper and Row, 1963), p. 126.

36. A Sufi tale is illuminating here:

> "I hear a burglar downstairs," the Mulla Nasrudin's wife whispered to him one night.
> "Not a sound," replied Nasrudin. "We have nothing for him to steal. With any luck, he might leave something behind."

Idries Shah, *The Sufis* (New York: Anchor, 1971), p. 94.

37. Augustine of Hippo said that "We come to God by love and not by navigation." Navigational disciplines do not replace the love but, as Douglas Steere infers, they can be means of letting ourselves be in the stream of that graceful love, encouraging ever further yielding and communion. "Common Frontiers in Catholic and Non-Catholic Spirituality," *op. cit.* (including Augustine citation).

38. For detailed approaches to journal-keeping, cf. Ira Progoff, *op. cit.;* George F. Simons, *Keeping Your Personal Journal* (New York: Paulist Press, 1978).

39. "Helping People to Pray," *New Fire,* 1 (1969), pp. 15–23, cited in Leech, *op. cit.,* p. 108, schematized for the Shalem directors program by Gerald May.

40. Ignatius Loyola once said that a "truly self-disciplined person needs only a quarter hour of prayer to be united with God." Cited in Gannon and Traub, *op. cit.,* Chapter Nine.

41. The classic "examen," as Adrian Von Kaam points out, need not

be "anxious introspection," but "transcendent self-presence." *The Dynamics of Spiritual Self Direction,* pp. 76, 246.

Examen can be done in many ways. For me, it involves pausing after the petition in the Lord's Prayer, "forgive us our sins, as we forgive those who sin against us," and reviewing my participation in life since the previous day. Where I sense anything willfully and destructively alienating in my attitudes and behavior, I lightly let these go in intent, allowing God's strength for reconciliation and compassion to melt these "hard" places.

During this review, when I sense moments of real grace that have flowed through a situation, I give thanks, so it is not only "closed off" things that are attended. I find it important to keep a steady, lightly touching mind through the whole examen, not allowing a "heavy" sense of possessive judgment to dominate. The point is to "see" what is there, gently *let go* what has accumulated that clouds our appropriate participation in gifted life, *accept* what cannot seem to be let go or understood yet, and *appreciate* those fresh breezes of the Spirit that have appeared.

For a more classic approach, cf. George Aschenbrenner, S.J., "Consciousness Examen," *Review for Religious,* Vol. 31, No. 1 (Jan. 1972).

42. Cf. comments in Chapter Four on scripture and spiritual reading. You may want to consider suggesting to the directee particular passages of scripture for meditation relevant to his or her situation.

43. Dr. Helen Bonny, a faculty member at the Catholic University and cofounder of the Institute for Consciousness and Music in Baltimore, has done extensive applied research into the opening impact on consciousness of particular kinds of music. Literature and tapes are available from the Institute.

44. Both the Jesus Prayer and Centering Prayer (as well as other forms) are described in my book, *Living Simply Through the Day* (New York: Paulist Press, 1977), pp. 91–98.

45. *Op. cit.,* p. 348.

46. "We don't really *do* anything. Prayer helps us maintain the Christ-consciousness and *that* is the power that heals. It communicates itself as love, freedom, and as everything that is needed." Thomas Hora, *Existential Meta-Psychiatry* (New York: Seabury, 1977).

47. *Op. cit.* for a more succinct discussion of stages, cf. Leech. *op. cit.,* pp. 157ff.

48. John Ruysbroeck speaks of this progress as a movement from the "faithful servant" to the "secret friend," a common metaphor with patristic and medieval writers. Cited in Underhill, *Mysticism,* p. 229. The Jesuit Raimundo Pannikar speaks of the movement from innocence to comprehension to apprehension/innocence. "The New Innocence," *Cross Currents,* Vol. 27, No. 1.

49. *Op. cit.*

50. James, (New York: The New American Library, 1958); Assagioli (New York: Viking, 1965). Also cf. Herbert Smith, *Pilgrim Contemplative* (Collegeville, Minn.: Liturgical Press, 1977).

51. Cf. Fowler's chapter in Thomas Hennessy, *Values and Moral Development* (New York: Paulist Press, 1976).

52. *Spiritual Direction* (Chicago: National Sisters Vocation Conference), p. 46. William Connolly (see next note) adds to this second list the

experience of Jesus: "Living by our conviction despite opposition, empathy beyond social/economic class, willingness to war against evil and stand for justice and mercy at personal cost, and willingness to leave the resurrection to the Father."

53. "Contemporary Spiritual Direction: Scope and Principles," *Studies in the Spirituality of Jesuits*, Vol. VII, No. 3 (June 1975).

54. "Marxism and Monastic Perspectives," Appendix VII of *The Asian Journal of Thomas Merton* (N.Y.: New Directions, 1968), p. 343.

Richard Drummond quotes the Roman Catholic theologian Consius: "All spiritual traditions are dimensions of each other and now individuals everywhere are becoming heir to the spiritual heritage of mankind." "Experience of God outside the Judaeo-Christian Context," *Spirituality Today*, Vol. 30, No. 2 (June 1978).

The Jesuit William Johnston speaks of the need for dialogue with other religions to help enlarge Christian partial knowledge of "the unsearchable riches of Christ" (Eph. 3:8). *The Inner Eye of Love*, (New York: Harper and Row, 1975).

55. This Eastern integral sense of the body's relation to spiritual development also is basic to traditional African spirituality. Cf. Mercy Amba Oduyoye, "The Value of African Religious Beliefs and Practices for Christian Theology," *African Theology Enroute* (Maryknoll, New York: Orbis Books: 1970).

56. For some particular exercises in Christian perspective, cf. my book, *Living Simply Through the Day*, and to I.M. Dechanet, O.S.B., *Yoga in Ten Lessons* (New York: Cornerstone, 1972), and *Yoga and God* (St. Meinrad, Ind.: Abbey Press, 1975).

57. *Op. cit.*, pp. 301–302. Ware refers us to a primary document of Eastern Christian spiritual direction, the *Books of Varsanuphius and John*, Containing some 850 questions addressed to two elders of sixth-century Palestine, together with their written answers.

58. Books are very secondhand sources for learning about spiritual intuitive awareness. Firsthand experience under guidance, i.e., careful oral tradition, is best. However, there are many written works that deal with such awareness in Eastern experience, though not many in practical terms. Here a few: My book, *op. cit.*, pp. 118–135. Two books by Lama Tarthang Tulku: *Gesture of Balance* and *Time, Space, and Knowledge* (both from Emeryville, Calif.: Dharma, 1977). Chogyam Trungpa, *Cutting Through Spiritual Materialism* (Berkeley, Calif.: Shambala, 1973). Gerald May, *Pilgrimage Home* (New York: Paulist Press, 1979), and *The Open Way* (New York: Paulist Press, 1977). William Johnston, *The Inner Eye of Love*, H. M. Enomiya LaSalle, *Zen Meditation for Christians* (LaSalle, Ill: Open Court, 1974).

59. These practices in substance, if not always in interpretation, were learned from lama Tarthang Tulku Rinpoché, head of the Nyingma Institute in Berkeley, California. This last practice was meant primarily for male-female pairs, but I have found it applicable to learning intuitive awareness in general.

60. This approach is far more "direct" then current Western Church direction fosters. However, the Eastern Church, again in keeping with its "desert" lineage, still appreciates it. Listen to this excerpt from a descrip-

tion of the spiritual guide by one of its most respected representatives to-day, Anthony Bloom: "I try to make rise from [your] chaos all that is divine, human, capable of entering into the harmony of the Kingdom of God." *Op. cit.*, p. 194.

61. It should be noted that relatively few in the Far East seem to be so conditioned and qualified, despite some Western romantic notions. True intuitive spiritual masters seem a thin lineage in every tradition, though some traditions clearly give more room for its cultivation.

7. *Group Direction*

1. Adrian Van Kaam, one of the most learned Roman Catholics in the area of spiritual direction in the United States, believes that such forms of group direction should be the norm in the Church, with one-to-one direction reserved largely for crisis times. "[Private] direction is less common, not available to most Christians, filled with risks and by no means necessary for every person who wants to grow in the life of grace." *The Dynamics of Spiritual Self-Direction*, p. 384.

Though I must respect his experience, I believe that spiritual friend-ships can be much more hopeful than risky and are worth much more at-tention in the Church's life. At the same time, his views do reinforce mine in this chapter concerning the value of group direction. The form I pro-pose includes more room for intertwining group leadership, sharing, and limited one-to-one sessions than those forms mentioned by Van Kaam (cf. Chapter XI, "Direction in Common," *Ibid.*).

2. Just as group therapy can be more valuable for some people, or at least an important complement to one-to-one therapy.

Eugene Geromel (*op. cit.*) discusses eight curative factors in group therapy and their relation to spiritual direction: instillation of hope, uni-versality, imparting of information, altruism, imitative behavior, interper-sonal learning, catharsis, and existential factors.

3. McCarty, Roman Catholic priest and member of the Shalem spiri-tual direction program staff, provides this list in his article, *op. cit.*, p. 864–865.

4. The cultivation of small group life, or course, is a frequent theme in the history of Churches. However, the careful cultivation of spiritual direction groups as I describe them here is much more rare.

5. Such disciplines are explained in more detail in my book, *op. cit.*, and in greater detail and context in Gerald May's *Pilgrimage Home.*

This last book focuses on Shalem's experience with different dimen-sions of intent, content, and leadership in such groups. It is the only book, to my knowledge, that provides a comprehensive theoretical and practical approach to this kind of group spiritual direction.

For an article on more *group* (as opposed to leader) guided spiritual di-rection, with a number of parallels to human relations groups, cf. Quentin Hakenwerth, S.M., "Group Methods in Spiritual Direction," *Review for Religious* (Jan. 1968).

6. Cf. *ibid.*, Chapter Nine, for further discussion of conditions for such groups.

7. I have experimented with different forms of subgroups, ranging from pairs to groups of five or six. On balance, I have found best preassigned groups of four people, mixed male/female where possible. These groups continue meeting with each other over a period of weeks or months, with a midterm evaluation where there is an option to recombine groups.

8. *Op. cit.*, pp. 101ff.

9. I extend this bonding to the whole group by asking them to share a little of their own reasons for coming to the group in plenary session. This is extended further in the subgroups where there is more extensive sharing of personal journeys and issues.

For some individuals, this sharing is very important. For others the "sanctuary space" for just being open in prayerful attentiveness is more important than the more "figuring out" sharing of the subgroups.

10. This assumption runs counter, I know, to much of the literature on group dynamics that emphasizes "participatory democracy." In intradependent, task-focused groups, such shared leadership I believe is crucial. However, in groups with an extradependent focus, my experience and that of other Shalem group leaders points to a different mode of needed leadership. This is not an "authoritarian" mode. The leader does not seek to control or authoritatively interpret the *content* of personal experience of members. Rather, he or she seeks to remain in charge of the *structure and process* of the group, providing a securing and opening framework for personal experience to be seen and appreciated more easily.

11. I also have asked if they have any particular gifts of leadership they might share with the group. It has been interesting to note that, despite much talented and experienced spiritual leadership potential among participants, exceedingly few ever mention anything in response. I interpret this to reinforce the theory that their primary need in coming to such a group is not to be in the driver's seat, as they are most of the rest of the week, but to be "cared for" by someone who allows them a different quality of being/perspective time.

12. The historic Ignatian thirty-day retreat (or shorter versions of it today) is not normally group direction. Though a number of people may be on it at the same time, each sees a spiritual director only individually.

However, there is a form of Ignatian retreat, called the "Nineteenth Annotation" Retreat (referring to this point in Ignatius's *Exercises*), that has been given through a series of guided group sessions periodically over three months while people live a normal workday at home.

13. Cf. May, *op. cit.*, p. 110, for further discussion of the value and process of coleadership, and to Chapter Five of this book for a discussion of male-female complementarity.

8. Bringing It All Together—A Program for Spiritual Directors

1. The practical fruit of one director's experience is seen in Dorothy Devers's *Faithful Friendship*, (privately printed; available from the Potter's House bookstore, Church of the Saviour, Washington, D.C.).

This is a twelve-week plan of suggested procedures to encourage

Christian growth and spiritual direction through the *mutual* direction of two people.

2. Though it is not focused exclusively on spiritual direction, this subject is seriously included in a long-term program now at the Center for Advanced Pastoral Studies in Bloomfield Hills, Michigan.

3. Cf. May, *op. cit.*, pp. 31ff., for further details of these experiments.

4. Adapted from the case method for pastors developed by James Glasse in *Putting It Together in the Parish* (Nashville: Abingdon, 1972).

5. "A Spiritual Director's Colleague Group in Washington, D.C." An as yet unpublished paper.

6. The Union is a joint seminary for six Roman Catholic religious communities. It also provides special ministry programs for laity, clergy, and religious. The Union is a member of the ecumenical Washington Theological Consortium, whose eight member schools provide open class and library arrangements for one another's students.

7. An ATS national advisory committee of theological school presidents later was formed in relation to a supplementary grant supporting one national and six regional conferences of seminary faculty focused on learnings from the program, and on issues of spiritual formation in seminaries.

8. One laywoman in a colleague group spoke to this point poignantly when she said, "We [lay directors] receive little or no support from the church community. Our confidence must come from those who come for help and from this group."

9. I have used the terms "spiritual director" and "spiritual friend" interchangeably in this study. However, in the case of the informal work of many laity, it might be worth making a little distinction. Many laity find others bringing up spiritual concerns with them as an aside during some other kind of meeting for counsel, socializing, etc. There can be more of a sense of spiritual conversation or informal advice seeking and giving in these cases than formal direction. Calling these "spiritual friendships" rather than "direction" relationships simply rings more true, whereas formal direction relationships can be called interchangeably friendship or direction with equal sense.

10. The reason for this requirement is to insure that a person is able to keep up with the material of a graduate-level program. One person in the first-year program had only two years of college; she has had no trouble in keeping up (and in fact has written one of the best research papers). We have not wanted to exclude gifted people with less formal education if at all possible.

11. The program is geared explicitly to Christian tradition. However, we didn't want to exclude those of other traditions who might want to learn approaches from Christian tradition. Nor did we want to include persons who were so defensive and narrow in their sense of being Christian that they would not be open to learning from other traditions as these might provide insight. As it turned out, all participants in the first-year program have been active Christians.

12. This normally means someone in the second half of life. However, we recognize that some people mature earlier, have much experience, and much to offer others. Though a few first-year participants were in

their early thirties, most were between thirty-five and fifty-four. The most important factor seen here in the first year's experience was the importance of the person being on enough of a confident faith plateau in life that no overwhelming personal turmoil exists to block presence with other persons.

13. This criterion has a twofold purpose: To help insure that a person has an arena to use significantly his or her developed direction gifts (including during the course of the program); to help foster awareness and support of the program and its intents by different religious structures.

"Ideally" means that it is not necessary, but helpful. A few current participants, markedly those who are full-time students, have uncertain bases for the future; most, however, have clearly defined ones.

14. Though I have tried to distinguish spiritual direction from psychological counseling in this study, I also have pointed out valuable psychological learnings about individual and group development that can sensitize a person to some of the possible dynamics at work in a situation. Based on our first year's experience, we have decided to recommend more self-consciously some basic supplementary work in this area for those without sufficient background.

15. The first year has shown this criterion to be particularly important as: 1) a way of helping to insure that a person has some sense of direction as opposed to general pastoral counseling, and as 2) a vital "apprenticeship" background. However, we have left it optional particularly for the sake of Protestant applicants, for whom such a sustained and focused relationship often is lacking in the current operational norms of their traditions.

16. A personal interview was held with applicants whenever possible.

17. One reason for this lack of black applicants may be the great many pressures on black religious leaders for concentration in other areas, combined with formal individual and group spiritual direction as I have described it not being a significant part of mainline black church Protestant tradition. Another factor, as a black friend has suggested, may be the frequently special place of the mother, aunt, grandparent, or other "elder" of the black extended family as spiritual counselor. This also may be true in the Hispanic community. However, as that family solidarity loosens in keeping with the increasing fragmentation of family life in American society, there may be increasing need for outside spiritual friendship. Yet another possible factor is our need to publicize the program more carefully in the black church community.

Black Americans in Shalem programs usually have been from Roman Catholic or Anglican traditions, where there is more of an established place for formal spiritual direction, as well as for apophatic tradition. However, these are not the traditions to which most black American Christians belong (except perhaps the majority of those of West Indian background). Shalem is planning special conferences on black American spirituality, where this area can be explored further.

18. Again, for Protestants the frequent lack of a tradition of sustained spiritual friendship relationships in effect puts many of them in a position of paving new ground in their church contexts here.

19. We had not thought the readings would be adequate for covering

content in the beginning, since the literature in spirituality and spiritual direction is inadequate in a number of areas. However, there is more than enough of value to read in the amount of time participants have available.

20. The bibliography also includes a few general references to penance, moral theology, liturgy, scripture, systematic theology, pastoral counseling, psychology of religious experience, Eastern religions, and devotional writings.

21. Cf. Appendix.

22. The complex history of this split I think involves primarily variations on the theme of its ancestral, late Medieval split symbolized by scholarly theologians on the one side, and the *Devotio Moderna* on the other (described in Chapter One). Protestant Pietism and in a different way Evangelicalism in their many forms have sought to uphold the affective/ devotional, while often university and seminary-based theologians have upheld the rational/theological. These all have had moments of overlap, but I think many more moments of division.

23. E.g., terms like spiritual direction, spiritual, ascetical, and mystical theology, discernment, charism, ecclesial, examen, prayer used in a more inclusive sense, mental and quiet prayer, etc.

24. The full bibliography contains about 300 listings.

25. Copies of papers will be publicly available in the Shalem library; some hopefully will find their way into periodicals.

26. As a symbol of our respect for the maturity of participants, we have refrained from calling them students. It is interesting to note that this is true also in the Weston and General Seminary programs, where participants are called "associates."

Bibliography

SELECTED BIBLIOGRAPHY OF REQUIRED
AND ESPECIALLY RECOMMENDED READINGS
USED IN THE SHALEM
SPIRITUAL DIRECTORS PROGRAM

I. OVERALL TEXT:
Leech, Kenneth, *Soul Friend* (London: Sheldon Press, 1977).

II. REQUIRED GENERAL READINGS:
Brockman, Norbert, "Spiritual Direction: Training and Charism,"
Sisters Today Vol. 48 (1976), pp. 104–109.
Connolly, William, S.J., "Contemporary Spiritual Direction: Scope
and Principles," *Studies in the Spirituality of Jesuits*, Vol. VII.
English, John, *Choosing Life* (New York: Paulist Press, 1978).
May, Gerald, *Pilgrimage Home* (New York: Paulist Press, 1978).
McCarty, S., "On Entering Spiritual Direction," *Review for Reli-
gious*, Vol. 35 (1976), pp. 854–867.
Steere, Douglas V., "Common Frontiers in Catholic and Non-
Catholic Spirituality," *Worship*, Vol. 39, No. 10 (Dec. 1965).

III. RECOMMENDED GENERAL READINGS (INCLUDING
SOME ASSIGNED FOR SPECIAL SEMINARS):
Aelred of Rievaulx, *On Spiritual Friendship* (Washington, D.C.: Con
sortium Press, 1974)
Barry, W., Harvey, A., and Connolly, B., *Initiating Spiritual Direction
I–III* (Cleveland, Ohio: Audio Communications). (tapes)
Barry, William and Guy, Mary, "The Practice of Supervision in
Spiritual Direction," *Review for Religious* Vol. 37, No. 6 (Nov.
1978).
——— "The Prior Experience of Spiritual Directors," *Spiritual Life*,
Vol. 23 (1977).
Bloom, Anthony, *Beginning to Pray*, (New York: Paulist Press, 1970).
Bonhoeffer, Dietrich, *Life Together* (New York: Harper, 1954).
Bouyer, Louis, *A History of Christian Spirituality*, 3 Vols. (New York:
Seabury Press, 1969).
Browning, Don, "Method in Religious Living and Clinical Educa-
tion," *Journal of Pastoral Care*, Vol. 29, p. 175.
Callahan, W. R. and Cardman, F. (eds.), *The Wind Is Rising: Prayer
Ways for Active People* (Hyattsville, Md.: Quixote Center, 1978).

Chapman, John Dom, *Spiritual Letters* (New York: Sheed and Ward, 1969).

Clebsch, W. A. and Jaekle, C. R. *Pastoral Care in Historical Perspective* New York: Aronson, 1964)

Devers, Dorothy, *Faithful Friendship* (Washington, D.C., private printing; available at Potter's House Bookstore in D.C.).

DeSales, Francis, *Treatise on the Love of God* (Westminster, Md.: Newman Press, 1962).

Edwards, Tilden, *Living Simply Through the Day* (New York: Paulist Press, 1977).

Egan, Harvey, "Christian Apophatic and Kataphatic Mysticisms," *Theological Studies* (Fall 1978), pp. 399ff.

Fleming, David, "Models of Spiritual Direction," *Review for Religious*, Vol. 34, No. 3 (May, 1975), pp. 351–357.

Fowler, James, "Stages in Faith," *Values and Moral Development*, Ed. T. Hennessy (New York, Paulist Press, 1976).

Geromel, E., "Depth Therapy and Spiritual Direction," *Review for Religious*, Vol. 36 (1977) pp. 753–763.

Hauser, Richard "Principles of Asceticism," *Review for Religious*, Vol. 38 No. 3 (1979).

Hora, Thomas, *Existential Meta-Psychiatry* (New York: Seabury Press, 1977).

James, W., *The Varieties of Religious Experience* (New York: Modern Library, 1936).

Jeremias, Joachim, "Being a Child," *New Testament Theology* (New York: Scribner, 1971), Ch. 18.

John of the Cross, *Collected Works* (Washington, D.C.: Institute of Carmelite Studies 1973).

Johnston, William, *The Inner Eye of Love* (New York: Doubleday, 1978).

———— (trans.), *The Cloud of Unknowing* and *The Book of Privy Counsel* (New York: Image, Doubleday, 1973).

Kepler, Thomas, *An Anthology of Devotional Literature* (Chicago: Baker Book House, 1977).

La Place, Jean, S. J., *Preparing for Spiritual Direction* (Chicago: Franciscan Herald Press, 1975).

May, Gerald, *The Open Way* (New York: Paulist Press, 1977).

McNeill, J., *A History of the Cure of Souls* (New York: Harper and Row, 1951).

Merton, Thomas, *Spiritual Direction and Meditation* (Collegeville, Minn.: Liturgical Press, 1960).

————, "The Spiritual Father in the Desert Tradition," *Contemplation in a World of Action* (New York: Doubleday, 1971).

————, *New Seeds of Contemplation* (New York: New Directions, 1961).

————, "Manifestation of Conscience and Spiritual Direction," *Sponsa Regis*, 30 (1959), pp. 277–282.

Muto, Susan, *A Practical Guide to Spiritual Reading* (Denville, N.J.: Dimension Books, 1976).

Nelson, James B., *Embodiment: An Approach to Sexuality and Christian Theology* (Augsburg, 1978).

Peters, W., "Spiritual Direction and Prayer," *Communio*, Vol. 3 (1976), pp. 357–372.

Poulain, A. F., *The Graces of Interior Prayer (Des Graces d'Oraison)* (St. Louis: Herder, 1910).

Reed, Bruce, *The Dynamics of Religion* (London: Darton, Longman and Todd, 1978).

Rossi, Robert, "Psychological and Religious Counseling," *Review for Religious*, Vol. 37, No. 4 (July 1978).

Setzer, J. S., "When Can I Determine When It Is God Who Speaks to Me in My Inner Experience?" *Journal of Pastoral Counseling* Vol. 12 (Fall–Winter 1977–1978).

Teresa of Avila, *The Collected Works* (Washington, D.C.: Institute of Carmelite Studies, 1976).

Trungpa, Chogyam, *Cutting Through Spiritual Materialism* (Berkeley, Calif.: Shambala, 1973).

Tulku, Tarthang, *Gesture of Balance* (Emeryville, Calif.: Dharma Publications 1977).

Underhill, Evelyn, *Mysticism: A Study in the Nature and Development of Man's Spiritual Consciousness* (New York: Meridian, 1955) Part II.

Van Kaam, Adrian, *The Dynamics of Spiritual Self-Direction* (Denville, N.J. Dimension Books, 1976), Part II.

Von Hügel, Friedrich, "Letter to a Confirmand," *The Spirituality of Friedrich Von Hügel* (New York: Newman, 1971), pp. 226–236.

Walsh, W., "Reality Therapy and Spiritual Direction," *Review for Religious*, Vol. 35 (1976), pp. 372–385.

Wright, J.H., S.J., "A Discussion on Spiritual Direction," *Studies in the Spirituality of Jesuits*, Vol. IV. No. 2 (Mar. 1972), pp. 1–51.

"Direction Spirituelle," *Dictionnaire De Spiritualité*. Vol. 3, pp. 1002–1214.

"Spiritual Life Handbook," *Chicago Studies*, Vol 15, No. 1 (Spring 1976).

"Word Out of Silence," whole issue of *Cross Currents*, Vol. 24 No. 2–3.

IV. SOME CURRENT PERIODICALS THAT REGULARLY INCLUDE RELEVANT ARTICLES:

Abba, a Journal of Prayer
Cistercian Studies
Contemplative Review
Crux of Prayer
Formational Spirituality
Journal of Pastoral Care
Journal of Pastoral
    Counseling
Journal of Religion
    and Health
Journal of Theology
    and Psychology
La Vie Spirituelle
Pastoral Psychology
Review for Religious
Spiritual Life

Spirituality Today The Way
Studies in the Spirituality Transpersonal Psychology
 of Jesuits Worship

The Paulist Press is publishing a series of classics in the history of Western spirituality. The Press also is developing a major new series on world spiritualities, including a new history of Christian spirituality.

V. OTHER READINGS

Doran, R.M. "Jungian Psychology and Spiritual Direction," *Review for Religious*, Vol. 38, No. 4, 5, 6 (1979).

Fox, Matthew (ed.). *Western Spirituality* (Notre Dame: Fides/Claretian, 1979).

Ladenthin, Thomas. "The Journal—A Way into Prayer," *Review for Religious*, Vol. 38, No. 2 (1979).

Newman, Matthias. "Letter to a Beginning Spiritual Director," *Review for Religious*, Vol. 37, No. 6 (1978).

Roemer, Judith. "Discernment in the Director," *Review for Religious*, Vol. 34, No. 6 (1975).

Schneider, Sandra. "Training of Spiritual Guides," *National Catholic Reporter* Cassettes, Kansas City, 1978.

Ulanov, A.B. "What Do We Think People Are Doing When They Pray?" *Anglican Theological Review*, Vol. 60, No. 4 (1978).

Wallis, Arthur. *God's Chosen Fast* (Ft. Washington, Pa. 19034: Christian Literature.

Whitehead, E.A. and J.D. *Christian Life Patterns* (N.Y.: Doubleday, 1979).